MW01253341

Consumers and Individuals in China

Breaking new ground in the study of Chinese urban society, this book applies critical discourse analysis to ethnographic data gathered in Anshan, a third-tier city and market in northeast China. The book confronts the – still widespread – notion that Chinese consumers are not "real" individuals, and in doing so represents an ambitious attempt to give a new twist to the structure versus agency debates in social theory. To this end, Michael B. Griffiths shows how claims to virtues such as authenticity, knowledge, civility, sociable character, moral proprietary and self-cultivation emerge from and give shape to social interaction. Data material for this path-breaking analysis is drawn from informants as diverse as consumerist youths, dissident intellectuals, enterprising farmers, retired Party cadres, the rural migrant staff of an inner-city restaurant, the urban families dependent on a machine-repair workshop, and a range of white-collar professionals.

Consumers and Individuals in China: Standing out, fitting in, will appeal to sociologists, anthropologists, and cultural studies scholars, China Studies generalists, and professionals working at the intersection of culture and business in China. The vivid descriptions of living and doing fieldwork in China also mean that those travelling there will find the book stimulating and useful.

Michael B. Griffiths is Director of Ethnography at Ogilvy & Mather, Greater China. He is also Associate Research Fellow, White Rose East Asia Centre; and External Research Associate, Centre for International Business, University of Leeds, UK.

Chinese Worlds

Chinese Worlds publishes high-quality scholarship, research monographs, and source collections on Chinese history and society. "Worlds" signals the diversity of China, the cycles of unity and division through which China's modern history has passed, and recent research trends toward regional studies and local issues. It also signals that Chineseness is not contained within borders – ethnic migrant communities overseas are also "Chinese worlds."

The series editors are Gregor Benton, Flemming Christiansen, Delia Davin, Terence Gomez and Hong Liu.

1. **The Literary Fields of Twentieth-Century China**
   Edited by Michel Hockx

2. **Chinese Business in Malaysia**
   Accumulation, ascendance, accommodation
   Edmund Terence Gomez

3. **Internal and International Migration**
   Chinese perspectives
   Edited by Frank N. Pieke and Hein Mallee

4. **Village Inc.**
   Chinese rural society in the 1990s
   Edited by Flemming Christiansen and Zhang Junzuo

5. **Chen Duxiu's Last Articles and Letters, 1937–42**
   Edited and translated by Gregor Benton

6. **Encyclopedia of the Chinese Overseas**
   Edited by Lynn Pan

7. **New Fourth Army**
   Communist resistance along the Yangtze and the Huai, 1938–41
   Gregor Benton

Consumers and Individuals in China

Standing out, fitting in

Michael B. Griffiths

Routledge
Taylor & Francis Group

LONDON AND NEW YORK

First published 2013
by Routledge
2 Park Square, Milton Park, Abingdon, Oxon OX14 4RN

Simultaneously published in the USA and Canada
by Routledge
711 Third Avenue, New York, NY 10017

Routledge is an imprint of the Taylor & Francis Group, an informa business

British Library Cataloguing in Publication Data
A catalogue record for this book is available from the British Library

Library of Congress Cataloging in Publication Data
Griffiths, Michael B., 1979-
   Consumers and individuals in China : Standing out, fitting in /
Michael B. Griffiths.
      p. cm. – (Chinese worlds)
   Includes bibliographical references and index.
   1. Consumers–China. 2. Consumers–China–Attitudes. 3. Consumers'
preferences–China. 4. Consumer behavior–China. I. Title.
   HC79.C6.G75 2012
   339.4′70951–dc23
                  2012013429

ISBN: 978-0-415-53572-4 (hbk)
ISBN: 978-0-203-09353-5 (ebk)

Typeset in Times New Roman
by Taylor & Francis Books

Printed and bound in the United States of America
by Edwards Brothers Malloy

Contents

Figures

Preface

Between 2005 and 2011, I conducted an ethnographic study across a wide spectrum of society in Anshan, a burgeoning "third-tier" city in China's northeastern Liaoning Province, seeking to understand how individuality in this context was structured and generated. My primary aims were critical, since my approach directly assaulted the myth prevailing in large parts of the extant literature that Chinese individuals are not "real" individuals; that they are not autonomous, altogether individuated social actors, but rather passive, "interdependent" entities, their identities entirely determined by their social circumstances. My aims were also methodological, since I sought to chart a "third way" between individual agency and the conditioning of social structure in the actual assertion of individuality, thus demonstrating that Chinese individuals are both agents and subjects of practical culture.

Borrowing from post-structuralist social theory, where acts of self-assertion are seen as always already informed by "discourses" of social standing and evaluation (Derrida 1976; Bourdieu 1984), I sought to demonstrate the interaction of those discourses in their articulation by applying a "critical discourse analysis" (Fairclough 1989) to the ways in which individuals in Anshan drew and managed "symbolic boundaries" (Lamont 1992) through judgments of "purity", "taste" and "worthiness" most broadly construed. My approach was distinct from studies of "individualization" in China, where the emphasis has been on the diachronic extent to which Chinese individuals must deal with the increased risk and responsibility arising from China's reforming collectively owned infrastructure (Halskov-Hansen and Svarverud 2010; Yan 2009a): these literatures make no attempt to show how individual agency is itself structured rather than just in various in ways "simply" constrained. My approach was distinct too, from cultural sociologies which have examined practices of "social distinction" in China in ways very similar to my research (Hanser 2008): closer to the epistemological concept Pierre Bourdieu called "genetic structuralism", my research intended in the first place not to draw out "sociological" conclusions about class, gender and so on, but simply to collapse individuals' modalities of consuming culture against themselves, thus showing how my informants' individual identities arose from discursive environments structured by relation to similar peers and distinctly different others.

This book presents the results of my analyses. The first chapter contextualizes the ethnography and raises the research problem from a critique of existing literatures. Chapters two to seven treat data gathered from informants as diverse as consumerist youths, dissident intellectuals, enterprising farmers and Communist Party cadres as a "synchronic system", a snapshot of the present, and disaggregate these into eight conceptually rich categories. The first six of these categories – authenticity, knowledge, civility, sociability, morality and personality, are developed in their "internal" and situationally inflected logics at full chapter length, each differently demonstrating the almost limitless capacity for Chinese individuals to take prior cultural constructs and bend these to their will. The final two categories – materialism and status, are for important reasons subsumed under a second stage of analysis which pursues the further regularities and modes structuring the assertion of individuality, that is, the cultural "grammar" describing the ways in which my informants differently made these categories their own. Specifically, chapters eight, nine and ten juxtapose practices of symbolic boundary management across the rural migrant staff of an inner-city restaurant, the urban families dependent on an industrial machine-repair workshop, and a range of white-collar professionals from the private and public sectors, demonstrating how "consumption" results in diverse but structurally unified outcomes.

"Consumption" here is understood not just in terms of buying clothes, watching television, eating hamburgers and so on, but as a metaphor that stands in for the essentially dual processes by which "individuals" internalize, diffuse and reconfigure the same locally and historically specific discourses through which marketers and corporate agencies seek to articulate their brand communications. "Individuality", accordingly, is understood as a locus not so much of separation, but of connection, action and "consumption", a nodal point of cause and effect where language and social interaction conspire to produce individual and collective identities.

Importantly, none of the categories abstracted in my research should be understood as real independent of my analysis and its interpretation by other minds; they do not "drive" practice in themselves and remain only partial descriptions of local social constructions. They are, however, as I attempt to show, representative of a universal function of the human understanding, which does exist, to which these categories give expression, and by which function these categories were derived. Indeed, insofar as my analyses document how the structure of Anshan society obtains in the process of individuals "consuming" the discourses my categories describe, the book speaks of something common to the researcher and the researched even as it also broaches a new way of approaching Chinese urban society. In this way, my research seeks to contribute to knowledge in a way not bound by the context in which it was conducted, but by mapping the first discursive principles by which individual agency successfully negotiates social interaction per se: I simply seek to show how people in Anshan are human, just like "us", but with situationally specific nuances. And, to the extent that my analyses show how Chinese individuals are "different", my book offers an interpretative platform for engaging those individuals in their consumption.

My wife, Yuanyuan, citizen of Anshan, warrants first thanks for standing by me while I brought this book to completion. Flemming Christiansen was the consummate doctoral supervisor and a privilege to work with. Gregory Lee, Victor T. King, and Nicholas Tapp made generous comments on earlier drafts of the manuscript. Yan Yunxiang, Jørgen Delman, Tom Gold, Dorothy Solinger and Lei Guang supported various funding applications. Mette Halskov-Hansen, Jeremy Clegg, and Sid Lowe advised me in other ways. The University of Leeds' Research Committee, the Universities' China Committee London, the Worldwide Universities' Network, and the Sino-British Fellowship Trust funded my research. Professors Zhou Xiaohong and Zhou Peiqin of Nanjing University Department of Sociology graciously offered me an office to write up, as did Christian Lund and colleagues of Roskilde University's Institute for International Development Studies. Toby Lincoln, Jesper Zeuthen, Hinrich Voss, and Derek Hird were collegial friends throughout. Final thanks go to my daughter, whose birth provided a much-needed perspective on "completing" the research; to my local photographic artist from Anshan, Gao Yingchuan; and to Kunal Sinha and our colleagues at Ogilvy & Mather, Greater China, for offering me a way to apply my research in terms of cultural strategy.

1 Introduction

A contemporary context

During the "Maoist" era (1949–78), individuality in China was remarkably standardized in accordance with the cybernetic rationality of Communist political discourse. Central government planners attempted to micro-manage every detail of the economy so that individuals' needs were largely stipulated for them by the State. Urban citizens depended on their work-units to distribute products to them in accordance with a market of scarcity regulated by rationing (Walder 1986); rural communities subsisted in abject poverty, their production systematically bled to feed the expansion of urban industry (Christiansen 1993). Urban incomes were meager and highly approximate across social and professional ranks. Consumption as an end-in-itself was regarded negatively, so everyone wore the same drab clothes and sported the same bland haircuts. No-one was encouraged to distinguish themselves from amongst "the masses" in any way.

With the "Great Proletarian Cultural Revolution" (1966–76), in particular, pluralism and individual difference in the populous became anathema, and "redness" the only social and moral category of significance (Kraus 1977). Social order broke down entirely as "individualistic" dispositions were exorcised through violent public "criticisms" and ideological "struggle", and warring factions of the infamous Red Guards persecuted and neutralized anyone who exhibited evidence of "bourgeois consciousness" (Chan *et al.* 1980; Walder 2009). Mao's ambition had been to make China self-sufficient and independent of other nations, so the commercial offerings of Western nations were strictly outlawed as capitalist enemy propaganda: Hooper (2000), for example, reports a case of a Chinese official being sentenced to five years in prison for, amongst other things, "having a fondness for Coca-Cola".

Nevertheless, and despite the egalitarianism and public subservience which disguised the imposition of "comradeship" over individual agency throughout this time, Chinese people still found ways to make space for themselves within this system (Davis *et al.* 1995; Yan 2003). Manipulation of status hierarchies in the pursuit of social esteem was very much alive, so long as manipulations conformed to categories ascribed by the State administration: "rural" versus "urban"; "worker" versus "cadre"; seniority in the Party (i.e. year of "joining the revolution"); rank in the salary system; which "tier" of city one lived in (provincial cities being seen as superior to prefectural and county-level cities), and so on, were all legitimately distinctive dimensions of social difference in explicit or inexplicit ways (Whyte 1975). Social and symbolic capital were traded by recourse to the underground markets and elaborate networks of personal relationships necessary to negotiate the State bureaucracy too, the ability to bend the reality of "the system" to the favor of one's patron, thus making your own career steps seem like sacrifices for the common good, being especially highly distinguishing (Yang 1994).

Material inequalities existed during the Maoist era too, even though this was explicitly against official discourse: senior cadres enjoyed "distinctive lifestyles" (Davis 2000: 3) behind closed Party compound doors, and the political power implied by access to consumer brands such as Panda Cigarettes or Moutai (a distilled wine) was widely recognized. Indeed, since Socialism was an essentially scientific experiment that depended in some large measure on the intellectual elite, even the outlawed "class" distinction configured by family background, formal education and social association was legitimately levered in "tactical" (Dutton 1998) ways to suit lurching shifts in State policy (Andreas 2002; Konrád and Szelényi 1979). For the overwhelming majority of China's population, however, upwards social mobility was prohibited to all but those who sang loudest from Mao's hymn-sheet, and room for individual interpretation of these commandments remained narrow to say the least. Consumption as a project of individuality was reduced to a "bare", highly homogenous, "minimum" (Dirlik 2001: 4).

It was not until after Deng Xiaoping's economic "reforms and opening" (*gaige kaifang*) were initiated in late 1978 that China began to change into a place where people were able to manifest their preferences in action and consumption more readily (Nee 1989). These reforms were challenged by the political Left, but when the Special Economic Zones that had been created as experimental havens for foreign direct investment around China's southern coast were given a boost in 1992, there was no turning back (Becker 2000). The government had struck a deal with the masses following a controversial democracy movement in 1989: the party would remain in power so long as tangible improvements in living standards were achieved year-on-year (Pieke 1996). Since then, China has consistently been amongst the world's fastest growing national economies, rapidly restructuring its stagnating agricultural and industrial base into a thriving mixed public/private economy founded on increasing global engagement and markets "open" to international trade (Garner 2005). By 2006 China's economy ranked fourth largest in the world in gross domestic product (GDP) terms, up three places since 2004 according to official figures; however, when the figures were adjusted for purchasing power parity China ranked second to the USA alone (Garner 2005).

This extraordinary growth saw the return of consumerism to China, which emphasized symbolic and status distinctions in ways not seen in China since

Republic times (1911–49). Historians have documented the impact of consumerism on the cultural orientation of "treaty port" cities like Shanghai and Guangzhou in the early twentieth century (Cochran 1980; Lee 2000; Gerth 2004); evidence even suggests that "consumers" used "brands" (Hamilton and Lai 1989) and "superfluous things" (Clunas 2004) to assert identity and social power as long ago as the Ming and Qing dynasties. But as the contemporary State encouraged consumer spending throughout the 1990s in order to sustain economic growth, there seemed little doubt that China was undergoing a "consumer revolution" (Davis 2000; Li 1998; Wu 1998) which promised Chinese individuals greater possibilities for self-expression than ever before.

Quite the contradiction of the Maoist era's Spartan norms, "conspicuous consumption" (Veblen 1954) – that is, spending on goods primarily for the purposes of display and prestige – rapidly became popular, stimulating "cultural shock" (Barmé 1999) within China and a flurry of worldwide business interest (Croll 2006). National retail turnover and the advertising industry grew at year-on-year averages of 15% and 93%–97%, respectively (Paek and Pan 2004; Hooper 1998a). However, when the hyperbole and agitation was laid aside, and China's massive population taken into account, the Middle Kingdom remained very far from the consumerist paradise international marketers imagined. Still today, China's GDP per capita remains amongst the lowest in the world, with hundreds of millions of its citizens impoverished relative to urban growth centers, and while Western observers have often been inclined to hope that the resurgence of consumerism heralds greater capacity for Chinese individuals to express themselves as such, the absence of thorough-going democratic reforms to accompany economic liberalization has provoked the observation that the promise of personal choice implicit in the new consumerist culture applies only to those who can afford it (Pun 2003; Zhou 2004). Moreover, to the extent that China is experiencing a consumer revolution, this has been accompanied by surging corruption, piracy, prostitution, and a notable decline in public morals: the "flies", Deng admitted, would fly in the "Open Door" (Yan 2009b).

As China prepares for a power transition in 2012, indeed, its leaders face serious challenges: the size of China's national economy may now rank second only to the USA in absolute GDP terms too, but its population is aging and gender-imbalanced; the coastal manufacturing boom is fading and the labor pool that fuelled it shrinking and demanding fairer wages; social instability rises year-on-year, driven mainly by urban unemployment and rural land-grabs; and while expansionist rhetoric projects confidence overseas, media muzzling and political arrests at home reflect central government paranoia (Perry and Selden 2010). The contemporary State maintains a firm monopoly over the reproduction of social categories, moreover, although Communism has been thoroughly jettisoned as an economic ideology. Not least, there is still the household registration or *hu'kou* system which systematically discriminates between China's "urban" and "rural" folk, and makes life especially tough for the estimated 150 million workers who migrate to China's cities in search of jobs each year (Wang 2005; Zhang 2001). Recent reforms to such institutions have done little to assuage the popular perception that access to social opportunities in China is divided between allies and non-allies of the Clientelist State (Zeuthen and Griffiths 2011).

Yet outside, or rather within these categories, China is actually quite pluralistic and "free" today, so long as you do not explicitly challenge party-State authority (Perry and Selden 2010). The central government is much less concerned to prescribe for and control its subjects' lives than to offload responsibility for citizen's welfare, prosperity and social advancement onto individuals themselves (Yan 2009a). Party membership per se is a much weaker determinant of life chances than it once was, and internal social mobility is increasingly fluid and diverse, with new forms of hierarchy manifested rapidly (Bian 2002). Correspondingly, Chinese individuals are not just divided by their country's sweeping changes, but rather position themselves in relation to these (Hanser 2008; Hooper 1998a). Chinese individuals find all manner of ways to make room for themselves within the new discourse of market reform and consumerism, ways which need not necessarily involve purchasing consumer goods and services, but can nevertheless still be usefully understood as "consumption" too.

Essentialist errors: raising the problem

To date, perhaps most scholars concerned with "consumption" in China have sought to inform multinational business engagement with China and pursued quantifiable measures of the size and form of consumer markets. This approach assumes that everything real can be objectively perceived and counted (Lowe 2001, 2002). Typically, scholars of this persuasion have also assumed an instrumentally rational theory of action, known as methodological individualism, which superficially affords individuals agency, but in fact only allows for a reified set of cognitive intentions prior to the social world (Arrow 1994). Flow-chart models indicating separate stages in chains of consumer decision making suggest that every situation must first be consciously problematized and a "free, rational choice" made in accordance with self-defined "aims", "goals" and "objectives"; only then do individual agents actually act, effectively doubling causality!

Assumed in early empirical sociology where it was demanded that social happenings were the result of the aggregated units of individual actions (i.e. an essentially numeric, economic theory of social interaction), individuals are supposed to act entirely out of their own "rational" agency, and are not swayed to act by supra-individual social or cultural determinants such as class, gender, and so on, in any way. Though advocates of methodological individualism attempt to fit "society" and "culture", or a "relational and network context" (quotes Bao *et al.* 2003: 736–37) into their models of reality, quite as if these were afterthoughts, the same failure to allow that so much of human practice is irrational, not at all purposive, and much more a matter of "practical coping" (Chia and Holt 2006) than of temporally and causally suspended choice per se, effectively absolves these advocates of all responsibility for asserting a particular kind of rationality over social actors. At bottom, there is no accounting of how social and cultural factors can be reconciled with individual agency (cf. Arrow 1994; Lowe 2002). Thus, where scholars cast individuals as cause-of-themselves, "consumption" is understood only in terms of "purchasing" – the only successful kind of action this logic designates for "consumers" – even though it is self-evident that there cannot possibly be any "consumption" in any place where any identity is alone (Marcuse 1964).

Studies that employ these approaches can therefore say very little about the actual lived dynamics by which social difference is generated, in China or anywhere else: though markets may be segmented in terms of their demographics (Walters and Samiee 2003), geographical distribution (Cui and Liu 2001; Fram *et al.* 2004), psychographic attitudes, values (Schmitt 1997; Wei 1997; Dickson *et al.* 2004), and so on, studies of this form can only ever trace where consumption has been.

In the particular case of China, this same order of epistemological arrogance (Gadamer 1975) has often been perverted along East–West lines in order to insist that Chinese consumers are not the rationally driven, self-determined characters described by methodological individualism at all, but are rather only passive subjects, identities only insofar as these are entirely determined by their societies. Almost invariably, wherever scholars set "private selves" against "public selves", and "personal identities" against "social identities" in typical social psychological fashion – quite as if the "core" Cartesian self at once divorced from the world can now be made to "possess" (Belk 1988; Eckhardt and Houston 2001b) all manner of other selves, each of which is equally absolutely divided from each other, some timeless "essence" (Stening and Zhang 2007) of "Chinese culture" (Yau 1988) or "Confucianism" (e.g. Bond 1996) (the latter in any case too often conflated to the former), is uncritically conjured to justify casting Chinese consumers as "collectivist" rather than "individualist" (Aaker and Schmitt 2001; Hwang *et al.* 2003), as "interdependent" rather than "independent" (Markus and Kitayama 1991; Singelis 1994), that is, further essentialist categories into which Chinese individuals are made to fit, each of which is equally taken to mean that "selves" of this peculiar "Chinese" type have a form of subjectivity defined solely by the collectives of which they are members.

These stereotypes of Chinese culture date back through early Western sociological engagements with China, through Weber to Marx, to Christian missionaries' early expeditions there: the radically different Oriental "Other" has always been a function of "Western" countries' needs to define themselves in their own autonomous and individuated terms (Said 2003). The expression of these stereotypes in terms indigenous to members of Chinese society themselves owes much to the work of Chinese sociologist Fei Xiaotong (Fei *et al.* 1992). Observing that Western models of human behavior applied poorly to the China case, Fei developed instead a functionalist model of

Chinese society structured by "networks" of social relations and sustained through the fulfillment of various social roles. Regrettably, Fei's search for "ideal types" and instrumentally rational motivations for action meant that he systematically overessentialized the "individualism" of Western cultures as the "Other" against which his narrative of "differentially associated" Chinese society was constructed, whilst simultaneously neglecting the complex social processes by which different forms of Western individuality are derived (Dumont 1992): while Chinese people were supposedly entirely determined by their social circumstances, the mere "egotistical" product of social concerns, Westerners were autonomous, transcendent and altogether independent from other social actors.

Francis K. Hsu, a "psychological anthropologist", proposed a similarly influential model here, whereby the Western person was "individually centered" and the Chinese person was "situationally centered" (Hsu 1953). He also proposed a "psychosociogram" (Hsu 1971) comprising a scale ranging from the "depths" of the personal unconscious, through one's most intimate expressible thoughts and feelings to one's intimate social relationships, then still further "outwards" towards more formal, utilitarian and less emotive relations with less familiar others, before eventually arriving at society per se and the world at large. The Asian concept of "personage" was supposedly differently located on this spectrum than the Western concept of "personality". Whereas the Western individual was understood as given, Asian "personage" was achieved by modifying behavior in accordance with prevailing interpersonal cultural standards (Hsu 1971). Hsu's model represented a considerable improvement on Fei Xiaotong, but his belief in a "core" personality prior to the conditioning of a naively homogenous culture meant that his spatial metaphors retained the illusion of a Cartesian mind and its object even for the "relational" Asian he sought to set against this (cf. Hsu 1985).

Unfortunately, essentialist readings of culture such as these have been widely accepted and taken to extremes, so that present-day cross-cultural management literatures read as if Chinese consumers are incapable of acting as such, but were rather more like bees and other insects supposed to share "hive-minds". For example, one paper in *Psychology and Marketing* has it that, "In a collectivist country like China, the individual is not a complete entity ... a male Chinese would view himself as a son, a brother, a husband, a father, but hardly as himself" (Bao *et al.* 2003: 736–37), thus representing Chinese consumers as somehow defunct or inferior versions of those "completely" individual agents, found, the same paper elsewhere avers, only in the "West". Another paper that offers guidelines for conducting research in China similarly wagers, "[Chinese] ... do not necessarily think of themselves as distinct from others, as having unique internal attributes [that is, abilities, traits, motives and values], and do not necessarily behave as a consequence of internal attributes" (Eckhardt 2004: 407); indeed, this latter paper even suggests that conversations with Chinese individuals should be actively avoided because, "in most Chinese contexts the appropriate unit of analysis is the group not the individual, as almost internally held beliefs, attitudes and values are the product of important in-group interactions" (Eckhardt 2004: 406), apparently oblivious to the sense in which internally held beliefs, attitudes and values are the ongoing product of social interactions for people everywhere (e.g. Goffman 1959).

Even where Chinese scholars have themselves attempted to drop the hegemonic trans-cultural model that "overwhelms" (Weick 1999: 804) cross-cultural management research (e.g. Hofstede 1991, 2001) and examined the world's cultures from the perspective of "values" "traditionally" linked to China (Chinese Culture Connection 1987), they did not dispense with their positivist and essentialist approach, so could not have been further from an analysis of Chinese people's actual cultural practices: the "Confucian Dynamism" with which Chinese were in this case stereotyped was just a more "active" form of methodological individualism (if such a thing were possible), just as "collectivism" is but a more "capacious" form of the same (cf. Chia and Holt 2006: 638). Similarly, whenever the idea of this peculiarly "Chinese" form of subjectivity has been used to mount half-hearted critiques of the individually centered Cartesian subject (i.e. as described above), contributors have been singularly unable to see that they reproduce the belief in a "core" subjectivity in their own methodology (Lowe 2001, 2002): contributors who invoke a little "Eastern holism" – some "contradiction", "paradox" and "ambivalence" – still typically perceive themselves as being able to "resolve" these contradictions, to "crack the reputedly indecipherable code", to reason away the contradiction and provide instead a coherent and definite solution that "smart marketers" must "help consumers" find (all quotes Doctoroff 2005: 1–8).

However, Chinese consumers are very well aware of the cultural "code" quite without marketers' "help"; indeed, they help produce culture even as marketers do; and although "Chinese culture" is widely spoken about in the most vernacular of everyday practices, Chinese consumers are only too well aware that there is no one set "code" that holds for all situations like a rational imperative. So let it be quite clear: the dynamics of social and cultural practice can never be captured by the essentially one-dimensional "dimensions" essentialist acolytes like to believe describe all the world's cultures (cf. Hofstede 1991, 2001), and scholars who suggest otherwise deny what they themselves actually do in order to obfuscate the overwhelmingly obvious fact that individual agents and the social world are indeed reconciled in consumption! Such scholars imply, and then quite ironically, that the "discovery" of a Chinese cultural emphasis on "interrelationship" as opposed to the division in which the power of positivism consists has somehow reconciled subject to object once and for all time!

This is the one impossibility that all such essentialists cannot possibly admit, so arguments are developed which persistently skirt over the most fundamental issue, back and forth from the "subjective" to the "objective" perspective, erroneously reproducing the same series of broadly parallel individual–collective, East–West binary oppositions without ever undertaking to analyze what individual consumer-agents actually do that makes them individuals. Inextricably, researchers are confronted by the question of whether the preoccupation with selling to "billions" (Doctoroff 2005) of Chinese consumers, a siren-song that has consistently wrecked Western business interests in search of illusory East Asian riches against metaphorical rocks since mediaeval times, predisposes marketers to assimilate their quarry and make them subject again only to the undifferentiating logic of consumerism. Indeed, the question is begged of whether the entire notion of the "free, rational actor" is itself a product of the humanist and industrial discourses of the "Enlightenment" era and all of the commodifying aspirations that have followed since (Foucault 1970; Rose 1996). As such, this book draws on critical philosophies in its pursuit of identifying individuality in China (Fairclough 1995; Weiss and Wodak 2003).

Idealist retakes: alternative agendas

There is, of course, a well-tried alternative to the entire empiricism-based approach to the social sciences criticized above: the Durkheimian approach. Social anthropologists inspired by Radcliffe-Brown and so on (e.g. Durkheim and Mauss 1967), take the collective, society, as the appropriate point of analytical departure, rather than individual actors, and may even discount individual motivations altogether, thus lending force to analyses of societies seen to continue before and beyond the individuals who temporarily occupy a status within them (Durkheim 1997). Francis K. Hsu, discussed above, was a key proponent of this school of thought as applied to China, but his modeling of Chinese social psychology versus its Western individualist "opposite" betrayed the vestiges of cultural essentialisms that were not to be challenged until the advent of postmodernism in the social sciences (see also Barth 1969).

In recent times the Durkheimian school of thought has found expression primarily through qualitative research, and has become instrumental in the development of "Consumer Culture Theory" (Arnould and Thompson 2005), particularly with regard to how such theorists think about societies, communities and groups, and individuals' roles within them. A broad agglomerate of perspectives from the "Continental" tradition of philosophy is harnessed to emphasize that reality is in every case meaningful for social individuals possessed of a unique interpretive capacity to construct it for themselves, that is, a subjective capacity, rather than as a set of "true, objective facts" about the world (Thompson *et al.* 1989, 1990). The methodological muscle comes from an anthropological tradition where "consumption" denotes as much the meanings inscribed in objects, symbols, and the human relationships formed around these, as it does the economic transactions surrounding consumer goods and services (e.g. Douglas and Isherwood 1979; McCracken 1990; Miller 1987; Baudrillard 1998).

Scholars of this latter field have retained a distinctly US-centric bias, however: only a smattering of top-tier journal articles examine contexts outside of

North America, and those that do examine emerging market contexts, such as China, only rarely refer to existing ethnographic studies of the target cultures they analyze, which would inform many of the management, marketing and advertising issues with which contributors to this field, who are ostensibly scholars, are concerned (e.g. Appadurai 1988). "Consumption", moreover, though understood interpretatively, is treated only in a narrow consumerist sense, the simple "opposite" of economic production as it were, a shrinking of vision which can only be a function of the isolationist disciplinary ambitions attending this territory: individuals are understood as free to "consume" in myriad self- and collectively determined ways, as long as they eventually pay for something somewhere, which wouldn't seem so exclusive if the scholars credited with developing this agenda were not plainly more interested in furthering their "pure" academic research agenda than informing real-life consumption. Even where cross-pollinated works on China have emerged in the form of business scholars who refer to Asian Studies specialists (Hung *et al.* 2007; Zhao and Belk 2008), or even cultural studies scholars "turned" business scholars (cf. Wang 2008), these works remain very much grown in academic marketing or social science theory gardens.

Thus, while the best of these "qualitative marketing" academics (e.g. Murray and Ozanne 1991; Murray 2002) successfully have pioneered new ways of approaching "consumption", an unfortunate side-effect of their experimenting is that articles of qualitative research couched in terms of positivism's atomistic and mechanical vocabulary (i.e. validity, reliability, etc.) have proliferated in social psychology-inspired marketing journals, where terms like "phenomenology" and "social constructionism" get bandied around by closet objectivists who do not understand that no amount of methods of "triangulation" will ever fuse subject with object except in terms of specific use, that no theory will ever do this except in its dynamic creation, and that the "quality" of qualitative research consists precisely in the unremitting and ultimately unrewarding struggle to abstract its objects from the practices that generate them! Indeed, the most pertinent observation is that it is only by way of making their research fit the parameters demanded by the need to enliven an intellectually banal discipline (i.e. academic marketing research) – making room for themselves within these parameters whilst not entirely escaping them (de Certeau 1984) – that the more critically minded of the "Consumer Culture Theory" scholars have reached out towards social theorists who still fall short of brushing aside the paradigmatic gap between objectivism and subjectivism in grand sweep, but who have long understood that bridging that "gap" is what consumption actually does (e.g. Dunn 2008).

Contemporary scholars concerned to deconstruct the interaction of China's Communist system of government and "Confucian" culture with market reform and the re-introduction of consumerism (e.g. Chen *et al.* 2001; Chen and Sun 2006; Ma 2006), indeed, that is, anthropologists, sociologists, sinologists and so on, have long recognized "consumption" and "identity" as fundamentally political problems, and sought to approach these problems in ways that stridently avoid the essentialisms that positivist and pseudo-qualitative approaches generate. However, although the perspectives developed from the ethnographic fieldwork that scholars of these fields tend to prefer yield far greater conceptual power than those developed from objectivist methods, scholars of this broadly defined second field have often been as guilty of denying agency to Chinese individuals as the essentialists. Typically, all sorts of objectifying caveats and qualifications are made to assert the scholar's own position without discriminating much between informants, the individual being taken precisely as an example of a type, of "the masses", and the stance taken in relation to subjects of research obfuscating the actual dynamic genesis of individuality beneath factual detail, theory, and/or narcissistic wordplay.

Xin Liu's *The Otherness of Self* (2002), for example, begins by structuring practices of "selfhood" in contemporary China in interesting and poignant ways, but then leads the reader into theoretical discussions as far removed from what Chinese are doing in the act of asserting themselves as can be imagined. Quite similarly, Frank Pieke's book, *The Ordinary and the Extra-ordinary* (1996) gives much less room to Chinese people's actual practices than he promises, between the large parts of his book devoted to showing that he "knows about" social theory and those "telling the story" of the 1989 Beijing democracy movement. Similar charges could be made of many of the methodologically approximate works in the field, even of Andrew Kipnis's *Producing Guanxi* (1997), which otherwise represents the finest examination of individual and collective identity formation and performance in China to date, because these anthropologists do not usually write for the agency of the individuals who inform their research, but for somewhat the opposite reason, for each other, to write about other scholars' writing, and to complicate the object of knowledge until it becomes a matter for sophisticated critique. Indeed, this latter internally referential disposition may also explain why scholars from this field have ignored those "Other" works produced in the business management disciplines, even though both bodies of literature are concerned with the same Chinese individuals – "consumers" or "citizens", however we choose to look at them.[1]

The privileged perspective social science brings to its object is perhaps most condescending than where scholars most explicitly seek to give "voice" to China's poor, underprivileged "subaltern" (Pun 2003) types. Scholars of a (neo-Marxist) "Frankfurt School" influence (Anagnost 2004; Dirlik 2001), in particular, maintain an explicit disdain for the commercial agencies that impact upon consumption, matched by a rather more implicit disdain for the consumption decisions of individual Chinese themselves. Social and cultural anthropologist Pun Ngai, for example, addresses her studies of factory workers in Shenzhen directly at the idea that the re-introduction of consumerism into China may have engendered greater agency for Chinese individuals to choose their lives for themselves, and finds that this was the newest "ruse of capital", "whereby the extraction of surplus value of labor is ... suppressed by the over-valuation of consumption and its neo-liberal ideologies of self-transformation"

(Pun 2003: 469). "Consumption" is thus treated not as a metaphor for what individuals actually do with social structures to make them their own, but as a metaphor that stands for the "domination" of "global capital" such scholars must find in any problem at which they look (cf. Pun 2003: 469).

Now, whilst there is much to be said about the exploitation of individual agency in contemporary China, it cannot be denied that many millions of Chinese have been rather glad to be "exploited" and "consumed" by economic reform. Indeed other scholars have drawn quite the opposite conclusions: Deborah Davis, for example, found that although her Shanghai home-owner informants evinced ample evidence of social stratification in their consumption practices, they offered a "reflexive and critical narrative that signified agency and individuation more than manipulation and domination" (Davis 2005: 708–9); when juxtaposed against memories of past political repression and material deprivation, Davis maintained, her informants interpreted China's "consumer revolution" in genuinely liberating terms (Davis 2005: 708–9). While Shanghai home owners probably are more likely to express a more "liberated" discourse than Shenzhen's factory workers, a more methodologically balanced approach would seek to afford analytical primacy to individuals' capacity to appropriate structures of power and authority even in sites of economic exploitation. Hoist with their own intellectual petard and noble ideals, in short, the scholarly projects that most aspire to "liberate" Chinese individuals from the clutches of "neoliberalism" (Kipnis 2007) nevertheless too often seem to make their informants subject even as they attempt to champion their "ordinary" causes from the "heights" of left-wing academic theory (Agger 1992).

Global forces: essentialist dialogues

Scholars from this broadly-defined second "sociological" field have, however, convincingly shown that Chinese people have themselves been complicit with the "West" in essentializing their own culture. Chinese Communism, of course, was not only anti-capitalist but also anti-imperialist, tacitly but directly aimed at dealing with China's racist subjugation by foreign powers: Mao intended to build up an understanding of modernity not tainted by compliance with Orientalism and sufficiently differentiated from the "corruption" and "inefficacy" of the Kuomintang Party; pursuing Marxism and implementing a scientific "value-neutral" rationality with engineering precision was his way out. The reintroduction of consumerism after Deng's economic reforms therefore conflicted with the need the State increasingly felt from the late 1970s onwards to emphasize the "nation" in order to maintain its legitimacy (Unger and Barmé 1996). A Chinese leadership anxious to include greater China within their sphere of influence and prepare for the return of Hong Kong saw the underdog ideology of "catching up" with the West as negative and generated a new story of the historical evolution of the nation in which there was a continuous positive contribution to mankind.

Beginning with the "patriotic education campaign" from the summer of 1991 onwards, the State tacitly condoned the resurrection of the Confucianist and Taoist ideals outlawed under Mao for their "anti-revolutionary" emphasis on respect for traditional hierarchies and social harmony, and had these spliced into the Communist Party line as an act of identification which essentialized China's ancient past and played directly into the hands of Orientalism (Ong 1999: 63). This provided Western perspectives on Chinese culture with further credibility in China, meaning that essentialism was less nefariously imposed on the Chinese than manifested in the embrace of values and ideologies that allowed them moral judgments vis-à-vis the West (Ong 2005). This was the discourse brought together with Western financial interests in the 1990s to propagate the myth of "Asian Values", a notion premised on the promise that capitalism would flourish wherever inequality, lack of individual rights, and political oppression were excused as reflections of a set of Pan-Asian "values" that subordinated individual sovereignty to the social role in the family, society, and nation (Sen 1997). Implicit in the Chinese State's witticism "Socialism with Chinese characteristics", this discourse functioned to legitimate authoritarian regimes complicit with international business whilst ensuring that their markets remained open to foreign investment (Yao 2002).

These latter antagonisms were always framed in the literature by broader social science debates about the homogenization versus heterogenization of "global" capital markets and cultures (Hooper 2000; Dirlik 2001), and speculation about whether China's development would realize "alternative" forms of modernity (Ong 2005). In literature explicitly pertaining to "consumption" these discourses were manifested by an argument that raged out of all proportion from the late 1990s into the new millennium about whether Chinese preferred "Chinese" or "Western" themes in consumption (Paek and Pan 2004: 509; Zhou and Hui 2003). These arguments were precipitated by the observation that, by the early 1990s, while foreign firms and investors were discovering that China was vast, poor (frankly speaking), internally differentiated and resistant to foreign assimilation, Chinese domestic firms had fostered a new consumer "ethnocentrism" which reflected pride in China's rise on the world stage and were dominating lower-tier city markets (Ouyang *et al.* 2002; Wang and Chen 2004). Commentators reported a particular transformation in attitudes towards commodities of domestic origin following the NATO (North Atlantic Treaty Organization) bombing of the Chinese embassy in Belgrade in 1999, and again when a Chinese fighter pilot was killed in a crash with a US spy plane in 2001 (Dirlik 2001; Ewing *et al.* 2002; Hooper 2000; Wang and Chen 2004).

But the idea that China would conform to a homogenized model of globalization simply because Chinese individuals evinced a strong desire for consumerism as the poverty and austerity of the Mao era fell away, and for the "Western" goods and brands that had for so long been restricted in particular, was always misguided in its assumption that local consumers interpreted advertising images in the same way that advertisers intended, or in the way

Western observers did (Eckhardt and Houston 2001a; Zhou and Belk 2004). While China in many ways appeared to be undergoing a process of "McDonaldization" (Watson 1998; Yan 1998) or "Coca-colonization" (Ger and Belk 1996) compared to its isolation under Mao, the evidence on the ground was more complicated. Thus, it became necessary to conduct research which began by self-consciously striving to afford individuals agency, emphasizing the "local" in the "global" as well as vice versa (Eckhardt and Mahi 2004).

Stakeholders with interests in making Chinese people more like consumers in the West, however, had always been aware that in a place where people had risked their lives for expressing individualist tendencies, new forms of consumption would likely be interpreted in terms of increased agency. From the beginning of China's reforms, marketers wasted no time in documenting how exposure to foreign media content was related to "individualistic values" and "hedonistic pursuits" among youthful urban Chinese (Paek and Pan 2004: 493). Analyses of advertising content found that "Western" appeals held a position of symbolic dominance with values of "modernity" and "individualism" emphasized over "tradition" and "collectivism" (Chan and Cheng 2002; Tse *et al.* 1989). Similar research confirmed that younger, wealthier and better-educated Chinese enjoyed "conspicuous consumption", aspired to "self-actualization", and "worshipped Western lifestyles" (Wei and Pan 1999; Zhang and Shavitt 2003). Many commentators suggested the "one-child policy" was a factor enhancing "self-centered" tendencies (Li 1998; Lin 2001), but the broader Deng'ist "Get rich quick" vein of materialism was always recognized as an individualizing driver in itself, even by scholars who simultaneously chimed to the "Confucianist" mantra.

Stakeholders interested in making Chinese individuals members of intriguing traditional collectives at the same time as becoming more like individuals in the West – that is to say, always saw themselves as the "liberation" of a "repressed yet emerging need" to realize "what I want, what I like, and who I am" (all quotes Doctoroff 2005: 35, 100) in China. However, not only did this argument mistake individuality as the province of China's young and materialistic consumers alone (cf. Thøgersen and Ni 2008), much worse it mistook individualism for individuality! Further, it can only be assumed that the Chinese individuals subjected to these quantitative surveys agreed with scholars' implicit equations of "modern" and "Western" with "individuality", and "backward" and "Chinese" with "non-individuality" – a product of discourse (see also below) for all concerned. Seen through the haze of positivism, there was no methodological way possible for Chinese individuals to be all of these binary oppositions – "individual" and "collective", "modern" and "traditional", albeit in ways considerably different to the West.

Commentators of all stripes seemed to fudge this most important issue. Michael Dutton, a political scientist, radically simplified when writing: "Fashion [in China] is not constructed to mark out one's individuality, but to mark out one's success ... success is equivalent to choosing the popular product, making 'the popular choice'" (Dutton 1998: 273–74). Might it not be asked if

Chinese consumers were not positively "marked out" by making the "popular choice", how else they could possibly be "successfully" marked out? Li Conghua, a business commentator, sought to sophisticate the issue by maintaining that Chinese people "follow the tastes of the group", but within the group they seek to differentiate themselves from each other as individuals: "Chinese people", he concluded, "want to be the same but different" (Li 1998: 12–14). Tom Doctoroff, an advertiser, sought to nuance this insight with his "theory" of "Conformist Individualism", but while acknowledging that the "right" to individuality is the most crucial issue (Doctoroff 2005: 211), Doctoroff in at least one important sense skirted back and forth across the relation between the individual and the collective without attempting systematically to dis-aggregate this relation into its patterns of manifestation, thus essentializing China by appeal to the venerable sage, Confucius, as if individuality in the West meant doing whatever you liked!

In fact, as Doctoroff well recognizes, Chinese people find all sorts of ways of successfully "standing out" ahead of the pack without getting "shot down" (Doctoroff 2005: 102) everyday, in countless millions of daily situations and interactions that do not involve asserting oneself in overtly egotistical "indi-vidualistic" fashions. Even where "conforming" is understood as a way of "standing out" at the same time, however, we might still ask if the fixation with the relative legitimacy of "individualism" in China is a function of a predominantly Western, modernist, and linear logic which demands that our engagements with China be framed by the perception of its difference (Lowe 2002). Indeed, the point is that "strength of identity remains inextricably linked to external approval" (Doctoroff 2005: 82) everywhere, even in Western countries, where overtly "individualistic" differentiating actions remain subject to local cultural imperatives legitimating such acts (Wagner 1981). The issue of whether China is less "individualistic" than the West can therefore be left to cultural essentialists, and we can set about disaggregating the relation between Chinese individual agency and Chinese cultural collectives, showing how each is informed by the other.

Synthetic agendas: in search of a "third" way

Certain China scholars have attempted to nuance the paradigmatic stand-off in the cultural critique of consumption by arguing that because Chinese consumers are increasingly able to complain through official channels when sold shoddy or counterfeit goods, and to assert their individual rights under new systems of laws designed to protect them, the reintroduction of con-sumerism into China has engendered greater individual agency in its own right (e.g. Hooper 1998b; Ho 2001). Studies of this form have been metho-dologically approximate to those tracing the emergence of "civil society" in China (e.g. Brook and Frolic 1997; Hook 1996), studies that have always been attended by hopes of possible democratic reform, ranging from the skeptical (Schell 1989), to the more optimistic as China's reforms rumbled on (Davis 2000).

However, in no sense were any of these studies systematic of how individual agency was itself systematically structured. Rather they were case studies of how Chinese individuals struggle to individuate themselves against corporate and governmental agencies.

Quite similarly, anthropologists inspired by the work of sociologists Ulrich Beck (Beck and Beck-Gernsheim 2002) and Zygmunt Bauman (2000) have recently begun to document processes of "individualization" (Yan 2009a), where individuals are seen to "disembed" themselves from social categories (class, gender, etc.) and ties without necessarily re-embedding themselves into new, similar categories (Halskov-Hansen and Pang 2008; Thøgersen and Ni 2008). The "individualization" research agenda explicitly recognizes that individuality need not take the form of the atomized and self-gratifying self implied by positivism, and that the analysis of discursive forces need not produce a gridlock between free will and determinism (Rolandsen 2008: 105): its findings contribute the insights that any greater agency that economic reforms and consumerism have offered Chinese individuals has come with the burden of agency – that is, the having to adapt, the new demands on and new expectations made of individuals, and so on (Delman and Yin 2008); and that any sense in which China is indeed undergoing a process of "individualization" may still be a highly collective experience, since the individual challenge, risk, personal guilt and existential angst that new opportunities as well as constraints entail can provoke entirely new forms of collectives (Halskov-Hansen and Svarverud 2010).

Once again, however, aside from documenting areas of practice where this much more nuanced view of individuality is manifested, the "individualization" research program does not attempt to actually demonstrate that Chinese individuality itself is configured from the interrelation of individual agency with social structure. The primary concern in this research remains the diachronic extent to which agents in contemporary China are "individuals", and conclusions that Chinese are now acting as individuals "more" can really only amount to saying that they are now acting in ways in which they did not before, which is patently obvious, though the new ways themselves are nonetheless very interesting. The papers and articles that make up this "individualization" research agenda are therefore perhaps best examined as a whole, which does of course demonstrate a rich variety of ways in which individuality is configured from the structures of contemporary discourse, though this is still only to focus on where individual agency has been rather than a dynamic demonstration of agency's structuration per se.

At bottom, it does not matter much to Chinese individuals themselves whether they are more or less "individualized" than they once were: granted that individual autonomy is hugely important to Chinese individuals. Granted, even, that Chinese individuals are more "individualized" than they once were. Still, as broadly marketing-communications scholars Paek and Pan put it, "the key concern in the development of a consumer society at the turn of the century is no longer whether consumers recognize their sovereignty but how they seek for *distinction* in the consumerist culture" (Paek and Pan 2004: 496).

Notwithstanding the fact that Paek and Pan's formulation has an explicitly "consumerist" edge to it, an analysis is called for that concentrates on the internal workings of what Chinese individuals perhaps most do to make themselves individuals – the judgments and differentiations by which they position themselves in relation to one another, assertions which at the very point of instantiation will always be informed by the same structures that facilitate them, for these latter structures remain analytically (which is here to say ontologically) prior to all interaction, and thus significantly underscore analyses of "individualization".

In respects of the synchronic approach such an analysis would require, highly relevant work on China has emerged from sociologist Amy Hanser (Hanser 2004, 2005, 2008), but although Hanser makes a link between culture and society, meaning and power, anthropology and sociology, and so on, thus beginning with a theoretical and methodological impetus highly relevant to the proposed research agenda, Hanser builds specific sociological arguments about gender and class which remain of a very different scope and perspective: the proposed research would be quite different from Hanser's in that it would stick with this impetus, focusing first on the "internal", almost cognitive operations of discourse, only taking a more explicitly "sociological" turn when a framework for understanding how individual agency is systematically structured had been demonstrated. In many ways the proposed research would underscore Hanser's, just as it would also underscore the similarly sociological "individualization" literatures discussed above. Underscored, too, would be the consumerist forms of individuation Paek and Pan discuss above, since the proposed research would reveal the structures upon which consumerism in China should be best articulated if firms' offerings are to be most closely matched with consumers' projects of identity-making.

My research seeks to contribute, here, by borrowing from Structuralist and Post-Structuralist inspirations on "identity" (Derrida 1976), giving primacy to practice as a way of approaching "consumption". Although my research thus challenges most of the business literatures on Chinese consumers on theoretical and methodological grounds, emphatically, it does not seek to attack capitalism, commerce or consumerism in China per se. "Capital" will not be reified as if it had an agency of its own, and neither is my research concerned with the global division of labor (e.g. Chan 2001). Even as it pursues the analysis of an economy of power relations (Baudrillard 1981; Bourdieu 1984), my approach strives to avoid the characteristic condescension to ordinary individuals that so often attends Leftist intellectual agendas. Rather, I seek to chart a "third way" between the imperatives of the cultural collective and market on the one hand, and the autonomous agency of individuals on the other, disaggregating the "symphonic" (Jenkins 1992: 58) logic of practice into its patterns of modality and practical combination as these are manifested in one of China's most typical industrial cities.

Importantly, I do not presume to complete the insights my analysis should promote for social scientists and commercial practitioners in equal measure.

As maintained throughout, meaning cannot be separated from interpretation, and research that admits fertile grounds for sociality is far more valuable than commentary that in the name of "simplification" closes down room for critical engagement (Geertz 1975). Whereas practitioner literatures on culture, as a genre, pad out bullet-pointed "insights" with anecdotal and heuristic notes, my research recognizes that culture can be no more simply represented than language can. Practitioners seeking to successfully consume "Chinese culture" should not ask questions like "What do I do if … ?" (having been led to believe in the "code"), or "Can you give me a summary of Chinese culture", but would better analyze Chinese culture in terms of their own relationship to it, because the way that culture is successfully consumed shares more in common with the learning of a language than it does with the acquisition of a thing (Barthes 1972).

Language learners must of course acquire "grammar" (Chomsky 1965; Hjelmslev 1963) before their vocabulary can fully develop, the atomic internalization of lists of words being suitable only at the most rudimentary stage, so that vocabulary elements are internalized in the process of mastering broader, more fundamental "rules" governing how these are properly combined (Sturrock 1979, 2003). Rather than being like a "code" that "applies" in the situation, culture is therefore much more like a fluxing and multi-dimensional system structured by broad axiomatic principles within which there is a great deal of room for individual creativity (Ricoeur 1971). Axiomatic elements of the system may sometimes be directly opposed with one another in the actual instantiation of "vocabulary" elements, but this need not prevent the system as a whole from "cohering" over time (Sturrock 1979, 2003). Neither need this prevent cross-cultural practitioners from being helped to identify those key axioms in order to negotiate their experiences – everyday speech, we might note, need not be grammatically perfect for interpreters to understand the sense of it, unlike writing (Wittgenstein 1953).

My research contributes in just such a way, not with a checklist of "do's" and "don'ts", and not with tales of esoterica, but by reconstructing the deeper "grammatical" sense of the "language" by which individuality in my chosen context is configured from the analysis of what individuals actually do with the cultural system they inherit. That the "theory" derived remains only a partial grammar and does not pretend to account for the whole of the vocabulary logically follows: readers wishing to put this "grammar" to the test, must consume it in the practice of culture themselves.

Discursive consumption and symbolic boundaries

In post-structuralism, the very accentuation of individual agency in the social world is itself seen as a social construction (Derrida 1976): at the very moment of acting upon the world, individual agency is seen to be always already structured by the structures that constrain as well as enable it; conversely, and with every act of interpretation, "I" intervene in the "text" (Ricoeur 1971), actively bringing something unique of myself to the production of social structure. Metaphorically speaking, individual agency operates in the crux between the linguistic subject and the predicate, as the "subjective" and the "objective" interrelate in dynamic practice.

The matrix of possible meanings generated in this interrelation is perhaps best referred to as "discourse" (Alvesson and Karreman 2000). Discourse has no internal partitions or edges, a point largely lost on those who would narrow their understanding of "consumption" to only that discourse defined by reference to monetary expenditure (Firat and Venkatesh 1995). Nevertheless, we may still refer to discourses in the plural, as structured collections of representations. Indeed, all the languages, moralities, ideologies and classificatory systems by which individuals assert themselves may be referred to as discourses. Discourses may remain considerably collective in their aims and projects while individuals' consumption of them may be highly self-assertive, but discourses of "self" and of "others" can never be entirely reduced to each other since individual identity is cast upon individual agents by the very nature of the social world.

Where discourse is regarded as a metaphor for social life per se – that is, rather than as a merely linguistic or psychoanalytical notion (Lacan 1977) – critical discourse analysts (Fairclough 1989, 1995; Weiss and Wodak 2003) begin with the premise that meaning consists of a symbolic economy contested by more or less powerful actors (Baudrillard 1981; Bourdieu 1984). Where individuality is the issue (and in an important sense individuality is the issue), the concern is how individuality is legitimated within the social sphere. Across all "forms of life", to borrow a term from Wittgenstein, the individual is made a locus of value according to how prior discourses are improvised upon and put towards projects of personhood (Foucault 1972).[2]

In this way, Foucault showed how individuals were made subject even as they believed themselves to be free: every instance of self-assertion was seen also as a struggle to "define the situation", to dominate the grounds and assumptions upon which social interaction takes place. Discourse was portrayed as an all-pervasive, autonomous "governmentality" (Foucault 1988) which subverted both hegemonic and resistant agencies through their mutual interdependence upon it (Rose 1996), but this approach was charged with overemphasizing structure and domination at the expense of individual agency (de Certeau 1984: 45–60; see Baudrillard 1996). My research recognizes that just as there is no reason to prioritize an element of grammar over the sentence or statement that utilizes it, "consumption" is always also a form of production. As the term is used here, "consumption" is a metaphor for the agency by which individuals uniquely reconcile and appropriate themselves to economies of social and symbolic resources. The "consumption" that marketers and business people understand – that is, buying, using, or otherwise "making use of" (de Certeau 1984) consumer goods and services – remains very relevant here, since these activities are partially constitutive of the discursive materials that inform and facilitate individuals' practices and identities.

Pierre Bourdieu's sociology perhaps provides the most relevant theoretical point of departure. Whereas most sociologies of the political in the social remain caught in an internal positivist discourse about the "objective structures" of "class" and "strata" (e.g. Zhou 2005), my research borrows from Bourdieu's concept of "habitus", taking seriously his insistence that the structure of society consists in the consumption of discourse (Bourdieu 1984). "A structuring structure" and "a structured structure" (Bourdieu 1992: 53), "habitus" is that largely unconscious element of practice which reduces the transaction costs of interaction and "disposes" actors to cluster with similar actors within and across whatever "field" of cultural engagement occupies them. In particular, "habitus" differentiates actors by the "symbolic boundaries" (Lamont 1992; Lamont and Molnár 2002) they draw through judgments of "taste", "purity" and "worthiness" most broadly construed (Bourdieu 1984: 6; Holt 1997). "Taste classifies", as Bourdieu himself put it, "and it classifies the classifier" (Bourdieu 1984: 6; cf. Holt 1997).

With Bourdieu, my research seeks to disaggregate the "discourse of distinction" (Hanser 2008) as a synchronic system, a snapshot of the present, an approach which remains closer to de Saussure's original structural linguistics metaphor (Sanders 2004) than, say, Foucault, who was primarily concerned to excavate the diachronic evolution of subjectivity (though see also Foucault 1972). Though the historical perspective is the very givenness of discourse (Archer 1995), the analytical value of my research consists in the disaggregation of contemporary discourse, "path dependencies" to the various cultural "-isms" structuring the instantiation of individuality being for another project. The point is doubly important to stress, since when readers recognize elements of traditional Chinese philosophies in my research, they typically exclaim that the findings should have been grounded in "5,000 years of Confucianism", or some such comment, oblivious of the sense in which structure is prior to history (Archer 1996: 97).

A hermeneutic constructivism of "origins" of the disaggregated structures my research finds in Taoism, Confucianism, Buddhism, (Chinese) Christianity and Marxism, etc., would in any case be marred by the proliferation of pop-lit analyses of "Confucian Chinese culture" criticized above. Although "traditional" Chinese philosophy is replete with formulations about cultivating harmonious order between the private self and the public world, the reconciliation of cosmological contradictions in the "unity of opposites", and the pursuit of enlightenment via the "middle way" (Sun 2008), these are relevant to my research only as they arise in fieldwork and analysis. Chinese philosophies could also be relevant to my research insofar as early translations of Confucian, Taoist and Buddhist texts informed the development of dialectical philosophy in nineteenth-century Europe, of course. Indeed, the point still stands that insofar as Chinese individuals are individuals, appreciation of the sense in which the "subjective" and the "objective" interrelate in dynamic practice actually is more salient in China, meaning that "relational" essentialisms of "Chinese" culture are not entirely misguided (cf. Huang 2002).

Acknowledged inconsistencies in Bourdieu's theory, and the associated charge that his talk of "class structures" and so on still gives him over to an objective determinism in the classic Weberian sense (Dunn 2008: 60–65; Jenkins 1992; Schatzki 1996) are taken inspirationally, as a problem of method rather than of theory: the whole point of Post-structuralism is that it is only by showing how culture and its consumption is structured by largely unconscious, supra-individual forces that individuality can then be "found" in the subjective tactics of use, or consumption – of resistance, dispersal, and diffusion, and so on (de Certeau 1984), by individual agents who take those structures and bend them to their will. Any further theoretical stress on individual agency at the expense of structure is to risk succumbing to the market-oriented conception of the self-determining consumer as criticized above (Dunn 2008). Bourdieu allows that consumers can act against the dispositions of their "habitus"; his point is that so much of human practice is unconsciously determined in spite of individual agency, thus making the promises of freedom and universal opportunities of identity-making explicit in the scientific logic supporting consumerism highly dubitable.

Thus, my research joins the small but growing number of researchers who have followed the lead set by French cultural theorist Michel de Certeau (1984) in taking Post-structuralist social science beyond the constraints imposed by the narrowing of vision that Bourdieu and others inherited from their focus on European, North African and American cultures, and hunts down the "habitus" in contemporary China's vibrantly evolving consumer society (cf. Tapp 2010). To reiterate, my research asks not so much "what" the differences between individuals are, but rather how, when, and why differences are drawn. Only when the axioms of this discourse have been abstracted and developed in their "internal" and situationally inflected logics is it then asked how these axioms are "consumed" differently by individuals in objectively different positions in society, as the underlying "grammar" of the instantiation is fleshed out.

All this is to ask only one question: how do individuals manipulate their relationship with the world such that they are successful at negotiating social distinction? Having developed the perspective that allows us to ask this question, we can now turn to address this question in Anshan city, Liaoning Province, China.

To the field: Anshan city

A "rust-belt" city in the heartland of what used to be known as Manchuria, Anshan was a place of little broader significance until the Japanese established a steel mill there in 1918. The full-scale Japanese invasion of 1931 saw Anshan's steel and mining industries become consolidated under a single Japanese monopoly known as Showa Steelworks, which for a while became one of the largest iron and steel production centers in the world. This steelworks was all but destroyed by the Allied Forces' bombing during World War

II, but was rejuvenated following the Communists' 1948 "liberation" of northeastern China as The Anshan Iron and Steel Company. Its name popularly abbreviated to Angang, Anshan's new steelworks were managed directly by the State-owned Assets Supervision and Administration Commission of China's State Council, a situation that afforded local government officials considerable power and influence relative to those in cities of similar size. The city had seen vicious fighting between Mao's Communists and the vanquished Kuomingtang, ensuring its legacy in Maoist folklore.

From the 1949 founding of The People's Republic of China, and 1978, the year China's one-child policy was enforced, Anshan's population swelled rapidly around its State-owned enterprises to around 3 million. Since the vast majority relied entirely on Angang for food, housing and other resources, the mass industrial lay-offs precipitated by the introduction of automated processes and partial privatization throughout the 1990s had cataclysmic effects on the local economy. Workers were offered paltry pension pay-offs or, for those too young to claim their pensions and ineligible for unemployment benefit, a meager stipend while they waited for retirement age, thus earning Anshan a reputation for social depression to complement the one it already had for environmental grime (Giles *et al.* 2006; Hung and Chiu 2003). Waves of social unrest were prompted throughout the region, not least in nearby Liaoyang, where the central government struggled to suppress worker protests at management corruption in 2002 (Lee 2000, 2007). Prompted, too, were huge numbers of both formal and informal entrepreneurial start-ups, a few individuals becoming wildly successful, most much less so, the most prosperous run by well-connected individuals who rented real estate property from Angang and sold services back to it from the premises.

Once an icon of Socialist productivity, Anshan rapidly became a society characterized by vast differentials in personal wealth. While former workers eked out a survival by any means necessary, the newly moneyed corporate and entrepreneurial class began to conspicuously consume luxury cars, foreign holidays, and a labyrinth of hedonistic new entertainment complexes. Faced with a rising contingent of angry "post-proletariat" (Won 2005) ex-workers, the local government had many of Anshan's shabby Soviet-inspired housing compounds leveled from the city center, making way for huge investments in shopping malls and upscale apartments. With the advent of the 2008 Olympics and the 2009 60th anniversary of the Communist Party's rule, in particular, entire swaths of dilapidated houses were demolished to make way for glittering consumer-scapes which now almost entirely eclipse the huge, monolithic frame of the steelworks still lurking in the belly of the city center. The strategy is to mold Anshan into a shopping and tourism centre for the whole region, thus making the systematic "redistribution" of State assets appear democratically accessible.

Today, Anshan's pollution is much more controlled than it once was, and though the city is still very much characterized by the erosion of collective social protection, the widening of social inequalities and the polarization of wealth, it has successfully cultivated a booming private sector and consumer culture.[3] International retailer Carrefour entered the market in 2008; Tesco was then under construction; several large domestic retailers have followed since. A new elevated high-speed railway running from Dalian on the coast to Heilongjiang Province in the far north will soon pass through Anshan's district "West of the Tracks", promising further economic stimulus in an area that still desperately needs it. Anshan's district "East of the Tracks" has always been regarded as more up-market than its Westward counterpart for its beautiful "219" park and lake-side housing; Lishan in the north is similar in social and economic constitution to "West of the Tracks"; the scenic "Thousand Mountains" district features sprawling new developments in commuter-belt housing and leisure outlets which fuel urban consumers' emerging desires to experience the countryside as leisure (Griffiths *et al.* 2010).

In 2010 Anshan's total urban and rural prefectural population was estimated to be approximately 4 million, making Anshan the third largest city in Liaoning Province and the fifth largest in China's northeast by population. The dominant Han ethnic majority is supplemented by around 530,000 indigenous Man, Hui, and North Korean minorities, and an estimated 500,000 unregistered economic migrants from neighboring or distant counties (Anshan City Statistics and Planning Bureau). Material inequalities have been complemented by the (re)emergence of strongly contested cultural distinctions

Figure 1.1 Tracking trains. Photography by Gao Yingchuan

(Griffiths *et al.* 2010): no longer is it sufficient to merely have money and material goods in Anshan; the distinguished person today must be configured from other less tangible forms of value also (cf. Hanser 2008). China is, of course, a diverse market, but Anshan, recently listed by the Economist Intelligence Unit as amongst China's 20 fastest-growing cities (Access China 2010), remains very typical of the sorts of places that social scientists and international marketers most urgently need to understand.

2 Authenticity

The real thing

"Authenticity" is the first of eight discourses my analysis abstracted from the "language" of social distinction. Authenticity is an essentialist discourse of originality pertaining to truth and reality (Pine and Gilmore 2007). As Marxist theorist Walter Benjamin noted in the 1930s, the discourse goes to the very heart of the notion of an authorial self that individuates itself against the world (Benjamin 1968). Authenticity could refer to many things in the China context, from allusions to ancient cultural heritage, depictions of naive industrial fervor in Cultural Revolution propaganda posters, to the well-honed, earthy bodies that characterized the late 1980s "searching for roots" movement in literature and film. However, it is not my concern to address the meanings that authenticity might have for various individual and collective stakeholders in the first instance. Rather, my approach seeks to examine the axiomatic principles of a metaphoric activity immanent at the most originating order of agency's assertion in the social world, drawing out the relevance of these discursive turns to Anshan, and China in due course.

Explicit iterations of the Authenticity discourse proliferate as the common assertion that this or that consumer product is the "real" variant. The separation of "truth" or "reality" from any notion of attributed value is rarely possible in practice, however, and the assertion of a single, universal order – "the authentic", nearly always partisan and situational, serving only to justify claims to authority vis-à-vis alternative and competing valuations (Notar 2006). Consider, for example, that "Johnny", only son of a powerful State-owned enterprise official, says he buys clothes by his favorite brand, Esprit, because "although another person may have an identical product but one that is nonetheless fake, and no one else can tell the difference, I know myself that mine is real and that I am wealthy". Johnny thus posits that his product is the "real" variant, an assertion which, we are to understand, requires no further justification. While it is clear enough that Johnny refers to his purchasing power as a measure of his social distinction, however, it is also clear that because the fake he postulates is identical to his "real" product, and no one else can tell the difference, the notion of authenticity to which he appeals can only affirm a subjective measure of quality that functions to differentiate "less authentic" versions of this standard as inferior, dividing the "real" by degrees.

As the authenticity discourse is actually instantiated, therefore, the discourse pertains less to the difference between the "real" and the "unreal", and the "true" and the "untrue", than to what makes the difference between these concepts – the act of original individuation and its justification. This chapter interrogates the "internal" logic of this discourse, seeking to show that since the formal structures of subjectivity are also the limitations of discourse, the essential ambitions of authenticity cannot be sustained and must necessarily collapse into themselves in their actual assertion.

Free space

Discussion is grown from a dialogue with Gao Xiaofei, a 23-year-old woman from Anshan, where the concentration of dynamics pertaining to the Authenticity discourse is particularly strong:

> Hairdressers look like whores with their blonde hair; they look like poor people who work in massage parlors. They all think that if they've got blonde hair they're not only fashionable, but also different from other people: they think they have a unique individuality. They think make-up and blonde hair is a way to attract men. This is a way to hide their dark side; because they do this kind of work they're always feeling very guilty. Blonde hair shows that they're confident and have nothing to hide; it's like they're living under a mask. They're like a package: they're dirty on the inside but they try to make themselves really clean on the outside. They do exercise, sex, all the time, so they're thin. Like girls who go with "suddenly rich" men, these girls try to keep thin by not eating. Just like the "suddenly rich" girls, these girls will fit the package for their men. These men have no education, so they think blonde hair and strong make-up is attractive.

From the beginning of this excerpt Xiaofei seems especially animated by the way in which these "hairdressers" have dyed their hair "blonde". We might reasonably assume that these "hairdressers" are motivated to emulate Western hairstyles and beauty ideals (cf. Johansson 1998; Schein 1994), but Xiaofei does not make this angle explicit. Xiaofei is rather more concerned with the way in which this form of consumption marks these women as belonging to a particular type that she considers worthy of scorn. In Xiaofei's perception the assumption of blonde hair color reveals these "hairdressers" as morally impure, the bleaching of their naturally black hair allegedly being precisely about "masking" this impurity. Still further, by consuming in this way, these women are supposed to have "packaged" themselves according to a form preordained for them by others, by the "suddenly rich men"; and it is only in this essentially subservient way that these women can be said to be "different from other people" and to "have a unique individuality".

The judgment of authenticity as it is applied here, therefore, seems to consist in the tension between Xiaofei's personal capacity to apprehend the "reality" of these women's motives and social situation, and the state of these women's motives and situation as she perceives it: as impure and unoriginal.

Xiaofei continues in a similar vein:

> It's all about money. Before they were all poor, but now they try to show as much as they can, with digital cameras, DVDs, the latest mobile phone and so forth. This is because deep down in their hearts they don't want other people to think they are poor again. Something they can't change is that their inside is still poor; they can't package their spirit. In a big company, a lady won't dye her hair blonde because if she did it would make her status lower. These people don't want to package their outside; they want to package their spirit, to have good character, to improve themselves in the right way. Look at professionals: they don't make their hair blonde; if it's black it just stays black. Low-class people, like the massage girls, restaurant workers, and hairdressers, dye their hair and get tattoos; they try to look different, unique and cool. Better-class people have education, exercise, eat well and try to be healthy; they study and show respect to others. These others are just focused on the way they look and what other people think of them.
>
> But surely these people with the "spiritual taste" you oppose these others to also care about what other people think of them?
>
> Yes, but everyone in the world cares. These people care but they are confident enough in themselves. They care, but they don't really care: when they're buying clothes, they'll choose what they want.

Xiaofei is adamant here: though these women have the latest digital cameras, DVDs, and so forth, they nevertheless remain poor of "spirit", a purity of "inside" asserted vis-à-vis an "outside" that these women try to "make clean", but in doing so cannot help but emphasize their "dirty insides". That other category of "ladies" and "professionals", on the other hand, those women with whom Xiaofei implicitly identifies herself, are said to improve themselves in entirely different ways: these women won't "package their outsides", they'll "package their spirit", and in doing so, will somehow also escape social pressure. "They do whatever they want", Xiaofei tells us, for themselves: they "care" about what other people think of them, "but they don't really care".

The explanatory power of the (in)authenticity judgment as it is applied here (i.e. "really"), therefore, is supposed to indicate not so much that the negatively judged hairdresser women lack the sufficient degree of individuality that would absolve them of the need to emulate others, but that they *categorically* lack whatever agency validates those actions or statements that people "confident enough in themselves" have. It is not just that Xiaofei has apprehended these women as unoriginal, but that in doing so she has affirmed her personal perspective on the situation as accurate and definitive, and, accordingly, her belonging to a superior order of social existence.

In order to understand how such a categorical assertion can be possible, and then, indeed, how such assertions cannot be sustained, observe that Xiaofei's "hairdressers" would be categorically marginalized by Xiaofei's judgments even if they had not dyed their hair and that Xiaofei's purity of "inside" would presumably not be corrupted even if she were to dye her own hair too. The dying of hair and so on is not the issue: the issue is the way that constructions of an ontological nature are drawn upon to support the categorical legitimization of "authentic" individuality. Prior to any genuinely social sense of exclusivity and discretion in this discourse, indeed, is the observation that Xiaofei's own "inside" cannot admit the slightest invasion, least of all by being assimilated from within. For wherever Xiaofei invokes a purity of "inside" vis-à-vis an "outside", that is to say, a presence, a spatial metaphor, is made to come before a division.

The first metaphor fixes (Douglas and Isherwood 1979: 45); the second isolates (de Certeau 1984: xix). That they should come together, but one apparently "after" the other, means that a temporal metaphor is begged for too, but there is no reason enough to attribute one since the "passage" of time requires more than just an "inside" and an "outside" to it, as we will see below. At once, then, the form of Xiaofei's judgment both implies and derives that which Xiaofei's "hairdressers" allegedly surrender to the "package": essentially, the "inside" is furnished with a "spirit", as Xiaofei puts it, by the Other which actively attributes that value to it, which is to say that agency can only be held to account when it could have done otherwise.

Thus is the reconstruction of the Chinese individual from the wasted rubble of essentialism begun. For it is only by this principle of autonomy that agency can be constructed as a subject of discourse at all. In exactly the same way in which the weight of a lump of ice floating in water is perfectly equivalent to the weight of the water it displaces, individual agency must necessarily displace the Other who recognizes it as an authentically agentive self in discourse. From the very "beginning" (which is still not a temporal metaphor), discourse depends on multiple and distinct agencies.

The problem, of course, is that although Xiaofei's hairdressers are fully "fixed" within discourse despite being judged negatively, not only have they fashioned themselves in the image of a foreign order, but in doing so they also appear to have assumed a kind of existence quite unlike those who live for themselves. At once given by the form of Xiaofei's judgment, they are also constructed as having to consume in a way that reflects the pressure of other, more powerful agencies – "subsumed", as anthropologist Pun Ngai puts it, by the "suddenly rich men" (Pun 2003). Indeed, it is exactly as if any agency these hairdressers have is given to them only by the form of Xiaofei's judgment, while her own agency remains somehow independent of those she judges – fixed for herself by herself. Yet, although it is clear enough that Xiaofei fixes these women as impure of "inside", it is not entirely clear exactly where she fixes them: they seem to be located somewhere between where they themselves want to be, and where those who judge them want them to be; not powerful, but not powerless either.

The key to the conundrum, perhaps, lies in the observation that whereas the hairdressers are judged to have an immutable impurity of "inside" – a dirtiness and poverty of "spirit" that cannot possibly be cleaned and enriched, those others with whom Xiaofei implicitly identifies herself are actually supposed to "package their spirit", as she puts it, to "improve themselves in the right way", thus somehow enduring whilst also changing. That is, not so much simply to say that mutability guarantees a more privileged form of agency than immutability would, but that the purity of "inside" itself is neither fixed nor isolated. Indeed, this may be why each of Xiaofei's judgments seem compelled to provoke and spill over into the next, ranging richly across different forms of condemnation without ever quite arriving at a place. It is almost as if the categorical form of Xiaofei's judgment entails that the hairdressers resist her denigrations even as they are drawn. As if, that is to say, the process of fixing is more important in the definition of authenticity than the simply "fixed" nature the assertion seeks to affect.

Solid sight

With this, individual agency's initial, though somewhat slippery, "placing" within discourse, the social and political dynamics by which this discursive "free space" is generated solidify in an explicitly "three-dimensional", though still not yet temporal fashion, as metaphors of presence further displace the Other, making the self, as it were, "more real" (Lacan 1977).[1] Consider that, in the excerpt above, even Xiaofei's hairdressers have what we might call a density of substance "deep down in their hearts", where they are somehow more real than at their "outsides". Social actors are, of course, everywhere judged for lacking this "depth", when it is judged that there is something about them not authentically present in discourse (Bourdieu 1984).

Seven of my Anshan informants used relevant variations of "emptiness" to position themselves against others in conversation with me; their judgments are synthesized into a single expression here, illustrating: one, the similarities in the way this metaphor is used across cases; two, how these metaphors tend to cluster with further metaphors foundational to the Authenticity discourse (see also below); and three, how it is precisely through these metaphors that the Authenticity discourse overlaps with the discourses introduced in the later chapters of this analysis:

> They follow the tide; they read the biographies of famous people and other dry and empty literature. They only pay attention to their external appearance and their inner being is empty. In their leisure time they often drink booze and indulge in loud and empty talk with their friends. Most have no point of view of their own; they drift with the tide. Their

innermost being is empty; they do not strive to move forward. They don't strive to make progress; they slavishly imitate and parrot others' words. Their bodies may be covered in famous brands but their behavior is vulgar; they may be heavily bedecked in jewels, but their heads are empty.

Of "emptiness" metaphors such as these, the case of an informant who found something distasteful about people "just going through the motions" best evinces that individuals are often judged negatively because it is unclear whether substance can genuinely be ascribed to them or not. It is in this that the authenticity judgment's utility consists, for we can never know for sure if agency can be faked. Certainly we cannot be certain on the basis of any observation, for agency, again, must always be assumed within discourse, the question of "reality" per se always secondary to this premise.

Beyond "space", then, the prevalence of visual metaphors in the data was remarkable. Some 24 of the 142 informants who provided me with written definitions of how "tastefulness" (*pinwei*) was opposed to "distastefulness" (*meiyou pinwei*) explicitly used "blindness" (*mangmu*) in their constructions, some using the metaphor repeatedly.[2] In the longer excerpt with Xiaofei above, "blonde" hair was supposed to "mask" the alleged immorality of the hairdressing profession (Hyde 2001). The overlap with "blindness" hardly need be spelled out: "masking" implies a secretive, deceptive and untrustworthy existence, whereas "blind" people are absolved of much of the responsibility for being "inauthentic" since they lack the intentional perspective that would grant them the right to "include" from an autonomous "place" all manner of things, "panoptically" (all quotes de Certeau 1984: 36 referring, of course, to Foucault). Insofar as all order is imposed on the world by making your own judgments, that is to say, "sight" is a necessary condition of making a legible "site" of agency's uncertainty in the "first place", so that agency is "seen" in discourse before it "sees" itself there too.

However, although the assumption of a plurality of "seeing sites" appears to be the necessary condition of discourse, those "readers" of discourse who are going to legitimately "write" discourse may not wish to be so transparently "placed". Indeed, though "masking" is usually an attempt to be inconspicuous, to "fit in" as it were, "masking" is clearly a useful form of consumption where it works. Consider Zhang Jiali, for example, rural migrant at Anshan's Lamb Buddha hotpot restaurant. Zhang says that "hypocrisy" (*xuwei*) is one of two words to define China right now. Hypocrisy, he explicates, "is what people speak: they can't speak what they really think". Zhang attributes this to the political order, which he illustrates for me by placing his fists one under the other descending and broadening outwards from a point at the top of a hierarchy: Zhang is unwilling to criticize the government on tape, a reminder that authenticity is a discourse operated not only through emulation, but also through dialectical processes of resistance, and often in the most covert sense of the word (Hanser 2008: 145). Indeed, and quite to the point, though the definition of "the authentic" in China is presided over by the Communist

Party's permanent veto on alternatives, all other "seeing sites" being subsumed under its own, the State's efforts to suppress discourse are only partially successful, and this, despite the fact that Zhang says the other word to describe China right now, is *nuoruo*, meaning "cowardly" or "weak".

Other players in the market of meaning may of course brazenly encourage consumers to become themselves the arbiter of authenticity, even as these rights are nonetheless sold to them at a premium. Clothing retailer "Jeans West", for example, exhorts its consumers, "Be yourself again; really it's better" (*zuohui ziji, zhende geng jingcai*), even as their billboard advertisements feature laughing, white-skinned Western models, which can hardly be encouraging Chinese consumers to be themselves again. When we learn that "Jeans West" was once an Australian-owned firm, now recently taken over by its Chinese supplier, however, this only serves to highlight the almost endlessly ironic form of the authenticity discourse. Indeed, the fact that "Jeans West" is Chinese might in the context of Chinese emulation of Western beauty ideals go some way towards explaining the ambiguity in the advertising proposition (Johansson 1998; Schein 1994)! Authenticity is thus shown to be less a thing-in-itself than an inherently unstable process worked out between multiple and distinct agents, and as such, our analysis demands that the temporal dimension be given explicit attention.

Time's beginning

So far, individual agency is configured as a "three-dimensional seeing site" that can "see" the objects and other such agencies from which it is forever removed, that is, removed by discourse, not from discourse, but that cannot yet "see" itself and that cannot yet "see" in time. By way of addressing this problem, observe that negative judgments employing metaphors of presence, substance, vision and so on, often clustered with liquid metaphors to make constructions such as "blindly flowing with the tide" (see also above). In other such judgments, the liquid metaphor signified the collapse of categorical boundaries, as in the "inundation" (Lee 1996; Lee 2007) implied in exclamations like "The floodgates open!", or "They're everywhere!", the meeting of different classificatory systems often yielding judgments of this form (Ardener 1989; Chapman 1992).

In China's post-reform era, the terms "floating population" (*liudong renkou*) and "blind floater" (*mangliu*) have become thoroughly instituted amongst official and urban middle classes to describe the "flow" of an internally migrant rural population migrating to China's cities in search of work. The latter term perverts an earlier term *liumang* (hooligan) usually reserved for all manner of persons who similarly don't belong, from wayward criminal types to homosexuals and so forth (Chen 1998; Barmé 1999: 62–98; Gamble 2003). Indeed, Xiaofei's judgments about "hairdressers" (above) are probably motivated by the material successes of such "outsider" peoples in the city.

In some situations, "flow" is a highly positive concept in China; many traditional art forms, from *taiji* to calligraphy, follow from the cultivation of unobstructed flow. However, in the context of urbanizing contemporary China, this particular form of migratory "flow" (*liu*) is to be contrasted with the groundedness and rootedness of *tu* – the character for "soil" or "native" which is variously applied to signify "crude", "coarse", "unrefined", "rustic", "local", and so on, the root meaning of which is, of course, "root" – that which is fixed and categorically does not flow around (Hanser 2008: 15). Although we will think of time "flowing" past a "fixed" point, the contrast of liquid metaphors with the tu principle does not in itself explain how agency is constructed as a temporal self.

For this, consider that in an interview with the shopkeeper of Anshan's "Local Products Shop", a question is raised about the justification for the premium pricing of packaged pancakes (*jianbing*), which are virtually identical in substance to those widely sold around the city by farmers who venture into urban markets to sell their wares from the back of hand-pushed oven-carts. The "Local Products Shop" shopkeeper immediately leaps in to state in her in defense: "The workmanship is not the same!" The shopkeeper's friend then interrupts suddenly, as if he has the authority to do so, saying, "Can you compare in terms of hygiene (*weisheng*)? Incomparable! And moreover, you must think of the source of the product". At this, the shopkeeper comes back in right away to dispel any doubt, "You've also got to think of the prestige aspects of the product: we're an honorable, decent, authentic (*zhengjing*) company. As soon as someone discovers a problem, we're here to be found; but the cart-pusher … ", thus leaving no doubt that these products, this shop, and the people who work here are authentic because they are properly located, and therefore accountable, whereas the cart-pusher is not only constructed as generally inferior, but also quite possibly a dodgy guy, given to tricks and cons.

Just as with the case of copying, then, the crucial element in the authenticity judgment here is originality. In this case, the question is of the "source", since the trustworthiness and sincerity of both the product and its traders consists in the verifiable attachment to a physical place of provenance. It is here, in the distance evoked by this first recursive allusion "back" to the "place" of its initial assertion, that the temporal dimension of "Self" is configured, the first three dimensions being configured "before" temporality, and agency only hereafter perceiving of itself as the forward-facing and still spatial present, past which time is supposed to "flow". In discourse, that is to say, time's passage is subject to agency before agency is subject to time's passage.

The irony arising from the above example, of course, is that in another context the cart-pusher would be constructed as *tu*. Here, though, out of place in the city, he is constructed as *liu*. Doubly ironic is that the "origin" that validates the "Local Products Shop" and its products is in fact the same countryside place from which the cart-pusher emanates. How strange, indeed, that mass-produced pancakes in the "Local Products Shop" can be thought of as more authentic than those hand-made pancakes sold in the region for centuries!

Truth and reality, we might wager, are defined by reference to temporal priority. This would explain why earlier "versions" are often privileged at the expense of later versions where authenticity is in question, and why the primordial "truth" of nature is commonly asserted as authentic in contrast to man-made products.

Consider, however, that cosmetics multinational L'Oréal heavily promote their new product *True Match* in China, a foundation that aspires to blend identically to the skin color of the product user, thus creating a "mask" that integrates perfectly with itself: "Natural can be better", claims the advertisement, a ploy that could not possibly be any more brazen in its stealthy attempt to seduce. In this case, of course, it is the later "mask" that is valued over the natural and original, even though the latter aspires to assimilate the former exactly, but it is not clear when exactly the "inauthentic" order can be said to have successfully taken over and become "the authentic", or what can then be said of the reality status of the initial order as a result. Is the original order "the real", or is "the real" obliterated by its simulation so that there is now a "copy" without an original (Baudrillard 1994)? It seems self-evident that the later order should somehow be more real, but there is only the temporal dimension to refer to in support of this intuition; or rather, that is to say, there is only subjective ascription of value to the temporal dimension in order to justify our priorities.

Of similar relevance here, were comments made elsewhere by Gao Xiaofei (see above) about the value of "naked dress" (*luozhuang*), a form of consumption that involves wearing make-up without appearing that you are doing so. Xiaofei explained "naked dress" to me by recourse to the "substance" metaphoric and that mysterious purity of "inside" once again: "Some people wear make-up but look like an empty shelf; they make themselves up but there is nothing in their insides. Other women wear very little make-up but have the look of the girl next door, a close feeling." Xiaofei thus attests to a purity of prior presence that would be spoilt by any form of affectation, itself defined by reference to notions of pristine virginity as opposed to the refined and contrived. Note here, however, that the "nature" to which Xiaofei alludes is but a supra-naturally natural nature undemocratically given in its distribution: she herself monopolizes the attribution of value to the concept, and the postulation itself only serves to disguise the fact that the distinction she operates is the result of a cultivated disposition to apply make-up in a particular way – precisely what it pertains not to be.

Keep it real

The social value invested in authenticity, indeed, may be just as much about the belief that value accumulates over time as it is about "location" on a chronological axis or a "point" of origin per se; that is, where distinguished "space" is defined first by a reference to "time", a reversal of the discursive priorities outlined above. Consider that when I casually remarked to a student named Sui that I liked the hole at the knee of her jeans, Sui vigorously asserted that she had not created the hole herself: the hole was worn, not torn; she had made no extra effort to appear this way. Indeed, Sui was probably also saying that she didn't have these jeans because she was fashionable, but because she was frugal, where authenticity is defined in opposition to materialism, a distancing from the "facile" distinction to be achieved through consumerism, and an identification with the authenticity earned through persistence, struggle and endurance – a "Long March" form of distinction, say.[3] In this particular case, however, the fact that only one leg of Sui's jeans had such a hole meant that her "truth claim" remained somewhat in doubt, which just goes again to show that (in)authenticity is always as yet still being generated in multiple layers of assertion and interpretation.

This latter form of the Authenticity discourse, where purity is refined with extension over time, may be particularly relevant to the Chinese, who especially like to assert that "their" culture has been passed down to them, miraculously undisturbed across turbulent millennia – therefore retaining its purity – from the originating figure of the mythical Yellow Emperor, to unite present day "Chinese people" (*huaren*) everywhere (Duara 2004; Tu 1994). Invocations of a plurality of people joined by a purity of blood play have a particular salience in everyday Chinese discourse; essentially, such invocations function to maintain a rigid sense of both "internal" belonging and difference vis-à-vis "foreigners" (Pye 1993). Let us observe here, however, that this form of "consanguineous nationalism" (Fei *et al.* 1992: 120–27) evidently joins some Chinese in closer unity with the "source" of original purity than others. This need not be an argument about the dominant Han Chinese ethnic group's chauvinism vis-à-vis the nation's many ethnic minorities or the relative "Chineseness" of overseas Chinese.

Consider Yuan Liwen, for example, a well-educated and high-achieving journalist in her mid-thirties, who is enormously attached to her ancestors, she says. Yuan likes to go to the Jiangsu and Zhejiang area (*jiangnan yidai*) whenever she can, not for relatively inconsequential reasons such as sightseeing or shopping, of course – "not me", I am to understand, but because it is her "hometown". Yuan thus professes to be especially motivated by *xiangqing* – literally, the feeling or emotion of the hometown, familial source or ancestral origin:

> Especially where people are already a few generations away from their native land (*gutu*), they really like to go. They are sentimentally attached to the old hometown even if they've already left a really long time ago. China has an old saying that we are "derived from the same source" (*yimai xiangcheng*). This *mai* means blood vessels, the blood of one's ancestors. Foreigners emphasize genes, but Chinese people emphasize the origin of one's blood. In my bones I am a Yangtze River Delta person. The blood vessels of people from that place have been passed on to me.

Liwen makes these assertions in the context of trying to impress upon me that she comes from the ancient crucible of Chinese civilization, the Yangtze River Delta. She repeats several times that her father originates from Shanghai, but keeps resolutely quiet about her mother coming from Guizhou, a considerably more "backward" province in the popular imagination:

> From ancient times until today it, the Yangtze River Delta has been a place of trade and culture. There has been trade there since ancient times, and its culture, its land boundaries, and atmosphere are all really thick, including that place that many Europeans now admire: Wenzhou. My ancestors were all in this Zhejiang area.

Liwen has lived in Anshan all her life, but sees herself as essentially "not from around here". Rather she claims to be steeped in, and thus herself an extension of, the civilized traditions of a far-distant past. Explicitly, the longer the attachment, the more she is cultivated, and the greater the transcendence of the present is implied. Indeed, Liwen is clear that the value of the attachment only increases with longer separation: "Especially where people are already a few generations away from their native land, they really like to go. They are sentimentally attached to the old hometown even if they've already left a really long time ago." At once both attached and separated, therefore, the appeal to a "natural" attachment ("blood" and so on) only serves to mask the fact that Liwen's distinction is not at all as innate as it pertains to be. Though in another context there may equally be distinction in the process of refinement itself, here Liwen is of the origin – not only formed, but form itself.

Earth's end

To be cultivated or cultured of course takes time, and is thus a kind of "fixing" quite the opposite of *tu*, the spatial metaphor which we may repeat here means "soil", "local", "native", and so on. Yet despite the negative connotations of "backwardness" with which *tu* is associated in China's contemporary urbanizing era, *tu* can also be a positive notion, close to the sense of essential "Chineseness" that Chinese people like to think they share across space and over time. *Tu* is the soil in which grows the root that sites Chinese individuals in much the same way as the "blood" of the Yellow Emperor does (his throne of course being symbolic of a similarly fixed and eternal nodal point in the cosmological order), by connecting them to that fertile, life-giving "source" from which agency itself springs forth (Fei *et al.* 1992; Khu 2001; Tu 1994). It is no accident, indeed, that this *tu* is the same metaphor used for the "Local" of the "Local Products Shop": the same intransigent and eternal order is invoked – that which can never "flow" since from it all things flow. As we have seen, however, the spatial metaphor by which an entity is fixed within discourse necessarily implies a metaphor of isolation too, invocations of an order from which all things flow serving only to recognize some flowing things.

Accordingly, *tu* has another opposite too (i.e. in addition to the *liu* that means "flow"), namely *yang*, meaning "foreign" or "overseas" in a way that has a decidedly Western flavor in its usage (Pye 1993). Used less often than the *wai* used for "foreigners" (*waiguoren*), *yang* reinforces the grounding and exclusivity of *tu* by constructing its "outside". Thus, we might also think of the opposition of *wai*, meaning "outside", with *zhong*, for "center", as in the Chinese word for "China" (*zhongguo*), where China becomes the "center" in a way approximate to the consanguinity of *tu*, making for an inward-looking "seeing site" quite appropriate for our purposes here. Although a concept that apparently fixes the singularity of virtue in a central and centering fashion, *tu* also expresses a peripheral concept, the realm of the provincial and rural in its contemporary usage, so that the term necessitates a tension between the "center" and the "outside" in an interesting and ambiguous way (Pye 1993; Tu 1994).

The same expression, *tu*, applies in a further relevant way too, used to disdain categorical anomaly, such as where clothes or styles are indelicately matched, or where otherwise inappropriately conspicuous or gaudy consumption is exhibited – in a not dissimilar way to the collapse of categorical boundaries described in the "floodgates open" metaphor above (cf. Douglas 1966). It is not clear, for example, what kind of distinction our neighbor thinks his doorbell reaps every time it plays a loud and whining version of Beethoven's *Für Elise*, but this is judged *tu* because of the clash between the "class" imbibed in the classic work and its pitifully "crass" digitization, *tu* applying because of the breach of boundaries defined by the judging power. There is also the term *shanzhai*, which corresponds to the English term "kitsch" in the sense of a false, tawdry replica of the real; the term is most appropriately applied to China's counterfeit markets and the "bandit" operators who sustain them (Tse *et al.* 2009). The difference between *tu* and *shanzhai* is one of perspective: to recognize something as *shanzhai* implies an ironic, almost postmodern perspective quite the opposite of *tu*.

A look at the Traditional Chinese Medicine system confirms *tu* as a metaphor for "grounding" and "centering" functions (Farquhar 2002; Pritchford 1993), but here we would also have to acknowledge that "grounding" and "centering" are dynamic rather than static functions, operated through self-improvement practices known as *neigong*. *Neigong* translates as "internal work", but might perhaps be better understood (in Hegelian or Sartrean terms) as the "internalization of externality", one part of a metaphor for the relational nature of human practice; one part, that is, because anything that stands in for the same essential relation must be completed by its auxiliary. *Neigong*, accordingly, has a "dispersing" as well as a "centering" energy-function – the "externalization of internality" that has been referred to as "displacement" here (above). When seen in the light of its temporal as well as spatial dimensions, therefore, the authenticity discourse is revealed as characterized by an indeterminate ambiguity in itself. *Tu* is a metaphor for a site that signifies both the "inside" and the "outside" of discourse, intersecting the temporal with the timeless, and at once (cf. Bourdieu's "habitus").

Authenticity cannot be the grounded, pinned-down, ontologically exclusive concept that constructions of it aspire to be, but is rather defined in the interrelation between the logical possibility of the concept that the assertion evokes and the necessary element of uncertainty to its practical identification. Somewhere between the determinate "fixing" of the "root" and the indeterminate "flowing" of the "blood", constructions of authenticity depend on the echo of their Other.

True lies

The inherent instability in the definition of authenticity runs very close to the surface of everyday life in contemporary China, and the Chinese might be particularly disposed to "uncover the mask" (Brandstädter 2009: 4) in the marketplace of meaning. The constant fear of being cheated meant that consumers could be observed to carry their own scales to market as late as the late 1990s (Veeck 2000) and purchase receipts are still checked religiously for "errors" today. Advertising is viewed with suspicion, too, since many firms, particularly in the early days of reform, hugely exaggerated their claims (Chan and McNeal 2002); and stories about poisonous "bottled" (tap) water, counterfeit medicines and toxic cosmetics abound (Tse *et al.* 2009). In Anshan's "The Underground" (*dixiajie*) shopping precinct, counterfeit wristwatches and training shoes are passed off as authentic, and logos from international brands "translate" into areas entirely unrelated to the original product category. Indeed, even the name of this shopping precinct was probably "poached" (de Certeau 1984) from another of identical name and character, in Haerbin, Heilongjiang Province, studied by Amy Hanser (2008).[4]

This extreme malleability of "truth" cannot be acknowledged in China's official State discourse, but government leaders are probably much more concerned to address the popular perception that they foster this sense of "rootlessness" (Hook 1996: 8) with their omnipresent oversight of conceptual categories than they are with international demands for intellectual property rights protection. Certainly the perception of a singular, dominating order from which the vast majority of individuals are excluded is probably what implicates so many Chinese in these tactics (Pye 1996: 32–33): when "lip-synching" was banned in response to the outrage caused by the revelation that Lin Miaoke, the girl who sang during the opening ceremony of the Beijing Olympics, was in fact miming over a song recorded by another girl judged "not pretty enough" to perform for herself, the new law was justified as being "in the national interest" (Eimer 2008).

Indubitably, whether it be a beggar popularly famed for ploys and ruses (Dutton 1998), or the cunning entrepreneur "eight sides all wide and slippery" (Ambler and Witzel 2000: 93), many Chinese are positively tricky operators, stealth, deception, and even outright cheating (*pian*) being recognized as entirely legitimate insofar as they are necessary parts of outwitting others (Wong 2009): though the airwaves are full of tales of Socialist moral heroism, seizing the moment is what really gets you credit (Blackman 2000). Even where Chinese consumers have been encouraged to exercise their newly sanctioned consumer rights by taking traders to task over "inauthentic" goods and services, savvy individuals have demonstrated a remarkable ability to buy up all the stocks they know to be counterfeit and claim back the compensation that given stores must repay at a multiple of the sale price (Brandstädter 2009).

Arrival at this point in the analysis therefore warrants a more explicit examination of "legitimate inauthenticity", for it is easy to see that "inauthentic" actions can even be explicitly "good" where they work. There is, of course, the strategy referred to as "calling someone's bluff", or the "white lie", known as the "kind lie" (*shanyi de huangyan*) in China, where the lesser evil of speaking an untruth reduces the transaction costs of social interaction in some way. "Face" (*mianzi*), the Chinese concept of social esteem (Hwang 1987), likewise often turns on the issue of authenticity, as individuals present "versions" of themselves in accordance with the demands of the situation. Indeed, as field researcher I would often play the role of the "dumb foreigner", feigning failure to understand what was being said, or more often in fact signaling that I did understand just to keep up rapport with my informants. Indeed, it was not even necessarily a problem even if informants saw that this was what I was doing, because individual agents exploit "inauthentic" strategies for action all the time, the difference between legitimacy and illegitimacy being nothing more than the question of whether the action has been worth it.

Once this has been realized, it is not even beyond this analysis to see that two different versions of authenticity may be explicitly traded upon at the same time. However, there, as elsewhere, we will be unable to escape the fact that certain people will have more power to effect their manipulations than others.

The hyper-rural

Further consider, here, the "Local Products Shop", which profits by drawing upon constructions of the countryside as a place of purity and moral fiber in a way that invokes the same "originality" that the *tu* principle (above) does. In conversation with the shopkeeper, for example, we are told, "When seen from the perspective of science, local products are original (*yuanshi*) and have not suffered pollution" (*mei shouguo wuran*), that is, where "original" is as opposed to "refined" and shares semantic proximity with "pristine" and "untouched". Mentions are made of pure wild ginseng, "not like the transplanted stuff", and the shopkeeper waxes lyrical about "rough cloth and candles from places where the wind of reform has never blown". At the same time, she openly speaks her mind to my assistant, and in front of my assistant's mother too, on issues of intra-family relations, which strikes me as a kind of over-familiarity, and she answers all my questions about her business operations by reference to personal stories inflected with local references and a rural register of intimacy – "Why, only the other day I said to Little

Gao ... ", where Little Gao is not at all known to us. The shopkeeper thus gives the impression that she is as plain and simple as the products she sells.

When it is asserted that much of this particular kind of grape juice on the market at the moment is "fake" (*jia*), however, the uncertainty of authenticity leaps immediately back into play and the shopkeeper jumps to defend her shop by comparing her local product *Five Woman Mountain* wine with national domestic brand *Changyu*. Asked if a bottle of *Five Woman Mountain* is more or less expensive than *Changyu*, she replies that her product is "not expensive" (not a direct answer), "only twenty-something kuai" (being vague and playing down the price), before finally saying that she "can't speak for the whole country but the *Changyu* in Liaoning Province is not good" (recognizing that she has to qualify her claims slightly or risk being unconvincing). The shopkeeper thus evinces a highly tactical disposition, cultivated no doubt as the result of a life operating in the margins of social categories defined largely by others. Since she is herself so anomalously *tu* in this urban middle-class retail context and profits precisely by traversing and reconfiguring the symbolic categories that legitimize this over her own rural roots, her occupation is somewhat treacherous indeed. However, in a world of urbanizing steel and glass, this strategy works for her: her honesty, warmth and naïveté, if not entirely feigned, are skillfully affected to sell product.

Indeed, and still further, the "Local Products Shop" of course trades on another, alternative version of authenticity: a new or modern "real" of mass production and product packaging; an authenticity that "admits" that the natural and original real is "best", but that asserts that this can be enhanced in its essence through scientific testing, measurement, branding and so on. The only difference between the pancakes sold here and those sold by the lowly "cart-pusher" (see above), indeed, is that these are branded with the name "Intellectual youth pancake" (*zhiqing jianbing*), a ploy that explicitly harks back to the Cultural Revolution era when educated urban youths were "sent down" to the countryside to "purify" themselves through labor in the fields. Again, the shopkeeper's friend uses the term *zhengjing* (which can mean honorable, decent and/or authentic) to describe the source of production and packaging of these products, quite as if the quality of the packaging and the shopkeeper's own moral steadfastness perfectly justify each other. Literally, he says: "Real factory: real packaging" (*zhengjing changjia: zhengjing baozhuang*). No further or external validation is required, we are to understand: the product must be authentic because the packaging says so.

More explicit, less underhand, and altogether more strategic in his pitch, the shopkeeper's friend then raves at great length about how contemporary multinational Amway was founded on the basis of Traditional Chinese Medicine, intending that we understand that this shop's products are of the same order as Amway's: "Scientific deliberation will always be superior to crude methods. The Chinese method of just grabbing a handful of this and a handful of that, charging two kuai for this, charging three kuai for that, cannot possibly stand up to scientific development." He is immediately suspected of being a promoter of Amway products. "No", he says, "but I study marketing management", thus making it clear that he and the shopkeeper work a double act so that authenticity obtains in their shop because of their mutual investment in signifying that it does so. Indeed, to the extent that their packaging claims authenticity from within these overlapping discourses, their product legitimates itself!

Coarse grain

Further consider, now, on this same theme, that while this research was underway, a range of up-market restaurants were established in Anshan's central commercial district offering explicitly *tu* produce with explicitly *tu* marketing themes. Perhaps the most interesting of these is called "Modern Coarse Grain" (*xiandai culiang*), which was opened in October 2006 to join three other restaurants around the city with "coarse grain" names. This terminology invokes the opposition between "coarse grain" cereals and "fine grain" cereals, the former of which was all that common people ate before the economic reforms, when the "fine grains" were rare. After the reforms, "fine grains" became much more readily available, and "coarse grains" quickly went out of use in urban circles: "fine grains" were seen to be refined, in both physical and moral senses, while the "coarse grains" remained the food of poor farmers. Today, this discourse is inverting in what is not so much a return to "coarse grain" as a turning over of the values imbued in "coarse", as consumers assert themselves in new ways (Griffiths *et al.* 2010).

"More and more people are seeking coarse grain consumption", says the manager of Modern Coarse Grain, "because urban people are already used to fine grains of the city and want to change to peasant tastes". "Modern people already have high tastes", she continued, where "coarse grain" consumption was explicitly understood as a "modern", "high" taste. Indeed, when several seafood and vegetable dishes that didn't obviously seem to fit the theme were described as "high-level" (*gaodeng*) dishes suitable for the wants of "modern people", one of the chefs explained that it was precisely this eclectic range of healthy "green food" dishes (*lüse shipin*) under the overarching banner of "coarse grain" that distinguishes "modern" coarse grain from plain, old, ordinary coarse grain. Every one of the well-to-do consumers described their consumption in terms such as "pollution-free", "chemical-free", "healthy", "natural", and "pure", some also referring to a "return to the simple and plain" (*fanpu guizhen*) and a "return to nature" (*huigui ziran*), thus explicitly evoking a mythical source of purity. The implication, of course, was that these dishes were enhanced versions of the "original" coarse grain foods still consumed in the countryside, somehow retaining this essence whilst being purified of everything that makes them "coarse". All this, despite the fact that the serving staff refer to the cuisine as "rural food" or "rural family food" (*nongjiacai*).

China's institutionalized urban/rural divide notwithstanding, some of China's savviest farmers are cashing in on the inherent malleability of authenticity discourse too. Farmers living in the "Thousand Mountains" (*Qianshan*) scenic area to Anshan's east have transfigured their rough and ready peasant homes to cater to urban consumers in numbers unprecedented who have begun to explore the countryside in their newly purchased cars. While much of China's massive rural population is still struggling to establish itself in the cities, the irony that cash-strapped farmers in the urban periphery should be able to market themselves as farmers, and profit from prostituting their "authenticity" to cash-laden urbanites seeking home-cooked food in countryside settings is sweet indeed. Some have become rich beyond their wildest dreams without having to alter their homes from their original forms, save for the presence of signs reading "rural accommodation", "rural snack food", "farmer family farmhouse food", or "farmhouse courtyard food" – signs that transfigure the rural experience into an object to be consumed. Proprietors are only too well aware that the "authentic" rural experience is precisely what urban consumers are seeking, and present exactly the same cooking pans, smoke-filled kitchens, and "fire-beds" (where guests will warm themselves alongside the resident family in the winter) as their neighbors, features which differentiate their offering from throbbing out-of-town karaoke investments that pass as *nongjiale* ("happy farmer"), with their distinctly urban trappings and undercurrent of moral licentiousness.

Still other establishments, however, and one feels that it must be these establishments that the other, more "down-market" outlets are imitating, have revolutionized the peasant home, magnifying and concentrating the essence of rural life, bottling it, as it were, until it becomes almost unreal, or rather "more real" than the original. These homes present tidy wicker shop fronts, fairy-lit signs reading "rural food", and clean picnic tables lit by lucky red lanterns. Some have purpose-built accommodation facilities so that guests can spend a night under the starry sky. Even here, though, in these somewhat "less authentic" homes, the experience offered remains distinctly rural, and providers are acutely aware that moderate exposure to insects, dirt, and animal smells is exactly what consumers are looking for. One such host had it thus:

> This place is really straightforward, just like home. The city is formal, but out here you can do as you please. In the city you have to sit like this. But here it's relaxing. In the city you can't relax when eating, you have to "behave". Here, waitresses don't follow the customers; in the city, they wait and serve, making people feel uncomfortable. Here, they won't even come over to you if you don't ask. In the city you need to listen to the staff, but here you can sit whenever you want. This gives you a "home-feeling", relaxed; you can do whatever you like, not like in the city.

The host went on:

> Even the five-star professional chefs in the city can't cook the real rural food that we cook; they may add luxury sauces, but we get real chickens

from the hillside. We fry caterpillars out here, and little fairy insects that no-one in the city has ever even heard of. Goose, duck, chicken, pigeon, fish, natural, natural: all the animals that fly in the sky and all the animals that swim in the river, we have them all here to eat. The pork in the city can't even compare to the pork here. Here a pig grows naturally for one to two years; in the city it only grows for one to two months and is fed by chemicals. We only use in-season vegetables; we never buy artificially raised food from the greenhouse. So they're no competition; you can't even talk about us competing with them.

What is the fundamental feeling offered by the places like this?

It gives the urban people the feeling of being "sent down" in '66 [the Cultural Revolution].

Who comes here to eat?

City people mostly, with cars. They come from Shenyang too. Students from Anshan Science and Technology University too, in big parties. The customers are not necessarily rich since a table is only 1–200 kuai [i.e. Chinese yuan renminbi, or CNY], but with spare time and money. They are the leisure class.

Authenticity here, as it is understood by "real" farmers, is packaged and made available for middle-class consumers in a way that reinvents China's revolutionary rural past in a way that somehow intensifies the essence of the "original" even as the poverty, disease, and political violence is filtered out. Yet, by instituting this "copy" as the "real" in its contemporary invocation, the original is made unreal, forever lost, not only to time and to memory, but in its ontology, as the shared "root" that makes the Chinese still *tu* entirely Othered (Baudrillard 1994; Eco 1986). That is to say, the bodily integration of "authentic" countryside produce is a metaphor for the way in which contemporary urban consumers possessed of "modern" symbolic dispositions institute themselves as the real (Campbell 1987). These dynamics are therefore quite different from the way in which nostalgic interpretations of the Cultural Revolution were re-enacted in the first themed restaurants in the early 1990s (Hubbert 2005). Quite remarkable because of its concurrence with the largest and fastest urbanization in history, consuming the hyper-rural offers a way for those individuals so disposed to tap the quintessential root of their worldly beginnings, to taste their raw and earthy flavor in refined form (Griffiths 2009). However, once the recurring, amniotic memory of that first primordial reflection has been traced, the umbilical cord may then be cut again as these "Romantic" new middle classes drive away in their Mercedes (Tapp 2008, 2010).[5]

Return to the source

So! The race is on to be the first to rupture nature's hymen; the first to drive a stake into the utterly pure and unspoilt and make it subject, instituting "self" at the interface of all contradictions; the first, no less, to puncture the "original" divide between discourse and the "Real" (Lacan 1977); the first to "return to the self" (*huigui ziwo*) as a "self-determining" (*duli zizhu*), "self-controlling" (*ziwo kongzhi*) individual (all quotes Festa 2006: 11). The first, that is, because this boundary is always being pushed back: once "born" into discourse (in Lacan's terms) there can be no return to one's psychoanalytical origins and no escape from the desire for authenticity. The hyper-rural may invite those so disposed to take temporary refuge from the pace of contemporary signification in the placental "soil" and "blood" from which they were originally birthed, but out past the karaoke bars that usually pass for "happy farmer" (*nongjiale*) outlets and up into the "Thousand Mountains" range, there is no place and no when for "self" to arrive at, because "self" did not come from anywhere identifiable in the first place!

Authenticity is a socially constructed ideal. The postulation of "the authentic" aspires to various exclusive forms of located purity – certainty, origin, coherence, quintessence, and so on, but this only ever remains an ideal by definition. The postulation, indeed, can only ever conjure the question of what it aims to express: that which can never be adequately expressed; the very idea of that "self" which has no origin, and which could not possibly be located in or by anything else because it is "being-founded-upon-itself" (Baudrillard 1996: 79). This ideal cannot be sustained because a sign cannot be found that does not but only metaphorically refer to that which cannot be spoken of. However, the idea invoked by this sign (i.e. "authenticity"), though the invocation cannot ever effectively represent or express the idea, is actually necessary to discourse. Not in itself, of course, but for exactly the same reason as the newly moneyed Chinese middle class exorcise their attachment to their rural past by consuming coarse grain cereals – for its difference. There must always also be this "Other" condition of all discourse, the idea of its negation, an "echo" of agency before it was recognized within discourse and of the primordial relation between subject and object thus configured.

No! More than the idea, a sense even, of agency scrambling up against the walls of language unable to escape! The proof that "self" is produced in the interrelation between structure and agency lies in the observation that it is impossible to write about the internal structures of discourse without using the metaphors by which those structures are themselves constituted. Metaphors of presence, space, vision, and so on, as elucidated throughout here, demand to be used again and again. Apart from the almost unconscious repetition of the spatial and visual metaphors made throughout this analysis, it has been extremely difficult to avoid referring to the internal structures of discourse without using terms like "dimension", "aspect", "dynamic", and so on, the first of which is of course a spatial metaphor, the second of which is a visual metaphor, the third of which is a spatial metaphor that also connotes the "activity" of the Cartesian mind as it were, since these are the first discursive principles of the possibility of meaningfulness per se. Even "structure" and "construct" are of course spatial metaphors, as is "distinction", which connotes a division and a visual perspective too. If the term "metaphoric" is used to internally refer to internal referrals then this is merely tautological, indeed the only form of statement that can truly be true, thus quite proving the post-modern insight that you cannot use language to come between language and the world (Wittgenstein 1953).

All signs, including "authenticity", are socially constructed ideals, and none such can be sustained, because each contains within it the "echo" of their antithesis. Ideals add to themselves (as Derrida put it) the possibility of being replicated, such that meaningfulness is spun out by the infinite deferral of signification. There can thus be no end and no beginning, but only the instantiation itself. Individuals' social power, their legitimated agency or distinction, is reflected in the ability to reappraise, to redefine, not just to "take over", but to turn around, thus completing the meaning of "revolution" as that which breaks even as it revolves, and make of the structures that even the most "lowly" of persons must consume objects of desire, beauty, art even. In this, now, is my "Self" constituted. Here, indeed, I am.

3 Knowledge

The rules of engagement

The question remains: exactly how does individual agency manipulate its relation to the world such that the instantiation of individuality is legitimized? Still, this can only be achieved by successfully negotiating all the myriad socially constructed "rules" bearing upon the situation at once, of which Authenticity was just one example.

Knowing the rules is of great importance. Individuals can only make judgments about what they know about; on the other hand, it is precisely by discerning between "legitimate" and "illegitimate" judgments that individuals learn to manipulate the parameters for social power. Knowledge thus institutionalizes, granting access to the "right" to apply value judgments, and becomes forceful in its own right (Berger and Luckmann 1967). Institutional boundaries will be marked by "insider" differentiations and references, technical terminology, ideological apparatus and idiomatic expressions, such that the institution is lived in language, and functions to include and exclude (Foucault 1970). Similarly, institutional practitioners may be accredited with positive social distinction on account of an "institutional memory" ("the way things are done around here"), and "connoisseurs" will show that they can differentiate expertly within a given field (cf. Bourdieu 1984 and his notion of "cultural capital").

The ability to apply knowledge in value judgments is important apart from the knowledge itself, of course, because from the perspective of negotiating other's judgments, you can know about shared norms and standards but fail to demonstrate your knowledge appropriately at the proper time and place. This emphasis on efficacy is also why the "rules" underscoring institutions need only be a loosely shared set of dispositions to behave in more or less "normal" ways in response to more or less "typical" stimuli: you may even hint that you know the rules and others do not without ever clearly explicating their basis or integrity, the actual existence of the rules being nowhere near as important as their social construction (Bourdieu 1992).

Individuals do not simply "follow" socially agreed rules, indeed, and neither do they always break those rules ignorantly, but rather actively contend the rights to define those rules. Though it may be important to know about rules governing when breaking one rule "trumps" another rule, the rules of symbolic inversion and so on, these rules are no less knowingly bent to individuals' advantage where those individuals think they can get away with it. The question is therefore of whose notion of "knowledge worth knowing" holds and who sets the rules for others to follow. Further, since innovators are usually required to master prior rules before redefining them in ways which are eventually accepted by those who seek to stay ahead of social change, a still more critical question is how far individuals must conform to prior rules in order to find room for themselves within them (Wittgenstein 1953: 158–243; Kozinets 2002).

This chapter examines the situational and transient nature of knowledge as it applies in Anshan, China, showing how individuals emphasize different kinds of rules, but that these assertions are ultimately all expressions of the same practical logic whereby such rules are Othered even as they are instantiated.

Knowledge economy

The "legitimate" order of knowledge in China is unquestionably defined by reference to formal academic schooling and merit (*wenhua*), which was established as a valid route to success in imperial times. Scholarship was then closely linked to morality and leadership of the nation, and in theory the lowliest of farmers could have studied his way up to the right hand of the emperor (Kipnis 2011). Formal education remains enormously important in contemporary China thanks to Chairman Mao making formal education distinctly "illegitimate" for a while and sending most of China's youthful urban population "down" to "learn" from illiterate farmers during the Cultural Revolution. Today, and notwithstanding the state's frantic re-investment in education, still only 10.7% of China's population aged 15 or above have a post-secondary school education. Nevertheless, the ruthless competition provoked by the pace of economic growth, and the often intense demands parents make of their only-children (that is, especially since the introduction of China's one-child policy), mean that formal education is much less of an option for social advancement than in the West. Indeed, curious for a place where "class warfare" reigned for a large part of the last century, differences in formal education level have become important factors in the development of new discourses of "personal quality" (*suzhi*) (Murphy 2004; Fong 2007; see also the next chapter).

Formal education has always been valued in China for the skill, control and self-determination that the attainment of high-level formal qualifications requires. Today, however, formal education is perhaps increasingly valued less for its own sake, and more for the social status, good jobs, and high salaries into which this is perceived to translate. China, moreover, is no exception to the rule that knowledge worth knowing is everywhere converging to that defined by reference to capital markets, and though classical skills such as painting and calligraphy remain highly valued, the best education possible in the popular imaginary today is perhaps a PhD in an explicitly commercial discipline. The social value placed on formal education may even have diminished in recent years since China has millions more graduates every year than there are graduate-level jobs available, and mass media revelations have confirmed that high-demand jobs are often filled on the basis of personal contacts and political affiliations. Youngsters without connections must now develop "grey skills" (*huise jineng*) to negotiate all manner of arbitrary obstacles on their path to employment, including tests of their alcohol-drinking ability, mahjong technique, singing and dancing.[1]

Still, Anshan has many people who will say they "lack culture" (*que wenhua*) relative to the educated urban elites by which the official sphere is defined, even where their money-making skills are recognized. This is perhaps especially the case where individuals have had a rural upbringing, the significance of the urban/rural contrast inviting the comparison of the *tu* principle (meaning "soil", "local", "native", etc., as discussed in the previous chapter), with *ya*, meaning "refined" or "cultured", as in *wenya*, a term linked with the urban elite. Zhang Xiuzhen, the Anshan distributor for a US direct-marketing firm, apologizes for "lacking culture" relative to her husband's "intellectual" (*zhishifenzi*) urban family, using a term for "intellectual" understood not to refer to practicing intellectuals but to anyone with a university education.

For an alternative example of how the urban/rural divide functions to structure China's knowledge economy, consider that Grandma Liu, a neighbor of mine, is especially keen that I document she is from a "cultured family", and gives as evidence of her pedigree the fact that both sets of her grandparents were scholars in times when most women were unable to read. Those pensioners who currently get a much higher pension than her, I am to understand, "came from the countryside, had low culture and many children; all the high-level jobs went to poor farmers like them". Ironically, the only reason Grandma Liu was able to rise up in society, she explains, was because her husband, who subsequently rose to the ranks of Army General before he died in Mao's purges, came from a rural background. Somewhat surprisingly, however, Liu confesses that she in fact has "no culture" (*meiyou wenhua*) herself, since she never attained the certification that should have attended her studies: the Chinese she studied "from 1953–56" and the Russian she spoke for "three to five years" do not count.[2]

In the socialist era, of course, before Mao's purges, formal education was free of charge, an "entitlement" rather than a "privilege", and paying for it today is still a shock for many Chinese. Parents make immense personal and financial sacrifices to send their children to the schools of their choice (Fong 2008). Perhaps most believe a foreign education to be best, since the West remains where knowledge worth knowing is supposed to emanate from in the popular imagination, but attitudes in this respect have fluctuated in accordance with China's changing place in the world. China is not without a number of world-class universities of its own, but places are restricted to only the very brightest students of all, and perhaps only those genuinely in a position to compare – intellectual elites and so on – adequately appreciate this. A foreign education, on the other hand, is accessible to anyone who can pay for it, so it can easily appear that parents believe the amount of money they have spent on their child's learning is genuinely a mark of their child's knowledgeability, alongside their examination results and the names of the schools, universities, and countries in which they are registered.

Paying for education is a kind of consumption quite apart from the distinction achieved through knowledge, ability and learned skills. While tuition in skills based on individual artistry or creation such as piano or violin that are highly valued in China can be paid for, the purchase alone does not guarantee that you will master the skills taught. Accordingly, whereas some Chinese parents emphasize the price paid to enroll their child at an expensive, foreign-invested college as a mark of their distinction, or in order to justify sending their child to an overseas boarding school at a very young age, other parents emphasize sending their child to the "best" schools on account of their knowledge and ability, and may also emphasize their own role in nurturing that ability. Du Bin, for example, loves to talk about his role in his son's success:

> I told my son very early on that my own situation wasn't that great, and told him that he should aspire to more. I took him to see the workers at the Angang steel plant, saying: these are the workers. And then I took him to Beijing and showed him rural migrants in temporary jobs. I also took him to a high-level state-owned enterprise conference so he could make his own choice. At his primary school there were pupils around who clambered all over each other 'riding the donkey' and playing games; some were coarse and had bad habits. I let my son see and made it clear that games were only allowed if he first finished his homework. Then I taught him to sing since I believed it was important for him to have extra-curricular abilities too. My son was entered for a great many competitions so that when he won one he would have a feeling of super-iority and excel in other areas. A competition was held with the top 1,500 students from all schools in the city. My son achieved fourth place, promptly entered the best school available, and was consistently excellent at everything he studied.

"Knowledgeable" and "consumerist" logics cannot be entirely separated in practice, of course, because individuals may reap distinction of the former kind by demonstrating knowledge of the rules governing consumption of the latter kind without actually being able to afford to make distinctive purchases. Indeed a great many people in Anshan are concerned to reap distinction in just this way. Ma Yi, a music teacher in his mid-twenties, for example, never misses a chance to drop references to the latest fashions and styles, the availability of things, their cost and so on, even though his salary makes for less-than-premium purchases. Consumer goods firms in China, as elsewhere, moreover, can be observed to market their products by appeal to design by brilliant designers, craftsmen, and artisans, such that much of the distinctiveness that the consumer buys into derives from appreciating the earned skills invested in the product.

In still other cases, although consumers can afford socially distinctive choices, they do not know how to appreciate the "taste" into which they buy. Zhao Guangyao, who was fortunate enough to be one of the first generation to return to university after the Cultural Revolution, has heard that red wine is good for his health, but does not know that wine should be consumed within a couple of days of uncorking, so consumes it instead in very small amounts over many months! Zhao can be interestingly compared with his elder brother, Fang Jian, who was "just a soldier" in his youth, so he says of himself, but today practices photography at an artistic level and likes to reminisce about how he was able to distinguish the country of origin of every kind of loudspeaker in his long-since bankrupt hi-fi store just by the sound. Zhao is widely respected for the business acumen that has made him considerably wealthier than Fang.

In these situationally complex ways, knowledge is a factor of social difference that cuts across other factors such as wealth and formal education.

Knowledge politics

We are interested more in how individuals use knowledge to compete socially than in whether they "have" knowledge or "how much" they have of any particular kind. Observe how Chen Xueyuan, a retired Angang Steel employee, uses knowledge to make a particularly political point in response to my casual suggestion that he should be considered "comparatively knowledgeable" (*bijiao you zhishi*):

> Oh yes, I've got a lot of knowledge, really a lot of knowledge. Not being modest, I'd have to say I'm someone with really quite a lot of knowledge. You could use a Chinese expression "has read more than 10,000 books" to describe me. The knowledge I've gained from reading gets me regarded as obstinate, because my entire boundary of thought and ways of thinking are different from most people in China. Summed up, we could say the way Chinese look at problems is philistine (*shisu*). I really don't identify with these things. Rather, I'm galloping away in my own spiritual world. My knowledge is at this level, and the level of the people I am talking to is at this level. It's like they're speaking another language. Because I've read so many books, when I'm with people who haven't read much, our talk is as dry as dust. A friend of mine has really got culture; he has a doctorate, he's the only guy I can share my thoughts with.

Chen is evidently very keen to assert how his knowledge and reading has distinguished him from most people. As he portrays it, his knowledge has

Figure 3.1 Violinists. Photography by Gao Yingchuan

worked negatively to exclude him, exiling him to a "spiritual" stratum of existence shared only with his friend with a doctorate. He continues in this vein:

> The crux of the problem is entering the spirit of European humanism: scientific ideology. A world of correct judgment cannot be separated from study. Reading from an early age will cultivate a certain consciousness. A lot of people do not have this consciousness. A great many institute their own views and live entirely according to the customs of society. Chinese people have their customs, but scientific culture has no national borders. Having this kind of consciousness makes one really clever, and changes one from being ordinary to being extraordinary. Chinese popular culture tends towards the vulgar. Since the beginning of the sixteenth century, the Renaissance has been the most advanced kind of culture in all mankind. But Chinese people don't know. The only consciousness they have of science is a very latent one. Thank goodness I'm not like this!

Chen's agenda becomes a little clearer here. His remarks about "scientific ideology" and the universality of this are intended to provide a basis for his other comments and to solicit recognition and empathy from me. His assertions are also intended to target people who are interested in "philistine things", a materialism against which he asserts his own "spirituality". Though I have only asked Chen what he likes to read, he goes on, bringing in a wide range of citations that perhaps only those with a formal education would recognize, as if to reiterate that those from which he differentiates himself are indeed "speaking another language" – a different set of rules:

> Most people's thinking is still about burning incense to Buddha. I rely on my own study. I received the influence of Balzac, Pinder, Herbert and Hegel at a very early age. Many people, like the children in the countryside, have never read books of this kind. And there are some children, and their children too, who already have this kind of consciousness. Perhaps it is inborn. What I want to leave you with today is that scientific culture will always be higher than money and power. Do not respect money: you should despise money and power, and instead respect scientific culture. My daughter is only 12 years old but she already says to me that she doesn't want to be a business person, and doesn't want to be an official; she wants to be a scientist. The contributions that scientists make to humankind will always be greater than business people and officials.

Chen sees knowledge as the vehicle of human freedom, a project of unique individuality, and seeks to lever his knowledge in order to institute himself in relation to this problem. The "humanism" he proposes is intended to directly counter the "philistine" alliance of "money and power" dominating contemporary China (as he sees it). His comments about "Chinese popular culture" tending towards the "vulgar" are probably intended to address the way in which the single-party state encourages the rejection of such noble humanist ideals, instead splicing its adulation of Western industrial and economic ideals with a valorization of the "wisdom" of the "ordinary" people, their "everyday" practices and "folk" customs, a mass and popular mechanism contrived to bypass those so-called "traditional" and "elite" cultures that threaten dangerous ideas like universal respect for individual autonomy (all quotes Festa 2006). Chen later seems to put this beyond doubt when he tells me that, "The value of an individual person is not really the same in these developing countries. My wife understands the degree of respect that should be offered to every individual, but China hasn't realized it yet. Science has no rules, and no national boundaries. All persons are the same."

   Of course, projects of freedom through knowledge need not necessarily be opposed to Chinese customs. We can only surmise that Chen would be intrigued by the idea that all knowledge is the product of people "instituting their own views" and living "according to the customs of society". Indeed, we might note, for all the universality of his humanism, how easily Chen turns to a categorical essentialism in support of his argument: "Perhaps it is inborn".

Practicability

Of course, some Chinese do not privilege formal knowledge and assiduous, often expensive, schooling in the first place. For those to whom formal schooling is denied, an entirely different range of virtues may be espoused. Not least among alternatives is the exposure to a broader register of experience than formal schooling allows. Consider how Lin Yue, an Anshan journalist, makes these elements interact:

> China has loads of university students now. University education is not the same in China as overseas. We think that some content should be changed; in some aspects education is failing here. Besides, "persons with culture" (*you wenhua de ren*) are not necessarily those who have read at university, but at least you must have some sort of cultural level. University students are really pervasive these days, much more so than before. In the past, educated people were few and culture wasn't accessible to the masses. People's thinking wasn't very active. People were comparatively stupid (*sha*) and pursued whatever career they liked. Now the education style is squeezed into your brain; it doesn't allow the students to digest it; it doesn't let the students make the things of their schooling their own. Overseas graduates on the other hand can get a job in society when they've finished. In China, students speak a lot, but they do very little, and university students who have just graduated lack experience; they must temper themselves. After they've been in society for a few years they'll be outstanding, but some of them already think they're awesome. But they have absolutely no way to compare with us at work. Experienced people have far greater ability and really cherish the opportunity to work. Everyone must strive really hard otherwise they'll lose the opportunity to eat (*diule fanwan*). I think I've really got this ability.

Lin Yue had to make up her education deficit after the Cultural Revolution through a program of online vocational training. She asserts her practicability to differentiate herself from younger colleagues who have university qualifications but lack the "industriousness" and "experience" she stresses. Lin emphasizes her experience, too, making her age a virtue rather than a handicap, and implicitly identifies with a generational cohort, using "us" rather than "I" to oppose "them". Lin is also strongly critical of the state's social engineering ("squeezed into your brain"). She asserts that the state's methods actively deny students the opportunity to take the rules they are given and bend them to their own projects ("doesn't let the students make the things of their schooling their own"), which is precisely the sort of creative consumption she herself demonstrates: Lin takes up the dominant discourse that privileges the formal education she lacks and does her best to turn this rule to her advantage.

A great many informants made similar constructions to Lin. "Formal education is not enough", attested Du Feng, emphasizing his life experience in a way not entirely dissimilar to Lin: "Reading 10,000 books is not as good as walking 1,000 kilometers". However, Du does not like to highlight that he has no education to speak of, and is very keen to come across as knowledge-able in his outlook most generally. He takes pains to show me that he knows a lot about the army and its functions, ranges strategically across national policy, global, and current affairs, drops comments about international destina-tions, the importance of environmental management, the difficulties presently being experienced in the Olympic Games preparations, and so on, and clearly enjoys the opportunity to discuss the art works in his office, and religion too. However, this is ultimately a function of Du's resourcefulness rather than of "culture" per se, an ad hoc improvisation enacted precisely because Du feels that he lacks culture in spite of his success. Particularly on his mind are his well-educated brothers who have all become "high officials" in "formal enterprises" (*zhengui de qiye*), he says, betraying his perception that his own enterprise is a ramshackle, unruly, indecent affair.

Du, indeed, like many of the entrepreneurs in this study, seeks to trade his financial capital for what he perceives he lacks within the symbolic economy: formal knowledge. Though all the entrepreneurs I encountered took great pains to emphasize the value of practical ability over academic knowledge as far as their own achievements were concerned, without exception they sought to "cash-in" the wealth they had accumulated in return for formal academic scholarship and the acquisition of formal culture for their children (cf. Bourdieu's notion of "tranverse mobility"). Du would like his son to go to a good university and then go abroad, not to stay in Anshan. "Money isn't necessarily the most important criteria to be occupied with", he explained. "You can have money but not necessarily have culture. If I'd had an education I would have done much better than I'm doing now". Business people also all strongly emphasized the importance of their own achievements against what they saw as the "ille-gitimate" achievements of those whose success had come through cultivating cliquey circles of favors and mutual obligation – corruption and nepotism having widely fuelled the perception that "ability" (*nengli*) is not as important as your connections in any case.

For a still further example of how individuals will employ knowledge in order to compete socially, consider that my rural migrant worker colleagues at Anshan's Lamb Buddha restaurant (cf. Chapter 8) would excuse themselves from answering questions on account of lacking education, but would never-theless skillfully assert themselves vis-à-vis knowledge discourse when they could. Lin Chuan, for example, contended:

> People don't necessarily rely on knowledge acquired through education; but their brains are extremely quick, they can look into any problem they encounter in real detail. They can connect a problem with so many other problems, and converse about it, but we can't do this. For example: one plus one equals two. We only know it equals two, but they can make it equal something else. They can calculate, but our thinking is naïve. They

can think in really complex ways, but our brains are not the same. They have nine years of formal education, I have only three. So their culture is high. But it's not the same: if a real situation comes up they'll not necessarily be any cleverer than me. They only understand expert knowledge; they don't understand extra-curricular knowledge. So, actually, everyone relies on their brains to get on in society and cope with issues.

The analysis of these last few cases, therefore, demonstrates not only how individuals are differentiated by "what" they know, but how they are united by the practical skill with which they take prior discourses and turn them to their own ends. Individuals divided by "objective" differences draw upon knowledge discourse in ways which are more or less similarly shared with individuals from objectively quite different positions in society. Thus, we have the beginnings of the "grammar" that the later chapters of this book will seek to draw out.

Law and practical order

The Chinese might have an especially "pragmatic" (Blackman 2000) attitude to social rules and their negotiation. Whereas in many Western cultures the "rules" are fetishized as if they cannot be broken, and exist for their own sake, in most Chinese contexts social knowledge is aimed at judging rules and their manipulation in terms of the immediate situation. Every Chinese is ready to quote the expression, "The hills are high and the emperor is far away" (*shangao huangdi yuan*) to explain the disposition to find room for themselves within ruling systems, and the perception that those who set the rules are those who follow them least is widespread and entrenched. Chinese humor, indeed, famously involves laughing at the rule, rather than at those who fail to comply with the rule, as is the case in most Western cultures. Indeed, and distinctly contrary to those literatures that suggest Chinese people are the hapless slaves of more powerful people's rules (see Hofstede's concept of "Power Distance", for example), the sense in which the only "golden" rule in China is that every rule can be bent, is one respect, indeed probably the only respect, where the kung fu clichés are true.

Take the practice of driving in Anshan, for example, which is structured by a particularly reflexive relationship with the rules. "Legitimate" driving is codified in formal written rules, but the actual practice of driving is informed by a situationally flexible logic which can appear "lawless" to those who don't know its implicit rules. Whereas many Western drivers will "simply" follow the rules, having placed their faith in the system, Anshan drivers cannot have faith that other road users are driving according to the rules. Whereas, heuristically speaking, most Western drivers will only sporadically monitor other drivers to see what mistakes they might make, "simply" following the lights and the traffic signs under the assumption that everyone else is too, Anshan drivers will constantly monitor each others' positions and trajectories as they drive in and out of each other's space, continuously adjusting their behavior in accordance with each other's modifications, possessed of a shared understanding of a modus operandi where the formal rules are made into something entirely new (cf. Kirke 2010).

At other times China's road users more obviously contest the grounds on which this modus operandi is based. Pedestrians will step out without looking at apparently "random" intervals in front of drivers who would never pause to allow them to cross otherwise, even though the rules say they should wait at pedestrian crossings till they can be ushered across by red-capped, armband-wearing volunteers. They do so full in the knowledge that they are protected by laws which stipulate that drivers will be at fault if they knock pedestrians down. Some drivers will drive right at pedestrians, forcing them to push their manipulation of the system right to its limits.

Willful contesting of the rules is a very necessary form of self-expression in China, a kind of "flexing" of agency against social space and political structure, and a reaction to the relatively recent introduction of ever-more sophisticated forms of law, governance and surveillance. Take China's new high-speed "harmony" trains, for example, where passengers are corralled with a wide range of forceful and detailed instructions on how to behave, since the government believes the "rules" need to be explicitly spelled out: at every stop passengers are reminded not to smoke, not to run, to put their toilet paper in the basket provided, to speak quietly on their mobile phones, to be sick in the bag provided if necessary, to ensure that their sunflower seed shells are discarded there too, all the way down to minutiae such as "drink only in the designated area, and if you return to your seat with a drink, please ensure you have not overfilled your cup"! We might make the point that this situation is not so different from the strictures of the "nanny state" in present-day Britain, with the stifling "health and safety" culture that has been cultivated as a response to a litigating society, but we will not pursue this analogy further. The point we will make here is that right in the face of what seems to be quite a rigorous and exacting form of instruction, even those passengers who are not flagrantly breaking the rules themselves at least expect others around them to be doing so.

Take a flight in China, for example, where Chinese will strip off their seatbelts even as the flight crew explicitly reminds them to keep them fastened; notably many others will follow suit once one or two have led the way. Similarly, while most Britons will slavishly wait until the plane has completely docked before using any personal electronic devices, many Chinese will begin mobile phone calls as soon as the landing gear has touched down and they judge it safe to do so, even though these behaviors are explicitly against the rules. Jumping up to retrieve your hand-luggage from the overhead cabinet before the plane has stopped would be too obvious a "transgression" – though some do try to get away with this – but releasing your seat belt early is unlikely to draw sanction. International charter flights will see flight stewards try harder to "enforce" these rules on Chinese travelers, but in China people do not expect to be too troubled for this order of infringement. Indeed, the fact that so many Chinese travelers seem successfully to negotiate gross contraventions of the weight and size limits for hand-luggage in the first place is evidence less of simple "unruliness" than of a cultural logic where a certain amount of situational "rule-bending" is recognized and anticipated even where the rules have been made explicit and generalized by a ruling authority.

Forms of "insubordination" such as these can accrue significant positive social distinction in China, signifying the "ability" to circumnavigate the rules without getting caught out transgressing them. Take Chinese car drivers who refuse to wear their seat belts but still drape the belt across their shoulders without actually fastening it to avoid the 20 yuan fine if spotted by the police: the notion that you might as well just fasten your seat belt the moment you enter the vehicle is not popular because where the rules are instituted to address the "unsocial" element of society, intending to make everybody conform to the model of an "ideal citizen", like the Lei Feng character of Maoist propaganda, the contemporary significance of wearing a seat belt becomes no different from the imperative to memorize the latest eight-character Party-policy slogan. You have to show that you comply in order to avoid sanction (fines, exclusion, punishment), but actual compliance would be to admit that you were "unsocial", "bad", etc., and need the policy for real. Symbolic insubordination to rules imposed thus becomes an assertion of your legitimate individuality: you have the ability to break the rules because you are a "good steward" of your immediate social sphere; you don't need the belt because you are a "good enough" driver, a "good" citizen. In this way, rule-breaking becomes distinctive and socially legitimate, signifying that the rules need not apply.

Symbolic insubordination to rules imposed is probably highly beneficial to a society as socially and politically engineered as that of China. When I ask entrepreneur Zhao about the new law decreeing that long-term employees must have a permanent contract, he insists that this will have no effect on him. "Isn't the law the law?" I ask. "The law is the law", Zhao replies, "but China has certain characteristics". Zhao refers to the sense in which many Chinese people see the following of laws, rules and regulations as "foolish" compliance with measures one would much better find a way around – that is, where "honesty" is the best guarantor of failure (Wang 2006: 28). However, Zhao is also keen that I understand that there is no need for the law as an external sanction or intervention by the state, however minimal, at least in his case, since he has his employees' welfare personally in hand. When his workers are sick or injured, he pays for their medical expenses; when they are off work, they still get paid. Indeed, Zhao volunteers all sorts of unexpected additional financial assistance, but he cannot give his workers contracts because he has to compete in the same way that his local competitors do or he would go under. Zhao thus makes all these additional gestures to sustain his workers' loyalty, "plugging the gaps" in the "chaos" generated by the relative paucity of absolutely fixed rules. His point, of course, is that even if all bosses gave their workers contracts, these would be next to worthless in China compared to personal guarantees.

In other ways, however, this flexible approach to the consumption of rules presents Chinese society with enormous challenges. Zhao's wife failed her driving test along with 20 others that day, but all were given licenses anyway. "Johnny", a relative, did not even have to take the test since his father was able to procure a license for him through the appropriate connections. For almost every formal rule in China, it can seem that there are attendant modes of circumvention, and then still more rules about those avoidances, and still yet further evasions. Take the Sanlu milk powder scandal, for example, where infants across China were poisoned by toxic additives: all the "proper" procedures were in place to check whether the milk was fresh or not (the "rules"), including a protein test, so that milk-producing farmers (who lived so far away that the milk would putrefy before it could be processed) added what they called "protein powder" (i.e. melamine) to the milk (the "avoidance" of the rule), probably without any idea of its adverse effects: the presence of the rule was understood but the need for its basis was not appreciated. This situational approach to the consumption of rules even extends to rules that do not exist: foreigners conducting business in China regularly claim that their Chinese partners regard the assertion of rules that do not exist as a perfectly legitimate negotiating strategy (Blackman 2000)! Quite similarly, when Chinese academics joke that they can't do anything in their hyper-bureaucratic universities without an appropriate rule, they add that when there appears to be the absence of a relevant rule, this must be the result of a government policy that decreed it be so!

To repeat, it is as much the presence of rules that explains so much apparent "unruliness" as their absence per se. True to an extent, the introduction of new forms of law and surveillance in China only applies to those who cannot afford to transgress, so that if you are on first-name terms with a high-ranking officer in the local authorities you do not stop at the red light if you judge it is safe to cross, but you will still try to dodge the traffic cameras by braking momentarily wherever you can.

Rules and ruling

China's government appears to be well prepared to deal with the dynamic and relational manner in which formal rules work out in their practice and application. Central government policies are deliberately formulated at the central level with a view to their being modified at provincial level. The population, forestry, and ethnic minorities policies, for example, all vary hugely in their application across different regions within wide and explicitly stated guidelines set down by central laws and policies intended to allow for flexibility in the application of the rule. Similarly, though the salience of rule-breaking in China owes much to the fact that ordinary individuals do not have a stake in the single-party state's claims to rule, the government would not have tolerated the recent explosion of social media services if it did not think it had the resources to effectively manage its citizens' attempts to "avoid" its rules and circumnavigate its parameters on liberal speech: "avoidance" is built into the system. However, this "flexibility" incorporated into China's ruling system has notably failed to prevent the relatively recent development of a trend for subway station attendants or traffic wardens, airline hostesses or shop assistants, indeed almost anyone endowed with the slightest semblance of official or corporate power, to occasionally be unusually inflexible about their enforcing of "the rules" as a marker of their own "distinction" or status. For in a country where the ruling power remains unaccountable to society, the role of "enforcer" has an especially alluring caché, and as Chinese people increasingly develop a taste for modernity, individuals empowered to "uphold" the rules, but of insufficient rank to judge that the rules need not apply in the particular situation, are coming to evince the almost mindless adherence to the rules or rule fetishes that characterize some Western countries.

Consider, then, those management scholars who like to contrast "fluid, relational rules" negotiated between individuals and groups, which they take to be a model for Chinese society, with notions of fixed and legally binding rules, which they take to be a model of modern Western society, to explain why relationships are more important in Chinese business than contracts and so on. While these East–West rulings obviously have broad currency in this analysis, and no doubt this is what Zhao means when he obliquely refers to "Chinese characteristics" (above), statements of this essentialist form fail to capture adequately Chinese individuals' situational and dynamic approach to social rules, and misleadingly suggest instead that social practice in China is "governed" by a mysteriously "unruly" *set* of rules, when in fact Chinese people can be extraordinarily picky about the precise intricacies of laws and policies when this suits their interests. Westerners, for that matter, are no less compelled to take prior social rules and insinuate themselves into their constraints than are Chinese, the fetish of the rules that seems to Chinese eyes to characterize places such as Britain of course being just a different form of relationality. In each case, it is the presence of the rule that begs the question of its "transgression". We might even say that the formal rule is the necessary condition of its situational application – otherwise chaos really would prevail.

Thus, where Anshan graduate Xiao Qiang tells me that his Western-authored management textbook says that, "In the West, a red light means red; people cannot cross. But Chinese people will cross the road depending on their individual judgment of the speed of the cars at the time", these constructions merely evince how cultural "rules" formulated by people who have not usually actually practiced the culture they objectify are uncritically adopted by social actors even in that target culture and reproduced in essentialized forms. The simple fact that the other relevant axiom favored in management literatures contrasts Western "rule of law" with Chinese "rule by law" should immediately tell us that this simple linear logic is flawed, since this latter axiom contradicts the favored emphasis on fluid relationalism over legality. With similar practical effect, that is to say that "rule by law" only conjures an authoritarian state and fails to do justice to the dynamics of how Chinese individuals work things out in the absence of the "rule of law". Thus, and quite similarly, where Chinese consumer gurus appeal to "Confucius" in order to assert that China is "a rule-bound society where acceptance of conventional order is second nature" (Doctoroff 2005: 73), they can only be in any way correct if they allow for individuals' active role in social reproduction, since interfacing with rules in "clever" (Doctoroff 2005: 209) ways is just what consumers do.

Cultural practice is always informed by prior rules, just as prior rules are informed by practice, the tension between the rule and the agent who "consumes" being generative of everything meaningful about social interaction. This might be especially well recognized in China, where known rules for legitimate action are acknowledged as resembling a rough guide that must be applied warily from context to context, rather than a rigid "code". However, the notion that the Chinese are somehow more, or indeed less, "relational" than consumers elsewhere is a fallacy perpetrated by the positivist scientific discourse of the West, where the modernist illusion that all things are not in fact interrelated in their determination has a more sophisticated grip on thinking and action. Cultures are all relational, just in different ways, so that it ultimately makes just as little sense to speak of "more" or "less" relational cultures than it does of relational cultures versus non-relational cultures. Relationalism, after all, is not something peculiar and unique to China but a question of how we look at China from a certain perspective.

The logical implication is that the legitimate utility to break socially agreed rules must be evaluated in light of all other contextual apparatus bearing on action, much of which may be internally contradictory. Indeed, even where the agency of breaking the rules becomes a social asset, it remains the case that individuals can negotiate redefinitions of the rules only by referring to them in the first place. Thus, the assertion of the knowledge of social rules and the ability to consume them, or indeed the lack of these, must always be seen in the light of other expectations and regularities structuring practice, lest you dodge one rule yet fall foul of another.

My analysis therefore turns now to analyze the civility discourse, a logic that projects the notion of "rule" onto physical and social space, and in particular the social construction of intimacy and social distance as appropriate in different contexts and situations. I will then continue to examine the remaining "rules" I have abstracted from the "language" of social distinction. This done, I will be in a position to address the question of how all these "rules" are crystallized in actual practice, a process which will demonstrate not only how the tension between rules and the individual agents who consume them is variously reconciled in different social situations, but also from where the power to be able to "set" the rules for others comes.

4 Civility

Spaced out

This chapter concerns the boundary differentiating the private self from the social world of others as these are constructed in social space. As with the situational and transient constitution of the other discourses of my analysis, this chapter maintains that there are diverse and competing constructions of where this boundary lies: there is no set boundary; rather the boundary is drawn by persons who put it into use as and when needed in order to include and exclude. The question, then, is of the construction of intimacy and social distance as appropriate in different contexts and situations. Whereas earlier analyses have tended to overlook the situationality of this discourse in favor of models inflected with various forms of essentialism (Hsu 1971), my approach emphasizes the constructedness of these concepts as a first analytical principle.

Discussion begins with the observation that until the 1980s most informants of this study shared a very limited living space with at least four but perhaps as many as eight or ten family members. With China's economic reforms, however, the introduction of private home ownership and massive urban expansion, most families' living environments have become considerably less intimate in both total occupancy and person per square meter terms (Bray 2005). These developments, and the increased frequency of interaction with strangers who speak different languages and have very different behavioral norms, have increasingly provoked the perception of a "code" for operating in a "civil", universal and cosmopolitan public order.

China is a place where boundaries delimiting the intimate and the social sphere remain configured very differently to the contemporary West, however, and competing constructions of intimacy in China largely mirror the differences between China and the West in these respects. Essentially, China is constructed as occupying the local and intimate end of a situational spectrum ranging from spousal and familial relations at one end, through relatives, friends, colleagues and strangers (where the self comes into contact with individuals who represent other, separate, intimate spheres), in the middle, to the official, civic sphere of employers, government and the "global community" at large at the other end of the spectrum. The following analysis explores the "internal" structure of this discourse, acknowledging that many Chinese might take offence, but maintaining that offense is somewhat unavoidably the "nature" of the "beast".

Orifices!

Analysis revealed that judgments related to the comportment of the physical body itself, and in particular the opening and closing of bodily orifices – points of direct intersection between the most intimate and personal sphere and the social and public sphere – were especially relevant to the construction of civil boundaries. Relevant judgments were often also paralleled by a metaphorical dialectic between "cleanliness" and "dirtiness", whereby "clean" was equivalent to the private, intimate, or inside, and "dirty" equivalent to the public, social, or outside (Douglas 1966). Importantly, however, other judgments inverted this congruence of metaphors.

Behaviors relevant to the first iteration included urinating and defecating in public space, which, like prostitution and thieving (similarly judged "dirty"), were widely blamed on peripheral "outsiders" (*waidiren*) entering "central", urban space (Solinger 1999; Zhang 2001), and this despite the fact that most of the excrement, toilet paper and sanitary products that litter Anshan's wooded parks are dumped by urban residents and cleared away by rural migrant workers. In the public playground in "219 Park" a grossly obese and presumably urban-registered child urinates onto the ground in broad daylight, supervised by his elderly grandmother, his trousers and pants around his ankles in full view of bystanders, while adults squat to defecate just past the tree line.

People spit in China's cities, moreover, just as profusely as they do in the countryside, usually following a highly conspicuous effort to rally phlegm from the lungs, quite as if there is rationality at work whereby this is a legitimate strategy for asserting oneself. Some people spit many times in succession, or indeed regularly as they go about their daily business, without discriminating much between roads, pavements, the floors of public restaurants, super-markets, and offices, and spitting into the sink or toilet in their own homes. Being accidentally spat on is not at all uncommon. Blowing mucous from the nasal cavity directly onto the ground, with or without the aid of fingers and thumbs, is also quite normal. Some people will spit repeatedly into a bag throughout the duration of a journey on a cramped public bus, apparently with a view to sealing the bag as an act of "closing" (Krajewski 2009), only to then throw the bag out of the window to slake the sidewalk without consideration for passers-by. Some people claim these are acts of cleansing, to expel inertia, "a site of possible decay" (Krajewski 2009), and thus healthy, but this does not account for the lack of socio-spatial discretion.

For others who more acknowledge and anticipate the "gaze" of society, however, these practices are considered polluting – "dirty" because they cut through what are seen as important social boundaries and categories. While some individuals in Anshan cough and sneeze directly into my face apparently without a thought, for example, others find it proper to place a hand over the mouth. Quite similarly, other informants would say that their parents had admonished them not to pick their teeth with a finger, or to leave chopsticks protruding from the mouth, actions which draw attention to and interfere with the boundary between the body's intimate internalities and public externality. In exactly the same way, however, the handkerchief, a distinctly Western and modern import, similarly blurs discursive categories by contradicting the need some feel to "expel" and "close" by retaining a snot-soaked rag in one's pocket. There is therefore no right or wrong way in which civil boundaries should be asserted, and behaviors considered inappropriate in one context may even be quite permissible in another.

Internal body matter is of course considered fertile in some contexts, a site for new life rather than a pollutant; and yet a passenger waiting at Shanghai Pudong international airport blows his snot directly into the bin marked "inorganic matter" whilst neglecting the adjacent bin marked "organic matter". Babies in China, for that matter, do not wear nappies, but rather a kind of jumpsuit that leaves the "private parts" exposed through a hole. This would be unacceptable in the West where our childcare is so sterilized and fear of pedophilia so hysterical; in Anshan, however, many parents will simply lift their infant into an appropriate position so they can be relieved in their immediate public vicinity, which makes for much less dirtiness for oneself but not such a pleasant environment for others. Of course, reasons other than mere personal convenience are offered for this kind of baby-wear; an open bottom is preferable to nappy-rash, I am assured. Nappy sales are rising rapidly across China, however, suggesting that these practices may be declining as whole rafts of China's population reassess their views about exposing the body to public space.

The "civility" discourse as analyzed thus far, therefore, is shown to consist in a tension between a humoric medicine view where the openness of the body to the social sphere, expectoration and bare-butt babies are considered "healthy" and "natural", and a modernity view of the opening of the body in public space that is an extension of urban society's enforcement of "hygiene" as civility.

Animals!

Just as foods and liquids must exit the body, so they must be replenished. Eating thus emerged particularly strongly in informants' judgments of civil behavior. In particular, it was "eating anything" and/or "eating carelessly" (*luanchi*) that was found disagreeable, which is of course another breach of the "floodgates" governing the perception of classificatory boundaries (see Chapter 2, p.30): where one anomaly comes through, legions will follow. Of course, only "animals" will "eat anything", a judgment that constructs the uncivil "Other" as an entirely different order of existence; civility aspires to be especially rational, the "animal" metaphor lurking wherever incivility is defined as a lack of control (Fiskesjö 2012). The judgment is akin in form to the revulsion English schoolboys express at first hearing that the French eat frogs and snails; hence the animal judgment "frogs", which condemns the culinary system that the French like to think makes them masters of good taste (Chapman 1992).

In the Western tradition, certain animals have been deemed "unclean" for human consumption since Old Testament times (Douglas 1966), but many Chinese share a strong passion for eating "wild" animals, the rarity and high price of which translates into a marker of status as well as "healthiness" (Zhan 2005). The revelation that China's 2003 SARS (severe acute respiratory syndrome) outbreak was linked to the consumption of civet cat meat provoked a raft of new hygiene legislation in order to annul the risks to public health that such tastes entail. Indeed, it is people from Guangdong Province, closest to the SARS epicenter in Hong Kong, that Anshan people most characterize as being "willing to eat anything", in reference to the monkey, bear, reptile and insect delicacies favored there, as well as the internal organs eaten less in the north. Anshan tastes are therefore to China's "wild" southern cuisines what the English are to the French: the more differentiated the culinary system, the more there is potential for differentiating within it, and the more tasteful is the differentiator, while Anshan people, like the English, tend to find an opposing tastefulness in being simple, plain and straightforward (see the next chapter).

A further contrast in the construction of civil behavior emergent here, and one that inverts the purity of "inside" asserted in the cordon sanitaria, arises when Xiao Li, a 22-year-old Anshan woman, points out to me that the character for "dirty" (in modern Chinese) is identical to the character for "internal organ", the two meanings differentiated only by a tonal inflection in the verbal language. For some Chinese, a personal "purity" of inside can be enhanced by consuming the insides of other organisms for their vitality; for others, other organisms' insides should be avoided on account of high fatty acid, chemical and germ content. Similarly, there is the "folk" awareness that the healthiest animals to eat are those furthest away from the human gene pool, the rule being that animals with the least possible number of legs are healthiest: meat from animals that walk on only two legs, such as chickens, is considered healthier than meat from animals that walk on four legs, such as pigs and cows; best of all are animals that do not walk on legs at all, such as fish, prawns and shellfish. How this can be squared with eating centipedes and millipedes in China's far south is beyond me!

Hygiene in food consumption is an issue that comes into conflict with the "modernity" construction in China in the public sphere if not in intimate spheres also, and in ways that can interestingly confuse the congruence of the metaphorical oppositions articulated thus far. Some foods must of course be prepared to be healthy, whilst others need not be, introducing the contrast between the "raw" and the "cooked", a form of judgment that inverts the privilege given to judgments of the natural, unspoilt "purity of origin" discussed in Chapter 2, and which broadly parallels the opposition of "nature" with "culture", "animal" with "human", "rural" with "urban", and so on (Lévi-Strauss 1975). Grandma Liu, for example, a neighbor, condemns farmers as "dirty as hell" on account of not washing fruit and not cooking vegetables before eating them: "They just take a carrot, give it a rub and eat it; they don't peel it; they don't even wash it!"

Until sterilizing machines and vacuum-packed dining kits were very recently introduced to China, diners at even the best of restaurants would routinely ask for a pot of boiling water to wash bowls and glasses before eating; the excess water was usually cast onto the floor. Insisting on disposable chopsticks was also standard practice for the same hygienic reasons until environmental awareness was very recently flagged up as a public priority (Ikels 1996: 29). For the very same informants with whom I enacted these practices, however, hygiene also remained in other ways very much opposed to health, since their understanding of health was still strongly informed by a "traditional" medicine discourse often set explicitly against the scientific healthcare and modern cleansing agents increasingly recognized to do as much to weaken the immune system as to heal (Farquhar 2002). Indeed, the washing of bowls and using of disposable chopsticks was only normalized relatively recently in China, as a response to Shanghai's hepatitis epidemic in 1988, which probably explains why informants often seemed to have double standards in these respects: spitting indiscriminately on the ground, for example, but loathing the picking of the nose, spots, and scabs, for fear of infection. This tension in the discourse may also explain why my hosts in Anshan love to jibe that I am "always ill" because I am "too hygienic", in defense of the implicit accusation that their environment is "dirty" when I suffer stomach upsets in their company.

Still other Chinese have recently taken the pursuit of hygiene to an excessive degree, in the "jiepi" craze evinced by Chinese housewives concerned to defend their homes and families against germs from the public sphere. Widely discussed in the popular press as a form of obsessive-compulsive behavior, the term refers to the over-zealous washing of hands, the disinfecting of new objects brought into the house, the unnecessarily frequent changing of outdoors shoes for fear of a bacterial build-up, the washing of plastic shopping bags before re-using them, and the avoidance of contact with paper money, which is similarly supposed to be laden with harmful pathogens. The phenomenon is proliferating rapidly, as modernity ideals of cleanliness become increasingly instilled in the popular imagination on account of detergent company advertising and local government communications (see also below).

Ins and outs

Unhealthy or sick people, of course, may burden others with their care and possibly spread infection, so individuals have a civil responsibility to try to be healthy. Where civil boundaries pertaining to hygiene awareness are brought into the private or intimate sphere in China, however, this can result in problematic charges of pedantry, formalism or even selfishness. My hosts, for example, found it incomprehensible when they heard that my parents might agree to sleep in separate beds if one of them has the flu, in an attempt to prevent the other getting ill too, since "civil" concern for personal health is amongst the very last of things you should profess if a relative is sick in China. By a similar token, whereas in many modern homes it is quite negotiable that an adult may need to shut themselves away for a few hours in order to work or study, in China the shutting of an internal door for anything except the most personal of activities can be considered quite rude. Likewise, while Western children over a certain age will be given their "own" space to play, most urban Chinese children are too absorbed with supervised homework to be given much of their "own" space. Thus, while middle-aged Fang Kai was unconcerned to leave the living room whilst speaking loudly on his mobile phone, my efforts to study quietly whilst he slept during the middle of the day earned me no credit at all because he was not fundamentally attuned to such "civil" deference.

Indeed, my hosts would sometimes deliberately exploit my investment in civil discourse to indicate my exclusion from the intimate sphere. Having noticed that I preferred to eat with my lips together whilst chewing, and felt the need to avert my eyes when seated directly opposite him at meals three times per day, Fang Kai, again, flagrantly flouted the implicit idea that he should have to conform to my foreign norms, asking, "Why do you keep your lips closed?", "What use is it?", and "Is it because of the influence on other people?", whilst slopping and slurping noisily across the table. Fang, however, notably made the effort to wipe his mouth and guard his burping when eating with his friend Guan Hongliang, a man of high status and representative of the official, civic sphere, who himself only occasionally spoke with food in his mouth. There was another situation at dinner with Fang Kai, too, when a third person asked me a question that I could not answer verbally because I had food in my mouth. I answered noiselessly, making a gesture with raised shoulders and upward rotation of the palms as if to say "I don't know", but this happened while Fang's eyes were momentarily fixed in the bowl from which he was slurping, and he mistakenly thought I had not answered the question, before jumping in to repeat the question to me, since he thought this rude.

Speaking of eating, talking about the origins of the food we were eating whilst actually eating it, and "unsavory" topics of conversation at the dinner table most generally – indeed talking about bodily functions and animal parts and so on – were areas where once again there was occasionally explicit contention. Once it had been discovered that I would rather not think about cows' udders whilst drinking milk, for example, even the eating of human placenta (still widely available on the black market), and unborn fetuses (allegedly a favorite of the still much-reviled Japanese), were not off the menu for discussion, provocations which were justified by the fact that human placenta and unborn fetuses are believed to be extremely high in nutrition according to now illegal interpretations of Chinese medicine (Pritchford 1993: 322). Powerful assertions of "incivility" like this are perhaps quite difficult to understand from a particular modern perspective; though many of these behaviors are enacted in genuine ignorance of civil norms, they are also made in willful ignorance too, and in some cases the "opening of the floodgates" governing civil categories remains a resource for individuals disaffected by the trajectory of China's reforms to forge a social space for themselves.

At other times, however, it was precisely by others making a civil transgression in my presence that the "foreigner" was to understand he belonged to the intimate sphere. Long after meeting my wife's grandfather, I was assured that when I first met him he had tried not to speak too much because his wife had given him explicit instructions to try to "hold his wind". I was led to understand what a privilege it was that the grandfather, who "had held a senior position and received the best of gifts back in the days when nobody was corrupt", had altered his behavior for me, and then changed it back again once he felt that I belonged! In contrast to European middle-class households, therefore, where members are socialized to behave towards each other as if strangers in the civic sphere, certain Chinese families may afford more intimacy between their members and allow for belching, farting, ways of speaking and other behaviors that define the intimate sphere in ways also observable in some non-middle-class European families. In Anshan, the situational lines of inclusion, which are often to do with communal eating and drinking (see the next chapter), can be drawn such that friends and colleagues may be inducted into intimate spheres with a fart or burp as a waft of belonging!

P's and Q's

Intimacy, indeed, is actively encouraged in China, especially at the "local" end of the situational civility spectrum, where people are actively encouraged to get along with each other without ceremony (see the next chapter). As a foreigner, I am frequently told that I needn't say "thank you" (*xiexie*) so much. "We are family; you don't need to say thank you", and "English people are really polite" (*tebie limao*) are regular refrains. My most intimate relations know that I express thanks out of deeply ingrained habit, but new acquaintances can find it disarming, my excessive civility, to their minds, keeping them as strangers. Of particular potential for confusion is the fact that I cannot help but say "thank you" to my wife, which in a place where "thank you" is reserved primarily for the public, non-intimate sphere can signify a lack of intimacy between us (which is not the case). One can now imagine the dilemma, say, of secret lovers: if they fail to say "thank you" in situations where it is socially expected, they may reveal their intimacy to others, while by using "thank you" they are mutually undermining their relationship.

There is also a sense, however, in which one does not normally say "thank you" in China to people who are just doing their job, so it seems exceptional to my informants that I say "thank you" to the restaurant waitress for filling up my glass. Though one may comment positively on people's work if it is excellently performed – "recognizing" the serving person as human by saying "you're hard-working" (*ni xinkule*) – saying "thank you" in a service context in China usually carries an ambiguity of command, and in exactly the same way in which saying "please" (*qing*) has tones of subservience to superior status. A careful ear to the ground, however, will note that a more democratized form of thanks has begun to sneak into Chinese discourse in response to the ordinary and unexceptional exertions of others, perhaps as a result of Hollywood movies and exposure to foreigners. This tendency has been encouraged by the state, which is keen to make it seem that the consumption of culture is equally accessible to all, which of course it is not, since the whole point of saying "thank you" just out of politeness in China is precisely to demonstrate exceptional cultivation and personal quality. Indeed, wherever explicit expression of gratitude is required in China, merely saying "thank you" is never enough, with the *buyongxie* that the Chinese say in response every time someone says "thank you" to them ultimately signifying the meaninglessness and insincerity of words.[1]

The relationship between professed intimacy and actual behavior is complex in any case: a steel worker who kindly agreed to have me over for an evening excitedly exhorted me to "be at ease" (*suibian*) even as he over-arranged tables and chairs and tripped over himself offering me fruits to eat. In other contexts, indeed, this same "be at ease" is used to make negative judgments about people who do not understand civil requirements: when I complimented the general manager of a Western-style restaurant on the orderliness of her staff, the term "be at ease" was used to describe "outsiders" (*waidiren*) who don't do service well. Further, excess civility can of course be used to exclude even with the guise of intimacy, such as when a family friend I had not previously met asked me if he could serve me at dinner, as if to draw us together in friendship, saying "You're a guest". When I replied to this saying, "I'm not really a guest, thank you, I know all these people, have lived here for years and have recently become family", the man responded, "No, really, I'll serve you", as if disagreeing and asserting his somehow more profound intimacy with our "hosts", thus keeping the interaction between the two of us in the civil, non-intimate sphere. Foreigners in China are perhaps especially likely to be encountered primarily as "guests" in this sense, since boundaries demarcating intimacy in China are often informed by ethnicity (cf. Chapter 6).

Intimate relations in China involve serving each other in very different ways to that in civil relationships. While service to a "universal" norm in the civil sphere is supposed to benefit everyone no more than any other – that is, you must be public-minded and public-spirited, etc. – service in the intimate sphere is explicitly personal. Accordingly, there are other instances, too, where the perception that the public or civil sphere has been illegitimately brought into the intimate sphere can cause offence. If good hygiene, rationality, the necessity of being socially responsible, accountable and fair, defines the civic sphere to the contrast of the poor hygiene and self-interest which define the intimate sphere, then corruption, official nepotism, and corporate pollution are close in the discourse too. This is perhaps especially the case where there is such little trust in the official sphere as there is in China, where the public so often seems something of which to take advantage (Fei *et al.* 1992: 60). Where the boundary between the intimate and the public is perceived to have been breached by way of official corruption, for example, at once "opened" inappropriately, the boundary is perceived to have been equally as inappropriately "closed" to protect those who have failed in their civic duty. Thus, while there are competing constructions of where the boundary between the intimate and the public should lie, most Chinese agree that there should be at least some separation between the two in all situations.

Public sex!

Sex is a particularly interesting area of practice from the perspective of the construction of intimate and civil boundaries, since it is perhaps where self and others come closest, though there are of course many other ways to be intimate (Yan 2003b). Maoist times were characterized by sexual Puritanism, where even talking to a girl or holding her hand indicated an intention to marry, and "good" wives would walk a few paces behind their husbands in public to maintain propriety. In the contemporary post-market reform "open" era, however, it is easy to see how the exposure of your body can be entirely reappraised in certain relations: it is easy to see how "animality" can be desirable in sexual relations, for example. However, suspicions of sexual laxity or hyper-sexuality can equally easily arise from, say, women exposing too much flesh on the leg or around the midriff as they try hard to be "modern" (Lei 2003), so that the "floodgates open" metaphor returns again: "some women will do anything for money", said an attendant at a luxury health club, referring to the women who work in the "massage" area downstairs. A certain sexualization might even be quite necessary for Chinese women to compete in the increasingly internationalizing and cosmopolitan sphere: a more public display of the promise of intimacy is in vogue, and women have found it to their material advantage to cater to this need (Hanser 2005; Zheng 2008).

Quite similarly, in prostitution, where the intimate is actively consumed in the public sphere (Ding 2012), the prostitute is an ambiguous figure who "both wants to be a bitch and hang up a sign saying she is morally pure" (*you yao dang biaozi, you yao li paifang*)[2]: though the service purchased is perhaps intended to be fouler and baser in its raw "intimacy" than the interaction of spouses, the "whore" must make herself out to be a "clean girl" in order to generate business, and her comportment may be dignified by the decorum appropriate for a business deal right down to the additional charge for having sex without a condom, the ultimate prophylaxis between self and others

(Zheng 2008). Again, prostitution demonstrates the sexualization of the internationalizing and cosmopolitan sphere: newspaper advertisements promoting prostitutes' services in China will sometimes explicitly emphasize the "quality" of the staff in terms of them being university students, presumably in order to appeal to a more "civil" client, with those women plying the big-city markets for foreigners commanding the highest prices, thus further complicating the axis of the civil and the intimate (Xin 2002: 35).

Extramarital sexual intimacy, in prostitution or otherwise, of course remains explicitly deviant in discourse, but even within marriage there will likely be separate rules about how partners construct and deconstruct their intimacy from the public sphere that surrounds them. One would expect a proper intimacy rather than a stilted civility between sexual partners, yet these boundaries are negotiated in complex ways, actors graduating "in" and "out" according to mutually defined terms.

As such, the gendered and sexual dimension of bodily posturing emerged as important in the construction of civil behavior, as when a middle-aged woman bent to attend to something at her feet, thus forcing her bottom directly towards my face for a prolonged period of time, apparently entirely without discernible shame! Though more than one female informant told me about the importance of sitting with your legs crossed, rather than apart, in the Anshan branch of the international supermarket Carrefour, a woman held a young girl (though surely old enough to know better?) over a waste-bin to pee, her legs splayed wide apart against her chest to reveal her vagina to every customer arriving at the top of the escalator! "They just don't know", said a presumably wealthy, middle-aged man of the changing room assistants in Anshan's luxury Euro-health club, who were apparently unaware that customers might prefer space to shower and towel away from the immediate gaze of several same-sex attendants. The man's comment was supposed to indicate that we shared a similar way of thinking in this respect, a rare act of "intimacy" shown in an environment where fellow customers preferred instead to act indifferently, that is "civilly", in accordance with their own perceived status and their perception of the international sphere, rather than express the intense interest in my being a foreigner that most people in Anshan do.

For these customers in Euro-health, however, it was perfectly acceptable to walk about in the changing rooms with their private parts dangling and swinging about, to make full-frontal naked greetings, to converse and even to touch, quite without fear of any adverse judgment or homophobia, and this in a manner quite unlike the loutish assertion that only too much testosterone might generate in males in similar situations in the UK (Farrer 2002: 60). In the UK, of course, while in the company of unfamiliar, naked, same-sex adults, you are supposed to posture yourself with a complex mix of eye-contact aversion and general economy. In Anshan, however, many men seem to feel little compulsion to avert their eyes to the ceiling above, left or right into empty space, down to mind their own business, or indeed anywhere but the regions of my private space even whilst I am using the urinal! This latter behavior can probably be accounted for by the interest in foreigners' physical constitutions; I doubt Chinese men enact this kind of behavior between themselves to a comparable degree. However, the stripping off of shirts in public, or the lifting of the shirt to expose the abdomen in order to cool down, again forms of distinctly male assertion quite different from the needy and aggressive showing of skins that certain sorts of males will perform in the UK, are practices so sufficiently status quo in contemporary China that the central government has found it necessary to launch a range of "civilizing" counter-measures nationwide (see below).

Take a stand

It is rare to hear people in Anshan publicly challenge what they perceive as incivility: the avenues, institutions and fundamental rights to complain about uncivil behavior do not exist or are largely ineffective outside of major cities. "We're used to it", and "There's nothing that can be done", are ubiquitous refrains. Many people complain in private, however, signifying the frustration that reality doesn't add up to supposed norms. Complaints were made when a neighbor lit a fire-stove in a communal corridor and spattered boiling hot cooking oil over the tiled flooring regardless of the smoke and wailing fire alarms. Complaints also followed the advent of the recent dog-ownership craze, since residents coop their mutts up to bark night and day no matter that they live in close proximity to non-intimates. Other gripes concern food waste and litter thrown from windows high above the streets in residential areas.

From a particular modern perspective, many people in Anshan seem apparently oblivious of the trajectories of other people negotiating public space around them. Supermarket aisles, train stations and other crowded public spaces can be especially challenging. Anshan's citizens must also suffer noisy construction works throughout the night, high-intensity techno music for the elderly to exercise by at the break of dawn, and fireworks extravaganzas in residential areas to commemorate every wedding, funeral, and new restaurant launch. Many of these disruptions are now outlawed in Beijing and other large cities on the grounds of disturbing the elderly and infirm, but not so in Anshan, so that more developed cities can clearly be seen to lead the way in the transition up the sliding scale from the intimate towards the civil sphere, from the local to the cosmopolitan, as a new form of judgment becomes normalized.[3]

Not complaining can be distinctive in itself, of course, for individuals who make a civil virtue out of restraint. In the UK, "holding a civil tongue" means to exercise a particular form of control where one avoids unthinkingly speaking one's mind in public, especially on intimate and sexual matters. In Anshan, however, it is far more legitimate for people from the external sphere to interrupt in the intimate sphere in the first place. Answers will be publicly demanded to questions about matters which in many other places would be thought private: it is not at all uncommon for a stranger or new acquaintance to ask a string of questions such as, "Are you married yet?", "Why don't you have any children?", "Do you have an illness?", etc. Relevant, too, is the way in which I find myself remonstrating with my hosts for discussing personal or family matters as we pass through the threshold of our home: lowering my voice is deeply learned and habitual, but both my hosts and our neighbors seem subconsciously mindful that until recently people would leave their doors open throughout the day and neighbors could come and go as they pleased. My hosts are also unconcerned to hush their voices when laughing at potentially injurious judgments about uncivil others: they do not seem to see that I am really judging negatively, and that I intend this to be a private matter.

Indeed, Chinese people can be readily observed to be less concerned about offending non-intimate others even in the explicitly civil sphere: Chinese delegates at conferences can often appear less inclined to lower their voices if compelled to speak at the same time as the principal speaker than Western delegates consider acceptable. Yet, although many Chinese do not register the "polite" cough, prickly glances or (if absolutely necessary) "tut" of the tongue variously expected to be enough to correct "uncivil" public behavior in modern Britain, dissatisfied frowns and mutually acknowledged rolls of the eyes at third-party behavior are increasingly common as the finer comportments distinctive to the civil sphere become rapidly understood.

It is often Anshan's youths or young adults who try hardest to be identified with manners, perhaps on account of greater exposure to modern or international norms. "Sam", for example, doesn't like it when his wife interrupts him while he is telling me about how much he knows about music in the West: he doesn't react and makes her wait until he has finished even though I offer him an opportunity to break off the conversation to attend to her by deliberately averting my eyes from his to her. Sam's wife has not been abroad. Sam also covers his mouth with his hand if he needs to speak when eating, something he has probably picked up in Canada as an overseas student, I imagine. Likewise, "Andy", who was schooled in South Africa, thinks it is good to have me as a friend because he can "learn manners" (*xue limao*) from me. Again, "Cindy" "liked the UK", because people were "more polite" and "opened the door" for her. Quite clearly these people believe that there is a certain set of behaviors appropriate and necessary for negotiating the cosmopolitan or international sphere that they are eager to re-enact in the cause of asserting themselves vis-à-vis their surroundings.

By contrast, it is significantly the middle-aged and older who lived through Maoist times when civil behavior was denigrated as "bourgeois" who invest least in competing through civil behavior. Those rummaging through racks of unpacked raw meats in the supermarket with their bare hands before wandering off to touch everything else in the store are also nearly always of advanced years. Age and generation are also nearly always a differentiator between those who find me practicing *taiji* in Anshan's woods and whisper a note of surprise ("foreigner!"), or even call "Hello!" (in English), and those who seem almost deliberately to disturb my space, walking right up to and immediately past me, before walking on by without any obvious qualms at all. "Either they don't have any education or they want to feel like they're the host, like they've got power", a young and relatively civil friend explained to me. There is an entirely different mindset and set of behavioral norms distinguishing more civil people from those less so, of which age and generation are important structuring factors.

Age and generation, however, are by no means the only factors structuring the discourse of civil behavior. There are those modernizing young sophisticates for whom barefacedly staring or pointing at foreigners are norms regarded as rude, but then there are just as many young people who evidently have not been schooled in the ways of civil behavior at all. Indeed, walking around Anshan's more downtown urban areas, you will see people of all ages occupying some vaguely delimited space in the streets outside their homes, hanging around in various degrees of undress, washing clothes, washing dishes, cooking and arguing, with the doors to their homes wide open to the public so that you can see and hear everything that goes on inside, yet entirely ignoring or not at all expecting any public gaze (Farrer 2002: 58). While Westerners and now many Chinese expect the private to be closed, secret and out of sight, for Chinese individuals bathing their bodies, breastfeeding babies, and even sleeping directly before the public eye, the sphere of intimacy remains distinctly within public space.

The civil behavior discourse is therefore quite clearly divided between those for whom intimacy and privacy are coterminous, and those for whom intimacy remains visible and not coterminous with privacy. There are many factors structuring the grammar of this divide aside from age and generation, not the least of which is formal education, but the difference is also a function of being wealthy enough to affect the civil sphere as a boundary between the intimate and public, or not. When we realize that the new and expensive homes in China's cities are constructed precisely to cordon off private utopias away from these lively and textured street scenes, and that the distribution of social space on those lively streets is apparently governed by the rule that the bigger and more expensive to repair your car is, the more right to social space you can claim, we must explicitly consider the question of civility as a function of economic and political power. For as China increasingly engages with the civil, international and modernizing sphere, the perception is rife that the intimate is rapidly being hollowed out of the public by private property and commodity ownership – that is, by the consumption that business practitioners most readily understand (cf. Elias 2000).

Breaking them in

By way of analyzing this problem, consider first this excerpt from Du Feng, owner of a luxury health club in Anshan, who is answering a question about the "responsibilities" (*zeren*) his firm has to society:

> China and Chinese people still have to go through certain process of adjustment before they can have a high degree of cultivation and high-level

quality-of-personhood (*suzhi*). Most important is that they must be educated. Anshan city is not the same as before: a good environment is being
created to cause those who don't understand civility (*budong wenming*)
and public morals, to force them to embrace civility. I'll give you a simple
example: if there's a person who doesn't understand civility, who spits
everywhere as he likes, and randomly throws dirty things around, and
you take him to the great hall in a five-star hotel, where the floor is really
clean, clean beyond comparison, and everyone is wearing Western suits
and leather shoes, he will be too embarrassed to spit on the floor. If you
have a clean environment you'll force him to behave.

Du clearly thinks that civil norms are Western, of the cosmopolitan sphere in
origin, and come at the cost of embarrassing people, and forcing them
to change their behavioral norms. He also seems to think civility is related to
top-end consumption: "five-star hotel", etc. Du goes on to say that from a
certain date members of his club will not be allowed to wear the loose paja-
mas currently provided, but must rather bring sports clothes, thus further
demonstrating that his understanding of civility is underscored by a particular
vision: "Sometimes, as soon as you are not careful, they 'open up'; opening
up is uncivil (*kaile bu wenming*), and not nice to look at. When doing yoga,
you've got to see the curvy line of your body. You must wear the right clothes,
not these baggy things. It doesn't look good for others." This essentially
materialist aesthetic, where individuals must look the part as well as behave in
certain ways, goes beyond the simple adherence to rules about not spitting,
etc., because it is a total vision of an alternative reality rather than of any one
particular behavioral adjustment. This aesthetic is highly salient in China,
and is why questions about "sustainability" or "green" consumption will
return answers about not spitting and so on, as well as recycling, emissions
reduction, etc.

Discourse on *wenming*, the term that Du Feng uses for "civility", has
crystallized in the contemporary era in approximate parallel with discourse
on "quality-of-personhood" (*suzhi*). The precise meaning of the latter term is
little agreed upon, its utility consisting precisely in the flexibility of its application, but suffice to say that low *suzhi* is often cited to explain uncivil behaviors, and that uncivil behaviors are amongst the first point of reference when
trying to define *suzhi*. Academics broadly agree that *suzhi* discourse has conflated ordinary people's "lack" of manners and "lack" of formal education
with issues of over-population in the countryside and the "lack" of progress
among the lower rungs of urban society (Kipnis 2007; Jacka 2009). The Chinese
State and its contemporary allies – that is, those who most stimulate economic growth – have been constructed as "supplement" (Anagnost 2004: 193)
to this "lack" in order to validate the single-party political status quo and
legitimize a paternal role in raising China out of the ranks of the unruly. In
the run-up to the 2008 Beijing Olympics, in particular, the Chinese government harnessed hosts of celebrities to nod their approval for acts of civil

deference, and plastered exhortations to "Welcome in the new trend of civility" on gigantic city centre billboards across the land. More prohibitive instructions about not spitting, etc., were posted in local newspapers and displayed in lower-key community areas.

Noting that this discourse has the effect of shaming lower-class Chinese persons into global cosmopolitan norms, scholars of a broadly Leftist disposition have attempted to lay blame for this mechanism at the feet of Western consumers, arguing that this discourse actively disguises the fact that the "bodies" (Anagnost 2004) of rural migrants and the urban poor provide the surplus of cheap labor that allows the accumulation of capital in the hands of the global elite and the flourishing of the Chinese middle class (Pun 2003; Yan 2003a). This "neo-liberal" (Ong 2006) exploitation is reasonably clear in the excerpt from Du Feng above: according to Du, Chinese people can only realize a "high-level quality-of-personhood" by being shamed at the altar of the "five-star hotel" and "Western suits" representative of capitalism, but while discourses of civility are used to excuse all manner of actions that unjustly constrain individual agency in China, there is nothing in Du's discourse to suggest that the goals of civility are mistaken, and nothing to suggest that market capitalism be opposed to social intimacy per se. The accumulation of capital in China's cities does depend in large part on capitalists' exploitation of rural-to-urban aspirations, and on the social aspirations of all non-elites most broadly, aspirations of which civility is often a part. While civility might be an important part of Du's sanitized vision of material affluence, however, civility cannot be "forced" on individuals at all, but only encouraged, because it is a transactional logic where disciplinary "costs" are matched by corresponding personal gains.

Breaking them out

By way of addressing this point, let us first consider Xiao Qiang, an Anshan graduate who is keen to speak the "language" of civility as a function of articulating his middle-class aspirations. Xiao is consistently keen to document that he is "competitive" above the level his call-centre job might suggest:

> On the bus in foreign countries, people will smile at each other to express their kindness when their eyes meet, is this not so? But on buses in China, when two strangers' eyes meet, they immediately hide away from each other. Why is this? Because there is a distance between people: really strange; a very indifferent feeling. Uncivil behaviors are universal here: spitting randomly, for example; or making lots of noise in public, upsetting people without the slightest self-awareness. These kinds of things really are a widespread. For example, when we get on a bus there's no queuing, making people feel real regret. In fact, Anshan also has this situation. What can we say about the universal situation in China right now? It's people's hearts; people's feelings are more and more indifferent.

No-one cares about strangers at all anymore; this is all unsatisfactory. Of course, there are many people who play on other people's kindness and empathy to cheat them. For example, beggars who use people's empathy to cheat them and don't rely on their own hard work to live; they only want to abuse people's kindness to cheat them. The result is that human feelings have become very, very cold. It used to be the case that, in China, when two people met for the first time, even if their only relation, their only link, was just a number or a QQ name,[4] or an email, they wouldn't break the feeling: it was group living. But now it's all cold, flat and lonely; so it's a tragedy, a real tragedy.

Xiao may be read as nostalgic for a social intimacy felt to have been lost in urban spaces: a very common notion for country people experiencing the breakdown of rural living and the transition to urban livelihoods. However, it is clear that he invokes a discourse of civility, at least in the first instance, with his references to public behavior in Western countries, and goes on to construct China as suffering a problem in this regard. Perhaps the most interesting observation to make, though, is that in conflating the discourse of civil behavior with an attack on selfishness, Xiao actually inverts the linear continuum in which this chapter has argued the structure of the civil behavior discourse consists. That is to say, it is not so much the spitting, the not queuing, or the making of lots of noise that bothers Xiao, though this is indeed what he refers to in the first instance, but rather the pronounced "indifference", lack of "human feelings" and lack of intimacy between people. Xiao, indeed, doesn't see civil behavior in terms of personal privacy at all, but rather through the prism of intimacy with others, precisely the opposite concept. The way Xiao mixes this judgment with the judgment of those who "play on other people's kindness and empathy" for personal gain and so on only reinforces this observation: while he continues to seek intimacy in the public sphere rather than in personal privacy, he remains unable to separate his judgments of civil behavior from judgments of moral character, a very different discourse altogether (see Chapter 6).

Xiao, then, is an excellent example of how the civil behavior discourse is structured by those for whom intimacy and privacy are coterminous, and those for whom intimacy remains visible and not coterminous with privacy. Xiao might realize that the ability to separate is the very principle of civil discourse, and that learning to seek intimacy in personal privacy rather than visible intimacy in the public sphere is a form of individuation very necessary for his social aspirations (see Chapter 10). However, until then, no matter how much Xiao inveighs against "uncivil" others, he is speaking the "right" discourse in the "wrong" way.

Of further significance here is that civil discourse is not the cause of the "feelings" Xiao regrets. Indeed, it is quite clear that everything "bad" he bemoans is the result not of civility but of incivility – precisely the opposite concept, although Xiao himself doesn't quite grasp the difference. Xiao is probably right that the underlying cause of China's spitting and queue jumping is the fact that Chinese act only out of personal convenience and self-interest when in public and have very little responsibility to society at large. However, although he seems to lay the blame for this lack of responsibility at the door of economic reform by pining for an earlier, supposedly more intimate time, there is nothing to suggest that popular discourses on civility, urban living, middle-class aspirations, or indeed market capitalism per se, are themselves in any way culpable here.

Responsibility for the lack of public morals in contemporary China does not lie with capitalism or neo-liberalism. Though China's "opening up" may have contributed to the perceived decline in public spiritedness, the further advance of global capitalism need not at all be threatened by Chinese people exhibiting greater civil courtesy towards each other. Civility, after all, isn't so much about whether you spit or not, but about the right not to be spat on if you don't want to be spat on; and manners, to put it bluntly, need not cost anything except respect for a "value code" (Anagnost 2004) that allows people to begin from a relatively universal starting point. Insofar as the Chinese State has promoted a set of social norms for civil behavior that offers as much potential for social aspiration as it does for marginalization, it should be praised, not least because such universalism has not been a feature of the prevailing Chinese political disposition to date. After all, many Chinese themselves don't have a problem with some people being richer or more socially elevated than others, or so the government now tells us: trading and accumulating money are Chinese characteristics. What Chinese people most can't stand are rich or powerful people, especially from the public or official sphere, who don't afford lower persons the same degree of civility that they themselves demand.

Because it is not only the rural migrants and urban poor with whom certain Left-leaning sectors of the social science establishment would have us sympathize who exhibit uncivil behaviors in contemporary China, of course. In fact, a less ideologically biased observation would note that youthful migrant individuals are now often more civil in their mannerisms than their urban hosts (cf. Jacka 2006), and this not because they have come under the spell of "neo-liberalism" or some such, but because they are improvising upon dominant discourses in order to get ahead, and collapsing the urban-rural boundary upon which civilizing discourses in China largely depend (see Chapter 8). Moreover, and as shown above, those people who do enact uncivil behaviors do not always do so as innocently as the social science Left would have us believe, but rather as tactics of self-assertion that suit their individual and collective projects of exclusion; and this even though civil behavior remains a very necessary condition for social distinction in China today, whereas until very recently you could still garner respect if you were a person of public rank or power, though nonetheless uncivil.

No, responsibility for the lack of public morals in contemporary China lies with the pseudo-Socialist Chinese State for repressing the evolution of a political environment conducive to equal respect for all persons to accompany its economic reforms (Yan 2003: 225–35). The State must level gaping economic inequalities and sufficiently provoke a more democratic notion of civil behavior amongst the population: democratic reform, indeed, need not mean civil anarchy as its opponents in the Party mechanically suggest, but the formal implementation of a mechanism by which individuals are as able as possible to universally access equivalent political rights. Markets have been consistently shown to aid in this regard, though there is little to suggest that they need do so inherently (Solinger 1999). However, there is nothing inherently wrong with aspiring to consume more like Westerners, to be middle class, urban or civil if doing so means that individuals may be increasingly afforded the prospect of equal rights.

The challenge of governing a market-based society is to ensure that personal privacy and individual autonomy are enshrined in civic institutions without individuals losing sight of their communitarian responsibilities and hollowing the intimate sphere out of "legitimate" society. The optimum fusion is of course precisely what the Chinese State promises in its fusion of "Confucian collectivism" with the market economy: that is, single-party, State-led economic development and omnipresent oversight of social categories. There might still yet come a time when China has much to teach the supposedly "civil" West about how to balance these imperatives, but this is also what will not be realized until the Chinese State is properly held to account by the Chinese people, and there are surely no "Chinese characteristics" that can prevent that, as the Chinese government must by now almost certainly be aware.

5   Sociability

Interrelations

This chapter is about how different personality types are constructed ranging from innate character to the protean use of diverse registers of social intercourse. In particular, the analysis concerns the self that competes by projecting a character amenable to friendship or social liking. The judgment analyzed here is therefore much more subjective and situational in its "internal" form than those "rules" articulated in some of the previous discourses, but a judgment that nevertheless describes a particular form of individual in the Anshan context.

For clarification, sociability is not a sub-set of knowledge (Chapter 3): if we think in terms of competing to achieve distinction, and the exercise of various strategies towards those ends, there is clearly a difference between "to know" as in knowing the rules and being able to apply them appropriately, and "to know" as in being known by others as a character. Sociability remains very closely linked to knowledge, however, because we must know the form appropriate for social interaction in different situations in order to generate good rapport with others. The sense in which it is important to know the "right" people is close in the discourse too, but "connections" is quite a different modality of social competition. Sociability should not be mistaken for the discourse of moral character elucidated in the following chapter either, because although a person considered morally good is usually also considered sociably likeable, and vice versa, the two concepts are not mutually equivalent: whereas sociability concerns the "self" as a social-psychological construct, the discourse of moral character, especially in China, is a discourse where "who" you are is defined first and foremost by what you do. Indeed, insofar as sociability concerns a judgment of "being" sociable no matter how this sociability is arrived at, this discourse shares a closer affinity with the authenticity discourse analyzed in Chapter 2 than it does with moral character, and this is perhaps especially so in the context of Anshan, as will be shown below.

Personal character

Contemporary Chinese, or rather the Chinese language, shares the concept of an "innate" character or personality (*xingge*) unique to the individual with languages elsewhere. Now, the extent to which personal character is truly "innate" or is entirely socially constructed itself is not my primary concern here; neither am I invested in the essentialist notion that the Chinese language did not traditionally have this locus of meaning (Elvin 1985). Suffice to say that in present-day China personal character often constitutes the locus for judgments of social transgression: i.e. "He can't help it, it's just his character". Indeed, I will argue in this chapter that while social psychology-inflected literatures on China essentialize Chinese individuals as having a low "awareness of one's distinct personality traits" (Aaker and Schmitt 2001: 562; Markus and Kitayama 1991), in terms of the construction of "innate" character individual agency is actually configured in an even more individualized way in contemporary China than in the contemporary West, or at least in an interestingly different, and still personal way.[1]

The first observation to make here is that despite the universal sanctity of the individual firmly enshrined in modern European political thought – that is, the very idea often set against the "collectivist" Chinese stereotype – the discourse of innate character in the West remains highly normalizing in form (Dumont 1992). Consider the UK, for example, where one of the biggest adolescent crises young people face is that they will be branded with a marker of abnormality. At school, it is utterly unacceptable to stand out as different from others, and if you are branded "freak", "geek", "nerd" or "perve", you do not say "I'm a nerd and proud of it", but rather do everything you can to conform. Even in the best of schools any marker of difference is subject to being highlighted, ridiculed and corrected as part of the imposition of a median or norm for identity – "piggy", "four-eyes", "skint", etc. In adult life, markers of character extremes such as "introvert" or "extrovert" are implicitly seen as "deviant", invisibly prefixed by a "too"; eccentricity is labeled "weird"; and work environments disguise brutal character assassination as affectionate banter ("taking the piss"). Indeed, there is a sense in which the very worst thing an individual can do is to try to opt out of this discourse, which would be understood as a weakness, thereby implicating all those present and instituting this mode of socialization. We might even say that the extreme individualism characteristic of certain elements of UK youth and counter-culture can be usefully understood as a reaction to this very strong process of normalization (Wagner 1981).

In Anshan, China, on the other hand, young people are not pursued by this same kind of angst, and neither are adults plagued by the same kind of insecurity. Though China's official education system is widely accused of striving to annul individuality through rote learning and so on, students generally feel it far less necessary to grind the individuality out of others in the cause of making fun, and individual difference in terms of "innate" character is far easier to negotiate. Social pressure certainly characterizes life in China, not just for school children but for hard-driven and existentially insecure adults also, but these are angst and insecurities of a quite different nature.

Take Chinese medicine, for example, where people are regarded as unique mind-body complexes, distinct, whole and complete within themselves, yet nevertheless in constant free exchange with the world of energy around them: bounded entities that are, rather than have, a certain nexus of traits separate from all other traits (Zhan 2009). From this perspective Chinese individuals are always considered more or less "damp" (*shi*) or "dry" (*gan*) than all possible others, axiomatic principles of discernment that serve to diagnose individuality within a matrix of such principles. Correspondingly, individuals are always more or less "sensitive to" (*pa*) "hot" (*re*) or "cold" (*leng*), similar principles of diagnosis, and it really doesn't matter which, but it is recognized that you will always either be "one who fears hot" (*parede*) or "one who fears cold" (*palengde*), both principles being understood as legitimate directions rather than extremes.

This discourse penetrates deeply into everyday life, proliferating in judgments about individuals' physically embodied constitutions and "tempers" (*piqi*); whether your "stomach" (*wei*), "spleen" (*pi*), "kidney" (*shen*), or "lung" (*fei*) is "suited" (*shihe*) to particular foods, practices and combinations of these, judgments given further definition by reference to additional axiomatic principles of taste: "sour" (*suan*), "sweet" (*tian*), "bitter" (*ku*), "hot" (*la*), etc. (Farquhar 2002). In accordance with this discourse, it is perfectly legitimate to accept or decline colors, dress styles, activities, environments, jobs and even relationships, almost anything in fact, in Anshan, just because these do or do not "suit" (*shihe*) your "innate" character or personality, and entirely without fear of negative social impact. It is understood in this articulation, moreover, that objects of consumption, at once tailored precisely to match, must be continuously regulated and adjusted, since in this sense personal character is never in fact "innate" at all, but rather defined by individual agency's interaction with its environment, the parameters for judgment always being continuously redefined in the actual dynamic context at the time.

Correspondingly, everyday discourse in Anshan finds almost no illegitimate extremes in terms of the particular mix of character attributes that makes individuals "them", and where a wife identifies her husband as "introverted" (*neixiang*), "liberal" (*kaifang*), or "conservative" (*baoshou*), this is seen as an entirely good thing, not as deviance from a norm, but as a statement of difference taken precisely as an indicator of the person's normality. Similarly, children who might elsewhere be pilloried at school for being "different" are recognized as uniquely valuable social contributors.

Magnanimous me

If we grant that the discourse of innate character finds so little by way of transgression in Anshan compared to the West, it is all the more the case that the organizing principle of the Sociability discourse is an openness and generosity of character. Keywords in the positive discourse include "huoda", "dadu", and "dafang", the root or common meaning of which can be summarized here as magnanimity. This self is outward-looking, engaging, open-minded, tolerant and forgiving of others. Correspondingly, the negative self in these terms is closed off and ungenerous of spirit, unforgiving and intolerant, miserly and worries about petty gains and losses. When asked what kinds of people she thinks are superior, aspiring young sophisticate Li Sha refers to someone in her class as outstanding: "He's the chairman of the student campus, people like him as soon as they meet him they like him; his personality is magnanimous (*daqi*) and carefree; you can be really relaxed when together with him." Li Sha contrasts this impression with someone in her student lodgings who is, "Awful: everything she does makes other people dissatisfied; she expects other people to do everything for her and always tries to get out of helping; her personality is lacking something".

It is important to see here that the opposition in the Sociability discourse does not correlate to a distinction between "good", outward-looking, extroverted characters and "bad", inward-looking, introverted characters; on the contrary, it is fine to be introverted in Anshan as long as you are willing to freely give of your character in whatever way you do. Migrant worker Xue Liang doesn't like going dancing with the other workers on pay day because he's "not very open" (*bu kailang*): he becomes embarrassed and "gets a red face". He won't sing at karaoke either, but his friends entirely accept this about him, and he about them. It is this acceptance itself, rather than being extrovert per se, that earns credit as good interpersonal rapport at the Sociability discourse.

"Openness" of character can only too easily conflict with the construction of boundaries between intimacy and the social in the civility discourse (Chapter 4), however: indifference is to civil behavior what magnanimity is to intimacy. Thus, while civility is constructed through statements like, "They're dirty, loud, coarse and vulgar", the antithesis is offered through statements like, "They're uptight, they can't relax; they're unfriendly". Literally, as it is said in Anshan, "They won't open up" (*tamen fang bu kai*), where this latter judgment is supposed to indicate an inability to "open up" as a function of an "innate" characteristic. Yet this close discursive proximity means that generosity of character can sometimes usefully smooth over a civility transgression too, such as on the occasion at dinner when we rallied around the host when dead insects were found in the drinking glasses: though we complained to the restaurant staff and insisted that the glasses were changed, we played it down like it was no grave matter, immediately moving on in sociable spirits; when the second set of glasses arrived also dirty my suggestion that we just drink directly from the bottle worked wonders since my hosts seemed to regard me as the locus around which face was to be lost or gained.

In respect of annulling social boundaries, the character given to cultivating good social rapport can usefully iron out status difference in the formal structures of authority too. In some social situations, when you are not in the intimate but the civic sphere, such as when meeting your boss, for example, it may be very beneficial to be reserved or "tight" in your projection of character; over-familiarity might be inappropriate though some staff will try to be on familiar terms with the boss in order to climb up the ranks. The boss, for his part, may insist on maintaining a distance thinking this fairer to everyone involved and more congruent with the demands of managing multiple people. The practical balance between formalism and informality is often much more complicated than such a simple dichotomy, however: a senior figure may profess to be "easy going" (*suibian*) but still expect to be given face, for example. An openness and generosity of spirit, demonstrated through exuberance or ebullience, will likely constitute a transgression in some situations just as excess formalism or pedantry will transgress in others, the extent to which form is required or relaxed depending entirely on actors' intentions at the time.

Indeed, for all the sense in which Chinese people in general, from a particular modern and Western perspective, can often appear objectionably rude, impolite and "informally" coarse in their presence and attitudes (as described in the previous chapter), there is also a sense in which some Chinese people can appear punctilious and "formal" in an almost hypocritical way about their social manners, possessed of a very strong sense of proper behavior in the situation even if these rules are ignored when it suits, and significantly less than magnanimous in their judgment of other people's behavior.

In any case, in China as elsewhere, the social construction is that "innate character" will dictate that individuals have only partial control over how they present themselves and judge others, so that sociability becomes about how people break the rules by character, and also how they use character to break the rules.

Drunken style

Taking others out to dinner provides perhaps the most relevant context for cultivating good social rapport in Anshan. Of particular import is the role of excess (Farquhar 2002). Formal etiquette holds, for example, that hosts should order more than his guests can eat, and that guests should not finish all the food offered as this would indicate that the host is lacking in his generosity, potentially a major loss of face (*mianzi*). An acute observation of dinners in the northeast, however, where individuals pride themselves on having "innate" personal characters especially disposed to cultivating good social rapport, will record that even at ostensibly "formal" occasions interaction consists largely in the spurning of these ritualisms reserved for strangers and (especially foreign) business partners. Once everyone is happy with where they have been seated (an area of practice which can sometimes be highly regulated by formality in itself), and the actual eating begins, formal form is quickly relaxed and an entirely different sort of social interaction is sought to bind the occasion. Though the host will pointedly order more dishes until everyone has eaten their fill, no-one is actively thinking about leaving some on the plate to give the host face – quite the opposite, in fact.

Eating in Anshan, both away from the intimate sphere and within the home also, is always an occasion of boldly expressed fellowship, where diners will continually encourage each other to "Eat more!" (*duo chi yidianr, a!*), and very likely consume excesses of beer and potent liquor (*baijiu*) to the tune of raised voices and general frivolity. It is precisely an abundant excess of social spirit and a collective dispersion of formalities that is affirmed in the exclamations, "It's all in the wine!" (*dou zai jiuli!*) and "bottoms up!" (*ganbei!*), as drinks are deeply indulged, if not by full glasses at a time. Outside of the intimate sphere, drinking alcohol with dinner is regarded as an essential lubricant to the mutual relaxation of form: unless you have a very good reason, refusal to accompany others' drinking is likely to be seen as a sign that you are unwilling to meet others on the same terms. Many people feign or exaggerate medical conditions to get around this imperative, excuses quite accepted because alcohol just doesn't "suit" that person. It has also become increasingly socially accepted not to drink because you are driving, now that this is strictly illegal, or even to have a subordinate drink on your behalf if at a formal occasion. Declining to drink is more legitimate in more intimate situations, but there the requirement for the relaxing of form is also highest, meaning that birthdays, weddings, Chinese New Year celebrations, and so on, are especially good fun.

The way drinking is conducted in Anshan, as throughout urban China, however, can seem overtly formalistic and quite the contrary to the relaxing of form, at least on the surface of things. Glasses are most often filled up in tandem with each other – that is, if I empty my glass, the others should drink up too and refill together (Kipnis 1997: 53–54). This practice is usually driven by males, but there are notable female exceptions. In less than intimate situations, where you are inferior or subservient in position, and especially where it is acknowledged that you want something from the other, it is expected that you must drink and demonstrate that the glass has been emptied by emphatically overturning it before setting it down on the table for a refill. If drinking on behalf of your employer, a relatively recent practice, you must accompany him in the toast then drink two glasses to represent him in response to everyone else's single glass!

At apparently formal occasions, you are also likely to have to stand to drink at every toast, though the manner of expressing your respects by tapping the glass on the table is widely in force where it judged that the rigid application of the rule is unnecessary. Even in the intimate sphere, however, if you do chink glasses together, you should always try to defer by chinking your glass below the others, even if from the seated position, so that your own glass is lowest, depending on age and social seniority; and if initiating drinking, you should always make sure to toast at least some other person, preferably the host, but possibly others present too, before drinking from your own glass, even if it is just a slight tip of the glass and nod of the head as form is mutually acknowledged and relaxed. Indeed, formality is actively joked with, consumed even as it is conjured, actors manipulating decorum in terms of situation and strategic intent: when one observes men stripped to the waist and challenging each other in strictly observed unison, piling up empty beer bottles below their chairs and so forth, the "form" for interaction is certainly about willingness of character rather than formality as such. The only general rule in such situations is that the heartier the situation, the more this "form for formlessness" has to be adhered to: as it is said in Anshan, "If friendship is strong, you'll drink till your stomach bleeds" (*gemenrtie, hechuxue*).

Not all drinking is legitimate in the first place, of course, the object of drinking not being, like it often is in some other countries, simply to get drunk. Outside of cosmopolitan middle-class markets, in places such as Anshan, drinking in China should preferably accompany eating and ideally some form of ritual "feast", usually indoors, and for best effect in order to seal an occasion, friendship or deal. Drinking on your own is seen to defy the point altogether, and drinking till you are out of control is considered quite shameful. Best of all is to drink to prove yourself as a test of strategic control, maintaining form whilst getting drunk, a sense of competition that accounts for ensuring that all others present enjoin in drinking to toasts made to you and the practice of pouring more drinks for others than for yourself. You will even be asked if you have drunk two, or two-and-a-half glasses thus far, and people make remarks that reveal they have made a mental record of how many glasses the others have drunk.

However, although many Chinese are especially concerned to ask "How many bottles can you drink?", or "How many bottles do you want to drink?", the same phrase ambiguously meaning either in a way that only exacerbates the tension somewhat at odds with simply drinking at your own pace without being monitored and competed against – it is usually less about the outright winning that matters in most situations so much as the participation: you get one over the others by being qualitatively more willing to drink, the actual quantity drunk being relatively inconsequential in the final analysis. Most people in Anshan would perhaps be more likely to boast in the strength of the spirit being drunk than in their actual drinking of it, or to boast in their fellow-drinkers' capacities rather than their own; indeed, people will compliment each other on how much they can drink even if they haven't actually drunk much. Thus, though there is always the question "How many bottles can you drink/do you want to drink?", there is very rarely the inane boast "I can drink ten pints" familiar to social drinkers in some other countries, each person's "drinking capacity" a respected factor of their individuality.

The undercurrent is a complicated interplay of all these elements, of course: considerable social rapport is reaped by stoking the fires of collective enthusiasm, but a sense of form is demanded throughout. Far from being formless here, you must ensure that your generosity of spirit appears boundless, but that you also ensure that the object of your friendliness knows this is directed especially at him or her.

True grit

Some Chinese invest in "competing" through a generous excess of personal character more than others, and certain sorts of Anshan people might be especially disposed in this regard. Consider that when my wife and I were invited for dinner at the home of a skilled manual worker from Anshan named Guo Jiale, we were joined by Guo's best friend Chen Dehua, Chen's wife, another couple, and the only-child from each of these families. As we sat on the floor to eat a large spread of red meats, washed down with lashings of cheap lager, Guo's discourse was awash with the use of expressions and terms such as, "Do as you please", "Don't be polite", "Open up", "Be open and bright", "happy", "cheerful", and so on, exhortations which served to create the impression that there are no boundaries to social interaction, as if all judgment and prejudice were suspended and all rules and form relaxed. These exhortations were regularly supplemented by formulations such as, "Whatever you want to eat, just eat it; whatever you want to do, just do it; whatever you want to drink, just drink it!", "We're buddies" (*gemenr*), and so forth. Significantly, we were drinking a beer specially produced for the Anshan market by joint-venture Shenyang-based national brand Xuehua Beer and local brewery Anshan Huarun Beer, a beer that has been spoken of in glowing terms around the city since its release in 2008, for its "kick" and "strong flavor" in contrast to the "light" (*dan*) and more watery beers that Xuehua markets around the country.[2]

After dinner, the women and children separated to the other end of the room, divided from us men by a curtain, at which point our interaction became additionally supplemented by statements such as: "We can say anything to one another", "We are brothers" (*xiongdi*), "We have a responsibility to each other", "We are in it together" (*zaiyiqi … huxiang …*), "We do what we like; we are free and unrestrained" (*zizai*), "We must have our freedom", "We don't change our personality for anyone", and so on, expressions that served to cement our male belonging through the unrestrained sharing of self-expression and the mutual flaunting of form, pretence, and the all-too-familiar rules of health – that is, "don't eat too much lamb", "don't drink too much", "don't smoke", and so on, commandments which were seen as "severe" (*lihai*) and somehow female in this context, perhaps because they came laden with the burden of responsibility. My wife was actually referred to as "severe" on this occasion, for intervening quite firmly to limit the amount I was eating and drinking, actions that were seen to cast a down-turn on an otherwise exuberant event because they prevented me fully expressing my character.[3] At this, the men present immediately pronounced: "Have another drink. As long as you are happy, everything's fine!" (*zhiyao ni kaixin, jiu haole*).

When I gave him the opportunity, Guo Jiale volunteered that he was "proud and cool" (*haoshuang*) by character, a key term in local discourse, and expanded on the meaning the term has for him:

I love to talk; my personality is proud and cool, frank and plain speaking (*zhishuai*). And my child is like me: playful and active. I say whatever I want to say; everybody knows this about me. I can't keep something inside myself: that's very reserved and not open-hearted. I've got to speak it out. I'm sincere and true, honest and simple. When I drink with my friends, I speak out with a proud look on my face. I'll stand next to you whatever the situation is. We are brothers together. Many people are fraudulent, crafty, treacherous; they make friends with you when you've money, but when you've no money they'll be gone. If you've no money and they still want to be friends with you, this is a true brother.

On another occasion, when I asked Guo how his personality was reflected in his material consumption (*xiaofei*), Guo pulled no punches in reply, showing how his generosity of character and the importance of being unrestrainedly true to himself were intimately factored together:

I don't like ordinary. Everyone wants money, I want money, but people's priorities are different. Others spend and save carefully, but I'll have whatever I like at the time even if I can't afford it. If I need seafood, I'll have seafood: I'll have seafood today. I'm still young, I need to express myself. Take my hair for example: it's different to everyone else's. Around here, no men have long hair. Mine has especially individual characteristics. My own style: my own desires. I like to play; I like to travel. But I have no time to go anywhere. I never save; I spend everything. I borrow money from my parents and friends and spend that too. I'm not afraid to spend. I don't worry about anything. I believe in fate. If I saved we would eat poorly and dress poorly. When I get to the point of being rich, we'll deal with saving then. Whatever I love, I just go and buy it.

Both Guo and his best friend Chen, who is somewhat quieter and saves his wages diligently, regularly indulge in excesses of eating, drinking and gambling together. Both are overweight and smoke heavily too. Guo admits he is "a bit greedy, a glutton" (*chan*). Both stress that health is very important to them, however. "I like to protect my body while I'm young just as a woman loves to protect her face", explained Guo. Then, speaking for the both of them, thus actively underlining their rapport, he added, "We like mutton, beef and pork, because we know that cows and sheep eat naturally healthy grass in an open environment, whereas pigs eat man-made food, which is unhealthy". Thus, Guo's projection of character is closely linked to his health, which he believes is bolstered by a masculinity tonic brewed of deer penis, antler, whole snakes, lizards and ginseng roots that he distils in maximum strength *baijiu* – an extremely strong liquor, with the aid of a friend who is a Chinese medicine doctor. Somewhat beyond the appeal to health, indeed, this potent tonic serves to boost Guo's virility, and it is ultimately this that is expressed in his gusto and extra helpings at dinner – competing in a way that nevertheless lubricates good social rapport (Bourdieu 1984: 191; Farrer 2002: 85).

The personal character given to this modality of cultivating good social rapport in Anshan thus has something distinctly masculine about it, and in exactly the same way in which there is something distinctly feminine about the "cordon sanitaria" discussed in the Civility discourse. What some people might find offensively "loud", Guo Jiale and his friends find "bright, candid, and hearty" (*shuanglang*), and this despite the fact that women in Anshan can be very generous, unrestrainedly expressive, and bold of character too. Thus, to continue the analogy with Chinese medicine drawn at the start of this chapter, we may now note that the discursive differences articulated here are similar to the binary Taoist principles of yin and yang, the former meaning "hidden, shady, secretive and feminine", the latter "bright, open, hearty and masculine", though the contrast is not as simple as one between "introversion" and "extroversion", as noted above.

Not all Anshan men seek to be identified with these local characteristics, however. Du Bin, for example, denies being "proud and cool", saying he's not like other men from the park who indulge in eating and drinking. Du knows his limits and believes he should stick to them: he likes conversation with "meaning and content", not just "laughing and mirth". Entrepreneur Fang Jian similarly tells me he should not be considered "proud and cool", professing a preference for a more gentile form of social interaction, but both Du and Fang, despite their espoused views, are in fact quite typical of the "proud and cool" character type so salient in Anshan, only distancing themselves from these highly expressive consumption behaviors as a function of documenting their awareness of where these behaviorisms constitute civil transgression (Hird 2009).

Let us note here, however, that even Gao Xiaofei, a 23-year-old woman who otherwise positions herself very much against brusque virile traits, also defines her character by reference to these same magnanimous, unaffected and, in this locally specific sense, "masculine" characteristics:

> If I want to laugh, I just laugh. If I want to eat, I just eat. If I want to speak, I just speak. I don't hide. I don't think the fact I eat, laugh or speak a lot is bad thing. I don't hide in front of other people. My behavior is the same no matter who I'm with. Some people will even go to the extent of suddenly behaving differently in front of their boyfriends: they won't eat cakes, they'll speak very quietly, if they're hungry they'll just bear with it, etc.

On another occasion, Gao Xiaofei raises this same nexus of meanings in a conversation about a male relative who is somewhat out of place in Anshan. The excerpt shows how this nexus of character attributes is claimed as innate to people of the region:

He is always going to the beauty shop to have face masks for his spots. His parents encourage him to have these beauty treatments. But this is not very Chinese, especially for a man. Chinese should know the healthy way. Face masks only help the external, not the internal. His body is weak. In many ways, the modern Chinese consumer is not very Chinese. I think the boys from Macau, Hong Kong and Taiwan are not manly. Japanese are especially short and have sick blonde hair; they're less manly; they've long hair and they're thin, with no muscle at all. And that sweet voice, my God, I can't stand it!

In these ways, in what amounts to a discourse of local or possibly even northeastern regional authenticity, individuals in Anshan, both men and women, assert themselves as tall and physically powerful, as unrestrained in both spirit and spending (*xiaosa*), as confident, robust (*shuangkuai*), plain-speaking (*zhishuai*) and forthright (*zhishuang*). They like to believe they are unreserved, easy with emotion, and wear their hearts on their sleeves (*shizai*). Their "straightness" (*zhi*) is explicitly articulated as a positive virtue and contrasted with the "roundness" (*yuanhua*) necessary to adapt to unfamiliar people and varied situations, which is in turn made the discursive neighbor of slipperiness, cunning and ambiguity (*jiaohua*). These latter negatives used to stereotype people from the comparatively wealthy south as the northeast's perceived Other, along with tight-fistedness (*kou*), meticulousness (*jingdaxisuan*), dishonesty, and shortness of height and/or otherwise physical weakness (*xiuqi*). Taiwanese men in particular are singled out for their high-pitched and effeminate voices; people from Shanghai, Fujian, and Guangdong for their financial shrewdness. It is said, for example, that where a southerner will buy a single piece of fish at market and take it home to eat alone, a northeasterner (*dongbeiren*) will buy a whole fish and share it with his friends. While a northeasterner will claim to throw himself unreservedly into new friendships, the southerner is supposed to be cold and indifferent: "slow to warm up" (*manre*).

This regional identity positioning is not quite as straightforward as the character northeasterners would claim for themselves, however, since people in Anshan jealously admire southerners for their proximity to advanced markets, international experiences and consumerist lifestyles, and reluctantly accept the counter-discourse from the south that labels them crude, coarse (*cu*), unrefined and provincial (*luohou*). Recognized, too, is that "roundness" can be advantageous in social situations where "straightness" could variously imply inflexibility, overt formality, social clumsiness and over-simplicity. However, it will not be allowed that Anshan people could be as "crafty" or as penny-pinching as people from the south are supposed to be: the whole point is that Anshan people are unlimitedly generous even though they're poor. Skilled manual laborer Zhou, for example, in many ways representative of the archetypal northeastern man, defines himself as a "poor big-heart" (*qiong dafang*), his capacity for unreserved generosity an important part of his understanding of what it means to be a "real man" (*chun yemenr*).

Thus, the northeast is not so much barbarous or untamed, metaphors reserved for China's far-western provinces, but buoyant and sanguine, gutsy and tough, vibrant and heterosexual, the "salt of the earth", as it were, as the very idea of "the authentic" is manifested in "innately" sociable characteristics.

Salt of the earth

Saltiness (*xianweir*) is perhaps an especially useful metaphor for analyzing the everyday social exchanges in Anshan, particularly since the saltiness of northeastern cuisine is opposed to the sweetness of, say, Shanghai cuisine. Essentially, in just the same way as a person from Anshan will, heuristically speaking, heartily attempt to lever as much food as possible into his bowl at dinner vis-à-vis citizens of China's southern cities who will pick over manifold tiny dishes, the Anshan character will also invest in every ordinary utterance the maximum possible intensity of "innate" sociability – a disposition towards the emphatic which can come across as coarse and abrasive for those accustomed to a more delicate palate. Everyday speech is littered with speech particles ending with the syllable "a!" or other response-invoking variants such as "ba!" or "na!" – that is, abrupt, snappy, and provocative verbal ejaculations intended to engage others and goad replies. Women of the region in particular manifest a caustic style of conversation inflected with particles that can almost appear intended to provoke altercation rather than rapport. "What are you playing at?" (*ganha wanryine?*), "What are you on about?" (*shuoshale ni?*), are constant refrains, the salty sense of which is difficult to capture in the written word precisely because this is a way of speaking. As a male taxi driver

Figure 5.1 Proud and cool. Photography by Gao Yingchuan

in Anshan once explained for me, "Northeast women can be especially burning (*huolala*); they've much more flavor than in the South" (*you weir, bi nanfang you weir*).

This particular character complex is often coupled with other forms of intrusiveness, as the same salty style of conversation takes an instructive form in expressions such as, "You ought to ..." (*ni yinggai ...*), "I tell you ..." (*wo gaosu ni!*), and so forth. Those same people who ask my girlfriend (now my wife) "Who does the cooking?", "Who does the washing?", "Ah, so that's what his contribution is" over dinner, are never short of suggestions for how we should conduct ourselves in terms of diet, health, inter-spousal relations, future orientation, and so on, interventions apparently intended to probe and resolve our camaraderie through oxymoronic friendly contestation.

There are further interesting dynamics here, too. If a bicycle and a car, say, prang in the street, highly confrontational and full-blooded exchanges of views will be immediately forthcoming. Rather than move the damaged vehicles to the side of the road for the benefit of larger society, the dispute will be enacted in the middle of the road, and others will be invited to become involved in what is essentially a private matter (Jankowiak 1993). Similarly, where a man and his wife argue fiercely in the street about personal matters, the party who feels most aggrieved will try to generate as much friction as possible, "adding chaos" (*tianluan*) to the situation in order to attract arbitration from as many other people as possible. I have already mentioned in Chapter 4 how many Chinese think nothing of intervening in other people's business, asking the most "private" or personal questions and so on; here, however, the point is to "intervene" (*zhaduir*) in order to play the "sage" or "hero" (*shengren*), as if acting under the presumption of some grand mandate to pass judgment and give advice on behalf of the whole of society. Only in this way, once huge reserves of emotional energy have been spent, is the problem at first inflated and yet dissolved into the social sphere in a way that enables all parties concerned to step down without losing "face" (Ikels 1996: 29–33).

Thus, when someone gets loud and apparently angry with you in Anshan, sophisticated sensibilities are of little use: you have to get even more loud and angry in response, investing the situation with equal, if not even more characteristic intensity, until the matter becomes everyone's matter and thus no matter at all. Violence rarely occurs in Anshan, and it is usually more bark than bite when it does, since there is a subtle balance of the choleric and the phlegmatic to local people, the choleric making the phlegmatic as fluid a substance as the spittle that lines the pavements! Much like seawater, or sperm say, the characteristics "innate" to people of the city reflect a high degree of saline suspension: both proud and cool.[4]

The price of friendship

Social distinction achieved through good sociable character can conflict in all sorts of ways with purposive intentions. Consumption relevant to cultivating social rapport is often instrumental, and can frequently require that a monetary price be paid to negotiate the judgment of generosity (Yang 1994). The "inviting" (*qing*) of another to dinner, for example, is nearly always purposive if only in the most general sense of being a polite and generous way of courting the other, but if you want to discuss a particular issue, or seek someone's assistance, it is expected that you will invite the other out to eat and you will pay. Of course, the more lavish the meal, the stronger the implicit tie between persons, but venues range from the plushest hotels to the lowliest snack shacks. Whoever makes the initial offer does so expecting to pay for the meal; the bill is rarely split.

Such situations can be highly problematic, however, since consistently consuming at another's expense is a significant negative of the balance between generosity and miserliness demanded by the judgment of good sociable character. Hence, the "right to pay" is contested in loud, public squabbles, pushing and pulling, etc. This can present a civil transgression for other diners, and is sometimes taken to the extent of fully engaged physical contact with hands placed all over the body of the other and shouting that can build to quite aggressive levels, either forcing money onto the body of the other or away in refusal: merely saying "thank you" is rare enough in Anshan. Most often, however, despite sometimes apparently extreme arguments, it is determined in advance who will in fact pay on account of seniority of wealth, age, or whoever called the dinner in the first place, the relative importance of these elements having been decided in advance by the protagonists, so that the "fight" is less about being generous per se than about competing through intensity of character (Fang 2003: 358).

Even so, there are expectations informing generosity, not least the obligation to reciprocate: favors accepted are usually expected to be returned, which is of course how networks of mutually exclusive ties or *guanxi* are consolidated and access achieved to all manner of political and extra-legal resources otherwise off-limits (Gold *et al.* 2002). It can be difficult to accept someone's generosity without concern for how you will return it in Anshan, and hard to treat someone without concern for the ramifications, especially if the other person is less well-off than you. Indeed, it is not usually possible for younger or junior people to invite older or senior persons to eat, which often presents a fieldwork challenge, since I would happily pay for a meal to have the chance to "interview" a subject, but older people will invariably offer an excuse for why they can't make it. If they accepted my offer, the implication would be that they would have to return it too (which they often are not in a position to afford), and by declining they not only avoid this obligation but also save face and keep the social norm in line.

Even on the occasion when it was possible to have a dinner with a substantially poorer person, Mr Wen, he insisted to death on paying: he would not let me pay no matter how far I tried. By having dinner with him, I had obliged him, and he had agreed to be obliged. On the other hand, on the even rarer occasion when I ate dinner with Mr Wen and entrepreneur Zhao, Zhao paid and Wen's struggles were vigorous but not nearly as vigorous as when trying to stop me paying for him! Others present explained that if Mr Wen was going to invite others to a meal, he would prefer to do it not on an ad hoc basis, but rather wait and call a big meal with all his family and friends and make a big show of his generosity in a rare orgy of excess. Still, certain people are expected to oblige each other, the system ensuring that only people of approximate social class socialize. Many middle-aged informants tell of not being able to maintain old friendships because the friends have an improved economic situation with which they can't keep up. Correspondingly, if you do not want to be obliged you can easily be seen as lacking in some way, and once involved it can be difficult to extricate yourself again. In the intimate sphere, however, it is understood that if you cannot give from the wallet then you must invest of the socially magnanimous self in whatever way you can.

Consider, then, the occasion where I had already spent money on cultivating a relationship with Fang Hua, a younger and less wealthy Anshan male, who felt a strong imperative to repay the favor. Fang asked two of his friends to join us to dine. Anxious to pay himself before anyone could mention it, Fang asked the waitress to bring him the bill in advance of time in a low mumble so I couldn't hear, and when the bill came he scrambled so violently to pay that he dropped his mass of coins and low denomination notes all over the floor. Since Fang's friends had made no attempt to pay, and evidently were happy for him to do so, he seemed somewhat over-keen to institute himself as being responsible for treating me, as if confusing the compulsion to show proper character with the issue of brute reciprocity and "face". He proudly told us after the waitress had left, "In the presence of my friends, I will definitely pay". Eventually my relationship with Fang became spoilt because we could not do anything together without him feeling obliged to "keep up" by inviting me next time to what he perceived as occasions of equivalent significance. Though I was quite happy to pay, or indeed to undertake shared forms of consumption that didn't require spending much or indeed any money, Fang was not at all happy for me to pay even slightly more often than him, and constantly clutched at opportunities to offer me drinks, cheap snacks and favors in what seemed like efforts to "make up" for what I had done for him.

Concern for "face" of this type is actually said to be characteristic of Anshan men, and Fang expressed the same characteristic in other ways, spending in excess of 100% of his monthly salary on clothes by sporting goods brands Nike and Adidas, for example, believing that these clothes were important elements in endearing himself to young women. Let me note here, however, that other Anshan informants have had no problem accepting my repeatedly paying for dinner or sharing the bill between us. Indeed, the self-defined "autonomous group" of men who exercise together in 219 park would always split the bill for dinner equally amongst them *AA zhi* (Chinese for "Dutch style"), since the cost of eating out in large groups was recognized as too great for any individual to bear, and "face" of that overtly competitive type seen was somewhat contrary to the meaning of the occasion. The intimate group of rural migrants discussed in Chapter 8 and the skilled manual workers discussed in Chapter 9 did much the same.

Essentially, Fang had mistaken the imperative to have a generous character for his desire to be seen as a man of status. His insistence that "courtesy demands reciprocity" (*lishang wanglai*) was ultimately symptomatic of our lack of intimacy, and the fact that he believed his "debt" had to be made up through monetized gestures only exacerbated the awkwardness of our inter-actions. To borrow from the local terminology, you could say that Fang had too much "pride" and not enough "cool".

Emotional economics

There is a lesson here for management gurus who stereotype Chinese social relations through the lens of esoteric rules governing reciprocal gift-giving and banqueting, etc. Good social character cannot be reduced to a rule, or a price, in Anshan. There are those more formalized mechanisms where you are expected to invite the other out to eat and pay and so on, and there are axiomatic "rules" or regularities structuring these (Yan 1996). However, there is also another, in some ways more primary modality, by which it is still not possible easily to accept someone else's generosity without concern for how you will pay it back, and still very difficult to simply treat someone else without thinking about the ramifications, but primarily because of affective rather than ritual considerations (Kipnis 1997: 105–15; Yang 1994: 312). These affections (*ganqing*) cannot possibly be paid back, but are only generated in the relationship between the actors involved (Yan 1996: 139–45). Good sociable character, though constructed as more or less "innate" to different individuals, is manifested as a factor of interpersonal familiarity and senti-ment: a logic which at least in its social construction is distinct from the formal and monetized principles of gift or commodity exchange.

Certainly keeping a record of others' obligations to you, calling them for-mally to "level accounts" (*suanzhang*) at times of your choosing is a social error quite the contrary to cultivating social rapport in China, and will likely spell the end of the relationship. This is of course quite different from Western countries where the transaction costs of a relationship are commonly divided up to the nearest economic unit as friends effectively treat their intimates in ways reserved only for strangers in China (Fei *et al.* 1992: 124–27). Indeed, some Chinese find measured reciprocity absurd, unnecessary, out of place and even onerous (Yan 2003b: 80–83), and not just because they have failed to follow "the rules", but because they don't believe these rules should have a ruling place in their relationships (Kipnis 1997: 156). There is little to choose, for example, between persons I would think most require a ritual token in order to achieve strategic influence thinking this least necessary, and intimates with whom I am already familiar in fact most expecting one! There is no hard and fast rule governing these interactions; rather there are only regularities and dispositions, the interface between instrumentally driven socialization and emotive modes of identification being worked out in context as a function of interpersonal intuition, or *renqing* (Wilson 2002).

In *guanxi*, of course, relations are often not intimate since *guanxi* is often about knowing someone who helps you influence someone unknown to you, thus placing yourself in a chain of deferred debt. Yet even within this less personal and more "politicized" (Yang 1994: 320) logic, the need for affective social character can actually be quite high: you behave as if your rapport with your more distant contacts is as genuine and sincere as your concern for your intimate relations; your gifts and favors, presented as heartfelt, function not only to facilitate but also to disguise the calculation involved, for just as protestations of affective character are always ultimately instrumental, conversely, instrumentality requires the appearance of affective character to make it palatable (Bourdieu 1977: 171). Thus, when "thanks" is expressed in China, this is not usually done as if conforming to a civil norm as is often the case in Western countries, where verbal expression of thanks is an important part of "manners", but rather in a somewhat exaggerated way, as an opportunity to express both gratitude and debt, the ultimately instrumental intent understood yet expressed as a manifestation of interpersonal sentiment. The result, somewhat surprisingly, since it goes against the grain of the local discursive construction, is that there is nothing necessarily immoral about having relationships with a practical purpose in China, nor necessarily impractical about having relationships without such purpose, since instrumentally driven and emotive modes of interaction are recognized as interfacing in context (Kipnis 1997: 8–9).

The tension we have arrived at here can only really be explained by reference to the sense in which distinctions between self-seeking motivations and emotive or otherwise "irrational" intentions tend to dissipate in actual practice (see also Chapter 7), and the sense in which Chinese tend to forge social bonds through economies of reciprocally accountable actions, whether completed or deferred (see the next chapter).

Still, we can still say here that in China's northeast, where people retain close demographic links to life in the agricultural communes and state-owned enterprises, social interaction is structured by a high operational reliance on characteristic enthusiasm. This is the case despite the intimate and the public sphere having already been quite divided by discourses of civility, as discussed in the previous chapter. As argued there, the organization of social space owes much to the sense in which Anshan people imagine the local as familiar and convivial versus what they see as the more anonymous and competitive societies characterizing China's more modern, urbanized and marketized coastal cities, where interaction with strangers is normal and, they imagine, social relations are more formal and utilitarian (cf. Hanser 2006). The fact, however, is that local contexts in China have rarely if ever been characterized by intimate ideals: certainly life in Mao's people's communes was hardly as harmonious as depicted in propaganda posters of the era and farmers had little choice but to conform to discourses of "comradeship" as an instrumental means of survival (Vogel 1965; Gold 1985). On the other hand, members of modern

Chinese urban societies can be observed to make recourse to "intimate" sub-terfuges to achieve instrumental ends too, so that the interface between the formal and the intimate has demonstrably similar utility in very different contexts. The idea of the "intimate, local" is, after all, just a myth seen from a particular modern Chinese perspective, with situational utilities of its own.

Even so, the remaining chapters of this book will progressively testify that Anshan individuals who invest most in exuberant social interaction tend to retain some immediate personal proximity to either the revolutionary Chinese countryside and/or the *danwei* urban infrastructure, and correspondingly, those who most differentiate themselves from these "innately" local character-istics when they find it socially advantageous tend to be more "well-to-do" men and women who benefit from anonymous modes of transaction such as mar-kets and contracts (cf. Hanser 2006: 477–82). Notwithstanding, or perhaps even because of the supposed "innateness" of exuberant characteristics to people of the northeast region, competing through expressions of "sociable" character will be revealed as a product of emergent structures of "class", where exuberance is a modality of reliving forms of belonging associated with the socialist era and class is defined primarily by reference to individuals' capacities to adapt to the new and individualizing discourse of market reform (Hanser 2006). Indeed, in the final analysis, perhaps individuals in China's more sophisticated and materially pretentious southern megacities are less generous and more instrumentally rational about social relations! However, this would only be to acknowledge that Chinese in modern, urban markets demand to be treated as having distinctly individual personalities too.

6   Morality

Goodness me!

The judgment of moral character aspires to be a measure of a quality beyond that captured by any of the other discourses of this analysis: a measure somehow independent of individuals' excellence at various kinds of performance; a measure by which falling short is supposed to render success at negotiating other modalities of social judgment irrelevant; a measure that may be constructed as present or absent in graduated degrees, but to which no other measure is reducible. These foundational aspirations are of course shared with the authenticity judgment discussed in Chapter 2. The two judgments are not reducible to one another, however, because, at least in Western cultures the judgment of moral character somewhat paradoxically aspires to resolve through social practice the idea which was only implicitly resolved in Chapter 2: the idea of a "goodness" independent of its relation to other things. At moral character, the discourse of social distinction is explicitly turned upon its head and directed towards a quality that supposedly obtains in individuals only insofar as they make the interests of others their own, in what we might call the social referent of morality.

The idea of an irreducible moral quality, however, is explicitly at odds with the central theoretic put across in my research – namely, that meaning and identity is a socio-historical product continually emerging from the judgments people make and the actions they perform. Moral discourse, my research maintains, functions to obscure the fact that individual agency is always rewarded for particular kinds of performance, and that the worth of all actions, and perhaps especially that of "selfless" actions, is contingent and socially constructed. We might even say that the "goodness" appealed to in the judgment of moral character is not only that which has been so completely institutionalized that it is no longer called into question, but that people assume there has never even been a question about it: moral character is a function of the most sophisticated of all (inauthentic) cultural technologies where fundamentally self-interested passions were first made subject in exchange for social recognition (Nietzsche 1994). Rather than ask whether this exchange was worth it, though, because it obviously was, and therein lies the point, this chapter seeks to reclaim the question of the exchange for individuals in Anshan, and China, where moral tension is configured very differently to Western cultures, and where the idea of a "goodness" above and beyond social discourse has not occupied anywhere near as large a role in discourse in the first place.

Proximity altruism

In the Christian tradition, being "good" or "bad" is ultimately a matter of the relationship between an all-powerful monotheistic God and a given individual possessed of an "internal" conscience (Mealey 2008). This relationship is absolute, since the omniscient Deity will know about things not even said or done yet, and will record any transgression in a ledger to be cleared on the final day of judgment; however, the uniqueness of this relationship is also what sanctifies individuals as ends in themselves, transcendent of earthly relations, and equal before God (Kant 1996). All persons are by definition "sinners", but will be redeemed by turning to God through Christ, who is supposed to have been God immanent in man, and alone capable of fulfilling the old Judaic religious law. A recidivist baddie is thus in a sense "better" than somebody who follows the narrow path of virtue. On the other hand, ostentatious denouncement of "sinners" is a sin, and being "good" means to embrace the outcasts, the harlots, tax collectors and traitors, the very opposite of the Pharisees' self-righteousness whose sin is to judge as only God can. This means that Christian morality has two dynamically interacting faces: first the judgment of moral character as a shared, social notion that implies self-righteousness and exclusion; and second, the imperative of grace for sinners, which is more sophisticated in easing relations between people, where people are given what they want/need even though they "don't deserve it" (Hauerwas and Wells 2006). Morality is configured in a similar way in Islamic tradition, too, where the same Abrahamic divine referent stands "outside" social interaction as the ultimate arbiter of moral judgment and the individual's moral worth is accounted for with similar eschatological legalism, though without the "guaranteed" salvation offered by the Christian messiah: rather less grace and rather more deeds.

None of this is so in China, however, where the millions of practitioners of all the world's major theistic faiths, including the many different branches of Christianity and Islam which have tried to nuance and sophisticate the relationship with Abrahamic divine referent, as well as Judaism itself, are somewhat complications to a simpler and more fundamental cultural construction, where there is no divine referent, where moral character is much less legalistically defined by an "objective code", and where individuals have no intrinsic moral quality. Moral character in the Chinese popular imaginary is determined primarily through the individual's social practice, and the judgment of "good" or "bad" entirely relational and situational in its construction.

In the Western Christian construction, of course, where the judgment of moral character is supposed to remain divine prerogative even though many people no longer believe in God, people simply believe the individual to be unique and socially autonomous, yet nevertheless engage in moral judgment of others in absolute terms (Dumont 1992). In China, on the other hand, the judgment of moral character is rarely absolute, and the notion of social autonomy reserved primarily for the negative judgment of others: heuristically speaking, the rights to legitimate individuality are realized only through your responsibilities to others, which is to say through networks of obligation (Fei *et al.* 1992). This earthly (as opposed to heavenly) reciprocity is of course what has allowed tales of "collectivism" and "interdependence" to flourish in the cross-cultural management literatures criticized earlier in this book. Categorically, though, China's particularly situational form of ethics does not mean that Chinese are any less free to act and judge as individual agents than individuals elsewhere. Indeed, the point stands that Christians are de facto as liable as anybody else to make moral judgments, and the insight into the Chinese case should make Westerners examine their own moral engagements, including academic research. If we are to have any argument here, it must be that Chinese do not set much store by the idea of equality and liberty for all, the ideal to which the democratic West overtly aspires. Or, more precisely, that Chinese morality is informed by a cultural politics that systematically denies individuals comparable agency.

This chapter argues that this politics determines that actions must take two major interrelating reference points in order to accrue moral value in China: first, a "good" action must have a highly altruistic social referent, serving as many people as possible – your community or collective, the Chinese nation, and so on, and the self last; second, a "good" action must serve first those people in your own intimate in-group or network – your immediate family, extended family, then closest friends, and so on – before serving others in close proximity, with rapidly decreasing priority given to those further away from the intimate sphere, to strangers last, who do not generally figure in moral action in China. I will refer to the first of these reference points as the "altruistic deferent", and the second as the "proximity law". The combination of these two principles in practice means that we may refer to Chinese morality as "proximity altruism".

The altruistic deferent

A morality with a highly altruistic social referent has characterized Chinese political dogma for millennia under the banner of Confucianism and is still very much the position enshrined in China's (superficially) Communist constitution. This discourse has huge purchase at the level of everyday life. Anshan parents will often remark that they want their child to make a "contribution" (*gongxian*) to the country or nation – the single-party State having of course skillfully conflated these notions with itself, and young people speak passionately about finishing school or university and "entering society" to "contribute" to its development. Elderly Grandma Liu has a particularly excellent reputation in these altruistic respects, she assures me, for "taking pleasure in helping others". She is not all self-effacing, as she tells me that various neighbors leave their house keys with her whenever they go away. She lists the households explicitly, before adding, "And I get the milk for my neighbors from the post-box every day".

Middle-aged businessman Zhao is understood as particularly "good" in this altruistic sense, I learn, because when the neighborhood committee wanted to install a security camera in the street to monitor for thieves and hoodlums, a whip-round was conducted to which he contributed "more than half". Moreover, Zhao recalls, having observed that the lamp in the bike shed was out of order on his way home late one night, Zhao went out and fixed it "even though I don't use the shed myself". Even 35-year-old worker Guo Jiale, who works for a private company and is in many other ways very obviously individualistic, is still acutely aware of the altruistic referent of doing his job well: "The product we make is still for the country; it's still a contribution to the country. This is united strength" (*tuanjie de liliang*).

This altruistic referent is often where the Anshan people most judge fault with me, since as a foreigner it is less the things that I actually do than the things I neglect to do that are found unacceptable. My failure to lift food into my girlfriend's bowl whilst eating, for example, runs the risk, I am assured, of others labeling me selfish, a bad boyfriend, etc., even though this behavior is not part of my cultural make-up! By a similar token, one day early in the research, others noticed that a spoon had been placed on the table next to my bowl of food; although someone else must have placed it there, it transpired to make it look as if I had drawn a spoon from the cutlery drawer for myself whilst neglecting to draw spoons for everybody else and I felt the unspoken scorn as I fulfilled the perception for my hosts that foreigners are selfish by definition (see also below).

The converse of this altruistic deferent, indeed, is that actions performed for the sake of the self alone are highly distasteful. It is understood that people are fundamentally self-interested: there is a saying, "If people didn't serve their own interests, the world would go under" (*renbuweiji, tianzhudimie*). Openly subscribing to self-indulgence, though, or appearing to put yourself in front of others in social situations, is declared unacceptable. Still today, aging self-professed revolutionaries will play on the negativity that remains latent in the Chinese word for "private" (*si*) in their judgments of business people as "selfish". Whereas in the West you might legitimately say, "If I don't make profit, someone else will", Chinese usually see right through this, acknowledging the exploitation even where this is also acknowledged as an effective strategy for creating wealth for society. Entrepreneurial behavior is highly admired in contemporary China for the fairness, level-headed decision-making, and self-control it necessitates (cf. the next chapter), the moral judgment and resentment of business people reserved primarily for those who do not keep within limits of propriety, who are unfair and excessively exploitative. Oddly enough, this has made for some positive popular verdicts for some rather corrupt businesspeople from the 1980s: they took more than their fair share, but this was justified by their "altruistic" contribution to the local economy!

From this particular perspective, consumption of material or hedonistic pleasures is understood as "bad" in Anshan. Material gratification is more acceptable today than it was under Mao, where frugality was everywhere lionized as an important part of good, moral character through rhetoric such as "Take pleasure in poverty" (*yiqiongweile*), but advertising themes such as "being good to yourself", or "treating yourself" are still much more difficult to negotiate than in the West. It is not that Chinese do not understand the individualist appeal in L'Oréal's personal hair-care products' tagline "Because you're worth it", but that the strap-line contains a sort of taboo transgression which makes the brand stand out in a thrillingly iconoclastic way, which in turn justifies selling the product at premium prices and paying to possess it! Indeed, the Chinese translation of L'Oréal's tagline goes some way to show why materialism has been so curiously successful in a "proximity altruism" climate. *Ni zhide yongyou* is actually closer to the logic of possession, as in "Because you're worth possessing it". In the English "Because you're worth it", on the other hand, the value is firmly centered on the individual, the "whatness" of the "it" somehow equivalent to something intrinsic about that individual. The translation is awkward, but there is something about the Chinese version that reflects the fact that self-interest is a difficult notion to legitimize in China: the "thatness" of the individual is only important insofar as the object is the center of value.

As well as altruistic service, active self-sacrifice thus becomes necessary to a far greater extent than in the contemporary West, sometimes causing considerable embarrassment to all around. Zhu Jun's elderly mother insists that we sleep on the bed in the master bedroom while she sleeps on the floor. The resulting fracas (very similar in form to the "fight for the right pay" discussed in Chapter 5) eventually results in us finding a room in a nearby hotel, but not before relations have been frayed to their limits in cross-wired attempts to give and save "face" – that is, where face is to be seen as of good moral character (*lian*). Indeed, people in Anshan can often be seen to seek to take over responsibility (*zeren*) for matters that are plainly outside of their remit of duty or personal capability in the pursuit of good moral character, believing that this earns them significant credit with others. You should stand up on the bus, allowing pregnant women, children and the elderly to sit – perhaps the singular example of good moral character that everyone in China seems to have at the tip of their tongues – and if someone offers you a place to sit you should vehemently decline. In Anshan, though, people will apparently behave quite irrationally in the cause of "duty", perhaps standing when there is an empty seat, or otherwise refusing the help of a third party on the grounds that their own hardship is somehow serving a greater good. It is not uncommon to hear people say things like: "If my hardship allows others to be happy, that's fine" (*wode xinku, weile fangran bieren jiu haole*), though perhaps not without an element of irony.

The conspicuousness of outward acts of altruism and self-sacrifice is balanced by "inner" moral control. Many Anshan people will appear to readily forgo realization of their own desires and satisfaction because they are of "good moral character", or even indeed, because they are "Chinese", the two concepts having been deliberately conflated in official and popular discourse. It is not that Chinese do not have personal desires, but that to sate them without first finding an altruistic social deferent is seen as crass and self-seeking. Hence the importance informants professed in qualities such as forbearance, frugality, chastity, and so on. Whereas in the contemporary West gratification means by definition that desires be fulfilled, in Anshan individuals are likely as gratified where desire remains unfulfilled, especially if there is a great amount of suffering in the meantime. Dying without consummation is perhaps a particularly meaningful motivator compared to the simple happiness of having desires met: in Anshan, the ultimate sacrifice reaps the ultimate reward, a form of asceticism that reifies and aestheticizes morality, so that the judgment of good moral character does not deny the benefit to the self but actively promotes it. Since self is always morally invested in others and vice versa, cultivating the self can actually be equivalent to cultivating others (see also the next chapter).

This is why one of the most intense forms of guilt I am made to feel in Anshan is for not looking after myself, for not eating as healthily as I perhaps might, for "enjoying myself", and so on, incriminations expressed with the same retaliation one would expect from vengeance. This is also why random acts of malice make very little sense in Anshan; rather, all animosity is deeply personal. Indeed, and by this same suspended logic, since actions have no intrinsic value apart from their being acknowledged by others, there is even a sense in which the doing of the good act is more legitimately highlighted for others to notice; that is, less imperative to defer the distinction sought away from yourself. Once your actions are negotiated as for the benefit of others, it is quite acceptable to declare yourself morally good as if moral character were an egotistical mark of distinction closer to status or the profligate deployment of a prestigious brand: moral "face" (*lian*) accrues as social currency in a way that is not readily seen as coarse and self-seeking. Certainly Guo Mingyi, the Anshan Communist Party member who has been elevated to nationwide fame since 2011 for his long track record of donating blood to hospitals and cash to impoverished children, seems legitimately to indulge public adulation as he addresses crowds and TV audiences. Doubtless a kind and generous man, Guo has been branded the "modern-day Lei Feng" after the altruistic role model of Maoist times.

Take Zhang, for example, rural migrant turned urban entrepreneur, who seeks to document her moral credentials: her altruism is to be declared powerfully since her moral ledger is to be accounted for entirely in the social sphere:

> I'll lend money to a friend if their parents are in dire need; then I'll not even think to ask for it back. I will give it; this is my duty. But I won't

lend it if they want to buy cars and houses. When this family encounters trouble, when the child has an emergency or when parents have an emergency, I cannot look on unconcerned. There was this one time where I intervened to save a friend's father who had a brain hemorrhage. He had to stay in an emergency room costing 5,000 CNY per day. I lent the family 10,000 knowing they had no way of paying it back. And then I got together with my friends to muster together another 50,000. This money has not been paid back even till today, but think, in the future when your friend makes a big profit, will he be able to overlook you? So, you can see I'm really responsible to my friends. They can think, no matter if it's a big thing or a small thing, a big matter or a small matter, I will come to help. When they really meet with something, they will come to find me and I'll do my level best. So amongst my friends I am considered good. Everyone says I'm really filially pious too; I can face my parents. My father always explained to me about the importance of moral spine (*zuoren*).[1] He said that if people were poor, they had to be clever, and never be shortsighted. I just take care of Mother's illness and wait on my husband's mother, and everything'll be fine.

Zhang must document that she has done her duty: she cannot have any moral capital in my eyes until I recognize the value of her actions. This is of course why she highlights at every turn the losses to her personal self: her actions are not credible as "good" unless they have taken something from her. Yet, Zhang is quite unashamed to admit that the anticipated reciprocal benefit she expects to gain from these acts is the point of doing them. This is what her father means when he says poor people should be clever: she should have a "moral spine" so that she will reap returns.

Thus does the "good" act bind in Anshan, holding others over to a duty to reciprocate. This is, of course, not to say that Anshan people are somehow fundamentally incapable of "selfless" actions, but rather that "good" actions in Anshan most often come with the expectation of reciprocity attached, and that those that don't nevertheless demand reciprocity. The corollary, indeed, is that it is very hard to do something "for free" in Anshan, the word bond quite capturing the sense in which autonomy has its wings clipped here. Indeed, this is again why material possession is actually quite acceptable within this moral logic: in this binding sense, those others comprising the network to which you are bound actually "belong" to the self (Eckhardt and Houston 2001b).

So, whereas in the contemporary West people have little choice but to believe in the modern necessity of self-sufficiency, self-determinacy, the need to be "smart" and so on, many Anshan people are used to thinking that they can invest considerable time and energy in "taking responsibility" (*fu zeren*) for others, time they could be spending on their own responsibilities, because somebody else from their immediate network is supposed to always be looking out for all the things necessary for their upkeep on their behalf. Whereas in the West you will ask strangers for help believing that they can straight-forwardly refuse if they do not want to be obliged, and that if they say "yes" they do so out of some immediate inclination without necessarily having expectations of reciprocity, in Anshan people will not likely ask for help at all, since to ask is to formalize a request for help that should already be forth-coming, and rather take moral offence. In short, wherever there is confusion over whether "yes" means "yes" or in fact means "no", confusion that can be paralyzing, you are simply expected to know that the right action is always the one that puts others before yourself, even if that can seem illogical and inefficient in the situation, especially to Western eyes.

The proximity law

The "proximity law" somewhat contradicts the imperative that a "good" action should serve as many people as possible by demanding that a "good" action serve your own people first. On the other hand, without this second imperative the strong altruistic referent would demand that all actions be reciprocated by everyone, which is ultimately to say that individuals would need to be recognized as having intrinsic value, which cannot possibly be squared here. The form of the "proximity" law is therefore very similar to the configuration of intimacy discussed in Chapter 4: a strong inclusion-exclusion dynamic binds people closely together according to a sliding scale of network density (Fei *et al.* 1992: 23) but also binds them strongly apart from other Chinese, so that the "collectivism", or "solidarity" (Chinese Culture Connection 1987) tropes positivist commenta-tors see in the strong altruistic social referent in Chinese discourse only hold water if active non-cooperation is recognized as a part of that, in which case these are probably not the right words at all (Fang 2003: 361). Indeed, the proximity law somewhat explains why the public sphere is so abused across China, since rather than having responsibilities to broader society, Chinese have "moral responsibilities" (*zeren*) where you are accountable first to the most intimate of your own in-groups or networks, but where in-groups or networks remain unaccountable to each other, except where the specter of "the nation" is invoked as the mother of all in-groups and "the people" are marshaled together as assertion against foreign powers (Pye 1990).

The extent of corruption in China's official institutions can also be explained by the fact that from a proximity perspective an action can be both "public vice" and "family virtue" at the same time (Blackman 2000: 6). For this same reason, the biblical "Good Samaritan" figure who helps a down-trodden man from a foreign land makes little sense in Anshan (Yan 2009b): you look out for sufferers in your own intimate network, and then you have to help out of an emotive sense of duty that becomes an almost rational imperative even if the sufferer is judged undeserving of your help; however, help is not usually either expected or solicited from strangers.

Indeed, helping a stranger can be interpreted as a sign of a guilty conscience in China. Certainly national soul-searching was prompted when a video posted online in October 2011 captured a baby girl being struck by a truck in a hit-and-run accident before being left to die in the street as no fewer than 18 pedestrians passed by. One of these pedestrians said in an interview that he hadn't felt the need to help because the baby wasn't his own child. The driver of one of the vehicles that ran the baby over justified leaving the scene by reference to the costs he would have incurred in compensation payments. Despite much public outcry, a large number of online commentators empathized with those who had not helped, admitting they would have done exactly the same for fear of getting into trouble and facing another "Nanjing judge" – a reference to a situation in 2006 when a judge in Nanjing ruled in favor of an elderly woman who had brought a lawsuit against a man who had stopped to help her when she fell over in the street and had taken her to hospital (the woman's family later accused the man). The Nanjing judge ruled that "Peng must be at fault. Otherwise why would he want to help?" His view was that Peng acted against "common sense" (Zhang 2011).

The proximity construction exists to protect and nourish, preserve purity and minimize risk, an almost genetic determinant of action where individuals are the essentially self-seeking "carrier" of the "family gene". Observe that the characters in the Chinese word for social "relations" (*guanxi*), which is perhaps best understood here as mutually beneficial intentions or care, happens to be composed of two characters that on their own can mean "close" or "closed", and "system", the boundary judgment demarcating "in" and "out" being subjectively centered, conforming to locally specific networks (Kipnis 1997). In just this same way, too, the word "everyone", which in contemporary English signifies a situationally and vaguely defined collective of people who are first and foremost individuals, translates most readily into Chinese as "big family" (*dajia*), an equally situational yet highly subject-centered "we" which by definition excludes as well as includes. Essentially, the Chinese word *dajia* stands in relation to the English word "everyone" in the same way as the Chinese exclusive term for "we" (*zanmen*) stands in relation to the Chinese inclusive term for "we" (*women*).[2] To get the same meaning of "every individual" in Chinese, you would have to say "*mei yi ge ren*", which nevertheless loses the situational collectivity implied in the English word "everyone", the comparison illuminating how Chinese language users appreciate the fundamentally self-interested nature of social relations and moral judgment.[3]

Thus, one time, early in this research, soon after meeting my girlfriend's parents for the first time, and in the middle of trying to express that I felt quite at home in Anshan having lived in China previously and didn't anyways feel particularly rooted to any particular place, I made the mistake of trying to say to my girlfriend that she was "my home" (*wode jia*), as in "home is where your heart is", a sweet notion in English. This was far too abstract a notion for her parents to glean through my bad Chinese and caused temporary affront: she was not "my home" but their family I was assured! Upon our later marriage, I was assured of being accepted as a full member of a vast web of familial relations, but since my roots remain regarded as profoundly incompatible, the splice entails that I will perhaps forever be the marginal native, with moral responsibilities and obligations to uphold, but without the authentic rights to belong (Farrer 2008).

Resisting "foreigners" (*waiguoren*) is of course to maximize the collective referent and lever the proximity law simultaneously (Barmé 1999: 254–80). Decades of state propaganda have taught Chinese to be hyper-sensitive about foreign "bullying", and people in Anshan remain highly suspicious of foreign criticism (Pye 1993). Proximity demands an enemy, so that the Chinese construction of moral character is to some large measure explicitly set against the perception of the West as morally vacuous on account of its polluting "individualism" (Yan 2003b). Anshan people are forever harping on about my Nan who lives alone, in good health, supported by nearby family and friends, apparently finding it incomprehensible that she might actually enjoy her independence (Thøgersen and Ni 2008). Also frequently encountered is the characterization of Westerners "kicking their children out of home as soon as they are 18".

Westerners, however, are equally complicit in this discourse: gripes about "uncivil" transgressions are routinely matched by claims that Chinese are the kindest and most hospitable of peoples, a perception that probably owes much to the sense in which Chinese feel a need to prove to themselves that they are capable of "selfless" acts; this, not least since foreigners "included" within proximity networks in a country which was for decades shut off to the world have always been "token" foreigners.

If you are a homeless person without family, an outlaw or outcast, however, it is quite possible to be the world's loneliest person in the world's most populous country, though doubtless these latter types of individuals find mutual belonging within their own networks of moral expectation too. Loneliness, significantly, is precisely what the "exiles" complain about, those overseas Chinese students living a life divorced in many cases to be endured only for the sake of the parents who made such sacrifices to send them there – that is, returning a "sacrifice" for a sacrifice. Almost invariably these students find their Western host countries "cold", "selfish", and "impersonal" (*lengmo*), while they themselves huddle together for "warmth" (*reqing*) in clans of ethnic brethren. While the degree of ethnic exclusion Chinese experience overseas must not be underestimated, Westerners in China seem altogether more capable of embracing the challenge of being the "lone foreigner" (though expatriates often huddle together in cliques too), hence the prevalence of the "teaching abroad" phenomenon, in which there is something of the challenge of self-discovery, enlightenment, and authentic self-becoming.

The strong "in" (*nei*) versus "out" (*wai*) boundary judgment the proximity law demands also accounts for the sense in which the discourse of moral character in the China context can appear strongly characterized by highly polar judgments of individuals as either "good" or "bad", in black and white terms, with very little room for people in between and shades of grey. Whereas Christians have to balance their moral judgments with confession of their own sins, at least many Chinese seem to instinctively believe they are righteous until given convincing reason to think otherwise: if you have satisfied the altruistic referent and the proximity law then why should you feel bad? This is why, in front of journalists' cameras, Chinese police can be observed proudly to hand over prisoners indicted for drug dealing to the state executioner without evincing a moment of hesitation or remorse, because they have "served the nation" or some such, which is precisely to say that accused criminals are less than human since they are judged to have failed comprehensively in this duty. Grandma Zhai, an Anshan neighbor, finds it purely a matter of pride that she once approved the execution of 30 people she believed were criminals: since she was herself promoted to a post at the Public Security Bureau on account of her own good "moral character" (*renpin*) and skills of assessing others' "quality" of character (*pinzhi*), why would she doubt her actions were righteous?

Criminals in China, for their part, can often be seen to be forced by police to confess their crimes (on television, at least), and to repent, since this is an important part of getting individuals to accept that they have done something wrong. Without the extraction of a confession and a repentant attitude, prisoners might only have the impression that "something has gone unexpectedly wrong here" (Nietzsche 1994: 56), and the sense of "shame" by which the boundary of the proximity collective is policed would not be provoked (cf. Foucault 1975). This is quite a different situation to morality in modern Western countries, of course, where the omniscient God and his manifestation in moral law means that you likely feel guilty before you have even been caught. Thus, although the Chinese are very proud of their nation, this discourse operates at a level of abstraction that somewhat overlooks the sanctity of the individuals who comprise it: compared to the contemporary West, the value of individual life is significantly relegated to the value of broader collectives, collectives that are delimited, metaphorically speaking, by the Great Wall, because moral worth can only be attributed to the self when the altruistic referent and the proximity law have first been met.[4]

In addition to the simple proximity law, your roles in relation to significant others are particularly important for good moral character in Anshan, as across China, a highly subject-centered imperative somewhat contrary to the self-denial of the altruistic referent. Your familial obligations as a husband, father, son and brother, and their female equivalents, are all immensely important, and deviance from these is particularly hard to cast in a positive light. Likewise, whether you are an employee, colleague (comrade), manager, boss, and/or party member, etc., your "responsibilities" (*zeren*) are taken very seriously. Children will hardly ever openly act against their parents' wishes, and parents will do virtually anything for their children, not infrequently to the extent of spoiling them awfully. Adults are equally concerned to buy their parents products that promote longevity and health as the parents are to buy things with which their children can study, and the "respect for the old and care for the young" (*zunlao aiyou*) are enshrined in contemporary law, along with similarly binding inter-spousal obligations (Davis 2000: 65).

In the case of my host family, five middle-aged women vie for the distinction of being a "good daughter", by trying to cook the best dish at family gatherings and best serve the others, starting with their elderly parents first. Those who can afford it will present expensive gifts, spurring the less well-off to harder, filially pious (*xiaojing*) labor in the kitchen. Yet even those who give expensive presents also have to put in their time on actions of demonstrable altruism and subservience to filial authority. Indeed, the fact that social roles are highly gendered, that women are expected to be concerned primarily for the family and home, and men for "taking responsibility" for working more and earning more, and this despite the "equality" of the sexes professed by the State and the attraction of independent careers and lifestyles, is no doubt also a factor of the almost biological form of the proximity law bearing on action. So, too, is the fact that family elders are instrumental in pressurizing young people into getting married as soon as possible ("So when are you getting married?"), and then into having children ("So why haven't you had a child yet?"); additionally, once grown, most parents expect ("hope" – *xiwang* – is the preferred term) their offspring will remain near to them, i.e. in close proximity, and the fact is that in many cases those offspring are happy to oblige.

Further to social role, the level of moral conduct expected of individuals in China also varies significantly according to various types of status, not least if your status is explicitly intended to maximize the altruistic referent. In these respects, the contemporary government official is an incarnation of the Confucian *junzi*, the gentlemanly scholar-officials who led society in imperial times and who were supposed to cultivate their own moral being for the good of humanity versus the "small people" (*xiaoren*) who were supposed to be petty, narrow-minded, self-seeking and materialistic.

Yet, these various moral imperatives – altruism, proximity, role, and status can come into interesting conflict in certain situations. One of China's popular old stories is about a waterworks engineer, Da Yu, who passed the door to his home without entering at three separate critical times (when his wife was ill, pregnant, and delivering his child, respectively), because he was needed to harness a flood disaster effecting 10,000 households. His obligation to the wider population was seen as even more binding than his familial responsibilities: the even greater good (Stafford 1992).

A similar point of conflict was marked in the aftermath of the massive earthquake that struck the Chengdu region in May 2008, when a school teacher was ridiculed nationwide as "Run-Away Fan" (*Fan Paopao*) for running from his school when the earthquake struck and then admitting afterwards that in his moment of terror he thought of saving no one except his daughter. Fan was publicly defamed as unfit to teach since his "proximity" concern should have been made secondary to the logic of the altruistic social referent which demanded that he save quantitatively more students. Fan attracted further public wrath sometime later when he tried to defend his actions on his internet blog, explaining that when life and death hung in the balance his thoughts were only for his daughter and he "wouldn't even have stopped to save his own mother", a boast which was found exceedingly distasteful even though sections of the public seemed willing to accept that self-preservation was human nature. Resisting the bullying of the media, Fan refused to retract these statements, professing that he was a "person who believed in freedom and justice, not some kind of self-sacrificing hero", thus bringing the politics underscoring proximity altruism starkly into view (Chen 2008).

Good sex and moral dilemmas

The essentially organic nature of the proximity law means that some of the worst "sins" you can commit in a climate governed by this kind of morality are those of a sexual nature. In most Western expressions of morality, sex is a prime measure of good character alongside lying, thieving, and so on. Both the Bible and the Koran feature two types of sex, the legitimate and the illegitimate: the illegitimate is so because it is seen as socially harmful and a "sin" against God: if you transgress and have illegitimate sex, you betray both your intimate in-group and your faith. Adultery remains far from acceptable in most Western contexts today, and the lines of judgment can be drawn very sharply in people's private moral judgments in large parts of Europe and the USA. However, in certain Western geographies and cultures, particularly those stoked by liberal-leaning popular media, if you are "unhappy in love" then almost everything becomes permissible; even sympathy for the adulterer becomes almost acceptable since it is recognized that the individual has "moral" obligations to themselves too. This is not at all the case for the majority of people in Anshan, however, where adultery is less about "sinning" in the first place, but about upsetting the almost civil gradations between the intimate and the public spheres: an almost bodily matter, much more situational than categorical, but nevertheless subject to strict prophylactic control. What might pass as "innocent" flirting between elsewhere already attached individuals in the West will likely reap the harshest of moral judgments from a certain Chinese perspective, and popular, State-sponsored media seek to reinforce faithful moral stereotypes wherever possible.

Some unmarried rural migrant women in the hotpot restaurant where I washed up dishes would not be interviewed on a one-on-one basis, stating that "Chinese cultural tradition" prevented them from speaking alone with a man to whom they were not married. Young, urban registered men in approximately parallel jobs explained this to me as a function of these women's backwardness, rurality and lack of education, intending that I document their own "modern" distinction. Almost needless to say, some married men in Anshan were not particularly willing to let me speak with their wives, yet this was also notably more the case for people of low status and education. On the other hand, wherever I have found that inter-sexual relations can be broached in China, most often I have been led through an elaborate, morally fringed "mating dance" where I have been expected to resolve all the contradictions for the female by making promises of commitment, marriage, future children, and so on, before the female, let alone her family, will consent. A merely philosophical approach to the question of whether partners will necessarily remain together will find me foul of the charge of "lacking a sense of responsibility" (*meiyou zerengan*), the catch-all sin (cf. McMillan 2006).

Commitment is therefore the sexiest form of social currency in China, again a factor of the proximity law impacting on action. Outside a local university, a sports car has *zhongcheng* in large Chinese characters inscribed upon its side, meaning "loyal", or "devotion", signifying a meaning quite at odds with the implicit lack of devotion and the promise of a ride with a quite possibly illegitimate lover that the same car might signify in the contemporary West! Despite the reversal of signifiers, though, the signified is nonetheless just as self-promoting in the China context. Indeed, in exactly this ever so morally laced way, hairdresser Zhan makes advances to my wife whilst cutting her hair (my wife reports). He says he still likes the friends he's had since childhood: "they are very true" (*zhencheng*), and "friends who can help each other, because when you want to start on your feet in society you need some friends". Apparently (again, I am told), Zhan's friends like him for two reasons: one, because he is "humorous", and two, because he is "really committed" to his girlfriend (*dui ganqing zhuanyi*). Is Zhan interested in other girls? "Of course not", comes the reply, and moreover, he wagers that if his friends think that he's really good to his girlfriend then he "must be a really good person to trust"!

Thus, in spite of all this chastity and piety on the surface of public discourse in Anshan, the proximity boundary is being transgressed in actual practice. The huge letters daubed on the walls of my residential compound read: "Community is at the center of my heart" (*shequ zai wo xinzhong*), and "I contribute to the community" (*wo wei shequ gongxian*). Immediately below these, however, are smaller signs advertising the services of "private detectives" to spy on spouses suspected of adulterous liaisons. Divorced wives of all social ranks tell stories of husbands who have "turned bad" (*xuehuaile*), "ran off to the south to earn money", and left them and their children penniless. The category *baoernai* is widely used to label those secret second wives who provide sexual favors whenever their wealthy patron happens to visit, in return for their keep. The second wife knows that she is just the secondary wife and so she is judged a little "bitch/whore" (*biaozi*). Similarly, "playboy" (*huahua-gongzi*) is used to indicate men who indulge in "play" (*wanr*), which is understood as the opposite of "responsibility" (*zeren*) since it involves what people in the West might quite permissibly call "casual sex" (Farrer 2002).

Complicating this discursive arrangement, however, is the observation that people engaged in "illegitimate" sexual acts may also feel "legitimate" moral obligations to each other, expectations that will be set against duty to prior roles, not only as spouse but against all the other familial roles too, so that if the transgression were to come out in the open it would "shame" (*chi*) the whole group. We may now imagine the case of the woman who bails her male lover out of a blackmail situation incurred over gambling debts but then requests the money back from his family and chastises them for being negligent of their duty; her liaison with him binds her to help him out but since she is bound to keep her affair a secret she is doubly bound to demand the money back from his family; the act of bailing out is expected of a lover, but her denial is even more expected so she has to make a claim vis-à-vis his family. Secrecy therefore stands above all other moral obligations in China: just as the "goodness" of an action consists only in its being explicitly acknowledged by its beneficiary, if sexual indiscretions are not revealed, the notion of illegitimacy need not apply (Farrer and Sun 2003: 19).

Indeed, in a moral climate governed by "proximity altruism", there need not necessarily be any sense of guilt apart from the fear of being found out, "shame" being manifest only in its revelation. Similarly, you don't "confess" in Anshan because there is not the same sense in which you should be shown mercy and absolved of "sin". Though the Christian God may forgive and forget, in China, a "face" (*lian*) tainted is tainted for life. The fact that extramarital sexual activity so often does not result in divorce in China is a function of the "responsibility" individuals feel to their families; especially where children are involved, not to forgive in this context would be considered selfish (Farrer and Sun 2003: 20).

If you are "found out" cheating on love in China, the results can be spectacular. When computer hackers drip-fed to the internet more than a thousand photos of "playboy" film star Edison Chen involved in sexual acts with a range of famous female Asian stars in the summer of 2007, the nation was rocked to its roots in a way that would have bemused the architects of tabloid scandals in the West. Edison was vilified for his promiscuity, hounded from his home in Hong Kong, and had to live abroad in hiding in constant fear for his life. The shame for the sexually prolific actresses involved (they were all fully aware they were being photographed) was so severe that despite multiple high-profile displays of repentance and atonement, film directors refused to employ the women since the market demanded that they be thought of as "morally" pure as well as attractive, talented, etc. Of greatest significance, however, was that the hackers in the "Yanzhaomen" scandal made no demands for ransom to any of the stars involved: otherwise inexplicably, as if the whole operation were a comment on the role of shame in China's "proximity altruism" morality, the hackers didn't want anything back.

Taking this argument to its logical conclusion, and especially if we further consider the almost physiological perspective to the proximity law, "illegitimate" sexual acts might even be thought of positively in China. In Taoist medicine, promiscuity is thought of as "nourishing", and there is an emphasis on cultivating essential energy (*jing*) from multiple sexual partners. Indeed, for all the attention on self-denial and moral self-control in Chinese discourse, at bottom fulfilling your desires is recognized as healthy. Anshan's lurid side-street massage parlors are marketed by appeal to "cultivating sexual health" (*xing baojian*) and "washing" (*xiyu*), and – the very real possibility of disease transmission aside – it is not entirely paradoxical from this perspective that the men who frequent these places are elsewhere doting husbands and fathers (Farrer and Sun 2003: 19–23). Further, there is also a sense in which sex with partners outside of your immediate network has been precisely what maintained the health of a group governed by the "proximity law", which would otherwise have had a very limited gene pool. Incest is of course the boundary turned in upon itself, which is why it is the "cardinal" sexual sin, and the hardest bend to morality's flexible fabric, in China as elsewhere (Douglas 1966).

Proximity altruism, after all, is an essentially self-seeking morality, a highly malleable discourse where social actors justify their actions by appeal to the same referents from different positions. Anshan masseuse Jiang says that her husband knows she does massage but doesn't know the full story: "He would be really upset if he knew; you have to understand the economic situation; my husband was laid-off from Angang; I do this for my husband and my son." Similarly, masseuse Jun says she left both school and her boyfriend to support her family: "I do this kind of work for my younger brother's tuition fees; of course my parents don't know; they think all my money is from an internship with a foreign company." In this way, provided that otherwise illegitimate actions are portrayed in accordance with the other "rules" bearing on morality, these justifications become entirely legitimate (Zheng 2008).

We might observe that even overtly unscrupulous types will appeal to the social referent of morality in order to secure a discursive edge and justify their actions, stressing the high personal risk and personal sacrifice made in order to achieve their worthy results. The gold-digger is of course "just looking for commitment"; whores, like thieves, "stick together"; sharks will stress the loans they offer as a service to the public; whereas gangs "provide employment". Morality is unequivocally the continuously evolving product of negotiation between different actors in the situational context, distinctly perspectival and practical in nature.

Good times, bad times

The moral order may be changing rapidly in contemporary China (Yan 2009b). Many people seem to perceive that the strong altruistic social referent in Chinese moral discourse is inverting to a radically weakened one, replaced by an emphasis on the consuming and commoditized self, a perception widely expressed in searing criticisms of the wealthy, materialism and the self-seeking youth (Ci 1994). Consider an example of this kind of discourse from an Anshan taxi driver:

> In the past people would just drop you round some dumplings, but not anymore. This is directly related to economic development. People nowadays have become bad. There's no help, no friendship between them. The police only know about fines, not how to help others. Young

people these days don't understand us; they don't know about Mao Zedong. I love Mao Zedong; I don't like Deng Xiaoping and anything he brought with him. Some people only have money, but nothing else. They've got no culture, no knowledge, no education; they don't know how to help others. I look down on them; they're bad, disgusting. If I had lots of money, I'd be completely different; I'd be virtuous and help others. People have no social responsibility, they're selfish, and only know how to consume, to buy the most expensive car or villa. I am completely different from these kinds of people. Helping others is much more important than being rich. I admire Bill Gates. He gave all his money away. People like Bill Gates in China are too few.

Thus, moral discourse is strongly inflected with cynicism. Whereas in the Maoist political era it was said, "Ridicule the whore, not the poor" (*xiao chang bu xiao pin*), today this expression is mocked and made to revert to its allegedly original inverse form: "Ridicule the poor, not the whore" (*xiao pin bu xiao chang*). The implication is that "whores" are using their "ability" (*nengli*) to make money in a comparatively "honest" way, which at least makes them better than those beggars widely accused of playing on "good" people's heart strings to trick them out of their hard-earned cash. The moral flux and opportunism of the contemporary era is also expressed in the formula: "Rich men will be bad, bad girls will be rich" (*nanren you qian jiu xue huai; nüren xue huai jiu you qian*). Indeed, it is probably only those who are sufficiently young, sufficiently old, sufficiently partisan in the sense of the "good Communist", or sufficiently wealthy to be secure in their naïveté who attempt to deny this increased flexibility in the moral order.

However, China is not yet ready to admit in the public sphere that those given to anti-social and self-seeking actions often get away with it and get ahead of the "altruistic" masses; this would be to explicitly acknowledge the fact that the morality of self-sacrifice for the collective social referent is being irrevocably replaced by a morality of the self. Indeed, many other individuals, and perhaps this tends to be those who have done better out of the reforms than their jealous peers, make alternative constructions to the effect that the altruistic social referent of morality is holding China back in its development. In particular, many adults complain about young people not being self-sufficient and independent enough, but only "selfish". Young people are of course unrealistically expected to be both independently minded and intensely filially pious, the latter imperative ensuring that the former is smothered by "proximity"-type effects.

Thankfully, and perhaps even as remedy, the "proximity law" may be softening to reveal a much broader collective referent. Even during the time my research was undertaken, the 2008 Beijing Olympics did much for China's consciousness as a member of a global collective. The Sichuan earthquake fallout, moreover, where charitable donations took on an unprecedented popularity across China, led commentators to document "the first time in recent history that ordinary Chinese have participated in a national movement that was not a protest against something – usually a foreign power": "Us vs. Them" changed to "Us without Them", "forging a new sense of modern identity without resorting to foreign scapegoats" (Forney 2008).

The earthquake was of course also a very good example of another kind of "Us without Them" – that is, the arousal in public sentiment aimed directly against government, a recent example of the "yearning for common decency" (Christiansen and Hedetoft 2004: 15) seen in the vigils in the German Democratic Republic before the fall of the wall, in the Belgian protests against the pedophile ring involving top bureaucrats, in Britain after the killing of Diana, and in the build-up to the events of 1989 in China's capital. This movement is no doubt part of what the Chinese State is trying to address in its "comprehensive personal quality" campaign, with all of its altruistic communications, recognizant that in a society where the strong altruistic social referent is weakening the proximity law only serves to foment selfishness and unrest in the population, which could in turn further foment popular political movements; hence the increasing ethnic protest China has seen at economic and social marginalization in Tibet and Xinjiang from 2008.

"Ordinary" charitable acts towards strangers (i.e. acts that are not part of a mass popular movement), which might perhaps have been until recently seen as a weakness in China, may now be on the up too, a new kind of distinction for those who can afford to feel sufficiently secure in their superiority. The success of film star Jet Li's "One" foundation (launched after his near-death experience of the Asian tsunami in 2004) evinces well that China's emerging middle classes may now enjoy what Nietzsche called "the delight of doing good" (Nietzsche 1994). Citing the State's reversal of their long-time suppression of organized charity for fear of autonomous civil movements, Li is clear that launching his foundation required the building of a culture of charity in a climate governed by what I have called "proximity". Not only have the "massive corruption and lack of transparency" (which again may be seen as functions of proximity) in China prompted Li to station his charity in nearby Singapore, but he self-consciously named his foundation "One" to reflect what he believes are the universal humanist values necessary to "change his country's attitude" (Bishop 2009). Though it cannot have escaped the public's attention that it is relatively easy for a multi-millionaire to say that "everyone can afford to give at least one yuan per month", this has not dampened a new-found nationwide enthusiasm for giving. Anshan entrepreneurs Liu Zong, Du Feng, and Zhao Guangyao all profess a penchant for charity and "ethical consumption" (Ma and Parish 2006) despite the otherwise morally dubious nature of their respective climbs to wealth in karaoke bars, saunas, and State sector-related business. "Blatant benevolence", after all, involves "the profligate deployment of resources" in just the same way as does Veblenesque "conspicuous consumption" (*The Economist* 2007).

Volunteering, too, in the form of collectively referential practices – tutoring students from impoverished families, neighborhood security programs and so on – have been shown to take on a stridently self-fulfilling form in the contemporary era, quite the contrast of the "forced duty" of Maoist times (Rolandsen 2008). A self-fulfilling form, that is, rather than a self-sacrificing form, the "good act" no longer expected to take something from the individual (Rolandsen 2008: 112). Recent years have also seen the emergence of moral complication in popular and mainstream movie culture: the "good crook" who faces off against the "bad cop" in the 2002 hit film "Nothing Between Morals" (*wujiandao*), for example, where proximity "black" and "white" are mixed to get grey.

Morality in China, then, may be moving from a politics based on proximity to a politics based on empathy with non-intimate others. Christian church communities, which of course sometimes play an important part in integrating the "exiled" Chinese visitors to foreign countries, and are communities that are supposed to embrace people without probing their character and credentials, and seek to convert by example, have an important role to play in this, so it is perhaps significant that overseas Chinese church communities have grown rapidly and have ever-increasing influence and connection with the equally rapid and genuinely huge Christian movement in China (Williams 2007). There, the Christian faith has been shown to be taking a form of syncretism, interestingly associated with modernization and advanced status, an almost fashionable endeavor, even as worshippers find belonging and shared identity with new forms of collectives (Madsen 1998). No doubt those youthful Chinese iconoclasts glamorized by writer Weihui in her popular cult novel *Shanghai Baby* (Weber 2002; Knight 2003) actually exist too: that is, those who believe they have a moral responsibility towards their own pleasure, towards breaking bonds and taboos in order to "realize the self", and who ruthlessly restrict solidarity to others who pursue the same aims.

The irony, of course, as a form of "post-Communist personality" (Wang 2002) dawns over China, is that it is only by first becoming more "selfish" – that is to say, legitimated as individuals – that Chinese people will be able to become more legitimately self-sufficient and more capable of moral compassion for those outside of their immediate collectives. Very difficult in a place where the moral self is only found in the altruistic and proximity social referents of actions, the Chinese will need to give something up without getting anything back in order to further find themselves. And this cannot in any way be a "bad" thing.

7   Personality

Personhood

This chapter is about forms of self-control and self-cultivation. As the word is used here, personality refers not to the social-psychological "who" of self described by the judgment of innate character discussed in sociability (cf. Chapter 5), but rather to an almost existential logic that somewhat describes what agency is doing through all the other discourses of my analysis – competing to assert, realize, or actualize the "self" within socially determined orders. This chapter describes a category of judgment and practice in a sense similar to the authenticity discourse (cf. Chapter 2), but quite without the foundational ambitions in which that logic consisted. Personality shares with the Chinese discourse of morality (cf. Chapter 6) the perspective that value does not consist in and of itself, yet whereas the morality discourse emphasizes that value accrues through reciprocity with others, personality emphasizes the value that accrues through exertions made first upon oneself and only epiphenomenally on the world.

Notwithstanding the fact that personality sometimes takes an apparently transcendent form, or that the ways informants make use of this discourse in order to compete socially are very often retrospective, this discourse reflects not so much social transaction, or even presence, but the motion resulting from a force. Much closer to the actual "playing" of the social "game" than its formal rules, the discourse analyzed here describes the logic immanent in the making sense of individuality through the articulation of discursive structures, rather than those structures themselves.

This means that personality cannot be as exhausted in its elucidation in isolation from dynamic practice as the others in my analysis, not at least without pre-empting many of the points reserved for the remaining chapters of the book. This chapter thus draws upon some particularly salient empirical manifestations and focuses on a particularly salient "field" (Bourdieu 1992) of empirical practice to identify personality as an analytical principle, before moving the analysis in the direction of the actual articulation of structure. This particularly salient field is entrepreneurship, a concept that in many ways wholly explains the self that competes through self-control and self-cultivation, especially in the context of post-reform China.

Intent and intentionality

In the first instance, the Personality discourse is perhaps best defined by its "constellation" (Levi-Strauss's term) in the Chinese semantic field. In its positive form, the "Personality" discourse proliferates in judgments concerning self-improvement and endeavor (*ziqiangzili*); enrichment (*chongshi*); purposeful application (*nuli*); strengthening (*jiaqiang*); making rigorous demands (*yaoqiu*) of yourself; the earnest pursuit (*zhuiqiu*) of personal ideals; strenuous effort (*chili*); determination and resolve (*juexin*); striving and struggle (*fendou*); hard work (*chiku*); going forward (*shangjin*); making onwards and upwards progress (*shangshangxin*); active application (*jijide*; *jijixiangshang*); self-reliance (*kao ziji*); single-mindedness and concentration (*zhuyi*; *zhuzhong*; *jiangjiu*); assertiveness; challenge (*tiaozhan*); the grasping (*zhua*) of opportunities; overcoming (*kefu*); conscientiousness (*renzhen*); concern (*guanzhu*); and the relentless and incessant (*buduande*) imperative of all these: persistence, perseverance (*jianchi*), and in particular the ability to tolerate, bear, and endure (*ren*).

By contrast, negative judgments in this discourse constellate around malaise; laziness (*landuo*); idleness (*dai*); slovenliness; decadence (*tuifei*); being disengaged and careless (*daiduo*); lacking attention to or overlooking details; lacking goals, targets, pursuits, purpose (*mubiao*); mediocrity (*yonglu*); sluggishness (*tuola*); lacking plans (*jihua*) and ambition (*zhuiqiu*); and leisureliness (*xian*), where leisure is equivalent to loafing about, fickleness, being easily distracted; and lacking "stickability" (*santian dayu liangtian shaiwang*), etc. A relatively random, but quite typical example of this discourse would be the contrast between pursuits of significance, such as reading, with television watching, which some informants saw as empty, time-wasting, devoid of application and self-refinement. As one Anshan informant had it, "Most of these people are wallowing in not using their brains; the kind of entertainment they fill their time with consists of, for example, playing mahjong and computer games; they are shortsighted and don't think to keep forging ahead" (*busi jinqu*). Satisfaction (*manyi*) can be a negative of this discourse, too, as can luxury (*shechi*), since the root construction is precisely that a kind of added-value accrues through the projective process that cannot be simply paid for and that can only be fully appreciated by the individual subjected to it alone.

Effort, of course, invariably features in the reflex reaction well-off people make when they find themselves confronted by the need to justify social inequalities: "If only the poor worked harder, and weren't so lazy, they wouldn't be poor" is a mantra that the promise of capitalism makes to its agents, even while it is recognized that effort is at most a necessary, not sufficient condition for success. Yet the whole point of the Personality discourse is that social discourse and objective reality are mutually constitutive, so that constructions about self-cultivation were conspicuously absent in the narratives of laid-off workers, who often seemed quite resigned to their fate (see Chapter 9). Anshan is a place where an awful lot of people of working age seem to sit around in large, often gendered groups, in the middle of the day, "just waiting for reform", as one laid-off neighbor put it. Yet, Socialism, as if it were a metaphor for this whole discourse in its own right, is remembered just as much for slow, sluggish, under-performing, innovation- and incentive-free markets as it is for labor. Similarly, self-cultivation was an axiomatic principle of Confucianism, so long as this meant social conformism.

Purposelessness is the "blindness" metaphor again (see Chapter 2, p.29), but here the emphasis is not so much that they have "come from everywhere" (the "floodgates"), but that they're not going anywhere. Whereas much of the temporal dimension to the Authenticity discourse concerns "timelessness" and the past-looking "origin", Personality has a very strong present-making focus even though the narratives that my informants constructed to compete through it were often retrospective in form. The modalities of self-cultivation are complicated and not limited to the kind of effort manifest in forwards and constant striving, indeed, because the capacity to withstand, which is said to be a virtue of rural folk – a virtue which like the wind-battered pines atop Chinese mountains is made of necessity, and one that justifies urban exploi-tation – is a significant positive of this discourse even though this is largely an agency acted upon. In this respect, the spirit signified by the image of a dead child's hand protruding from beneath a grave of rubble after the Sichuan earthquake, still gripping his pen, captures this discourse well. So too does the selection of an indomitable pig, renamed "Strong-Willed Pig" (*Zhu Jian-qiang*), which survived under the same devastation for 36 days on charcoal and rainwater, as China's most inspirational animal for 2008. The pig lost two-thirds of its body weight while trapped underground, but upon acquiring celebrity status became so gluttonous that it could not even raise its snout from its trough (Liu 2009)!

The causal complexity latent within this discourse is further explained by the observation that many relevant keywords in the discourse turn on the character *yang*, the root meaning of various compound forms including: supporting, providing, raising, maintaining, giving birth to, forming, culti-vating, resting, recuperating, and so on. Perhaps the most apt derivative is *xiuyang*, meaning accomplishment, training, mastery, self-cultivation and so on, a term that is often combined with *wenhua*, meaning "culture", to make *wenhua xiuyang*, or "cultural cultivation". Quite ironically, but nonetheless entirely congruent with the parameters of the discourse, *xiuyang* is also given a negative orientation in Anshan and used to refer to those laid-off workers who, ineligible for either unemployment benefits or public pensions, are paid a sum significantly lower than their previous salary until they reach retire-ment age. Often occurring in the discourse, too, is *suyang*, meaning an embodied accomplishment, attainment, and self-control, which uses the same *su* as in the *suzhi* meaning "personal quality" (Kipnis 2007: 307) and which is sometimes also prefixed with *wenhua* for a knowledgeable stress, or with *geren* for an individual or personal stress (Yan 2003a).

Peiyang, which means to foster, train, develop and nurture, and similarly *jiaoyang*, meaning breeding, upbringing, education, are forms of control more often explicitly aimed at cultivating others, but which can nevertheless be conceptualized as forms of self-cultivation when seen in terms of familial investment: the intense control over the offspring-cultivation to which many Chinese parents are given; the planning, monitoring, assessment, and comparison with other people's children in league tables, and so on; even lineage and status. *Jiaoyang*, incidentally, is also given an ironic twist, used to describe the "re-education" to which political prisoners are exposed in China. Further relevant terms include *qizhi*, meaning to have a certain manner, air, or countenance about you: that certain "something that comes from the inside to the out, something that you can't change overnight", as one Anshan informant explained, which can be marked in practices as varied as walking, talking, sitting, standing and so on. *Juzhi*, which means something like poise, elegance, grace, composure, and which is perhaps best understood as the result of *qizhi*. Also occasionally occurring are *taoye*, meaning "to shape character or taste", and *qingcao*, meaning intellectual or aesthetic sentiment, which is perhaps best understood as the result of *taoye*. A *verbal* relation to the world intended to achieve a particularly focused result is therefore the principle of the Personality discourse.[1]

We might usefully consider, here, those Chinese students who will study in the library for days on end, without a break, and without any sense of "I just can't study in the daytime", or any of the other indulgences that Westerners would likely allow themselves. Students with a thick accent at a particular foreign language school in Beijing, I'm told, get up early in the morning, "especially" (of course), and put a stone under their tongues to correct their accent: the idea is that the stone is painful and causes discomfort, forcing the students to alter their enunciation. I have met students in Anshan who will self-consciously practice their actions with their weaker hand, "because this exercises the left side of my brain". Whereas in some cultures it might be acceptable to drop out, to slack off, etc. – indeed it might be self-destruction rather than self-cultivation that is seen as desirable (drugs, self-cutting, etc.), any form of this is much harder to negotiate.

Take chopsticks, for example, often candidates for self-cultivation: no mere eating tools, these are often talked of as pure genius, exercising every muscle from finger-tip to shoulder and waist, as well as the nerves and brain. Everything in China, it seems, is more or less "good for cultivating the body" (*dui shenti hao*), this one imperative explaining all manner of positive self-investments, from choosing the right product from the supermarket, to control over food intake and exercise, to the exotic health-cultivation practices Chinese people perform in parks: the banging of backs up against trees and rubbing of bodies against playground apparatus, walking backwards and calling of animal noises, and so on. Consider, too, the extreme dedication of China's sports stars, and the stories of coaches and parents who zealously encourage pre-pubescent children into feats of the most ludicrous endurance (Brownell 2001), such as the young girl who swam across the Yangtze with her arms and legs tied behind her, urged on by her father (Coonan 2007). All these are examples of the same self-cultivating logic.

The question arises, therefore, of what it really means to say that individuals compete through self-cultivation. Why is it that when Gao Xiaofei sees a young child skateboarding on the street this is not understood as simply having fun, but as "developing the waist and legs"? Why is it that Anshan entrepreneur Zhao spends hours and hours in his second flat on his own, playing table tennis against a robot that fires balls at him only for him to return the serve into a net from which the robot is reloaded again, ad infinitum? The remainder of this chapter will explore this point in discourse in terms of its internal inflections.

Kung fu

All Chinese know the proverb: "As long as your kung fu is deep, you can grind an iron pestle into a needle" (*zhiyao gongfu shen, tiechu mocheng zhen*). The term *gongfu* usually refers to martial skill but can refer to all sorts of skills cultivated over time. In any case, it is recognized that kung fu must be continually refined in an ongoing effort of realization, the emphasis very much on the process rather than results even where the process is highly competitive, as is the case with contesting social distinction. This importance of being engaged in the discourse is to be compared with the importance not so much of winning but of being willing to compete: while trying too hard to compete can be a negative, just as self-importance is also, outright winning as an end in itself is similarly seen as crass and juvenile by those who are really in control. Heuristically speaking, holding the upper hand in the ongoing strategic battle is far nobler than merely having won. In just this way, whether it is table tennis, chess, or business, entrepreneur Zhao likes nothing more than to find his opponent's weakness and press that point over and over, but he is genuinely disappointed when his opponent eventually resigns to loss and calls a halt to the game. While there is genuine delight in honing his forehand smash, or in selling out his shares before the price drops and everyone else loses out, Zhao cultivates a kind of control exerted first upon himself before it is exerted upon anyone else, a control intended to perfect himself.

Yet even these most personalized of "existential" projects of control are nevertheless always social, since the world is always what "self" is projected onto. Similarly, although such projects are first about cultivating the self in and for oneself, they are not simply equivalent to a rampant individualism, though this idea is close in the discourse also. Control exerted simply to satisfy the self will likely fall foul of social judgment in China; and raw, unchecked expressions of power for self-seeking ends are never likely to be accepted by others, though they may be jealously admired where they work. Only the gods or immortals can get away with being wanton, but if your exertion is successfully negotiated as a contribution to society by conforming to ritual, role and obligation, such that your action is seen as the right thing to do, so it can be reasonably expected of you, then your exertion just because you can, because you are able, because you are being the best you can be, becomes entirely acceptable, and you become good, a positively distinguished presence within the social sphere.

Indeed, cultivation of the "self" in this sense is a compulsion that cannot be avoided: individuals simply must be competitive if they are not to be found guilty of the negative judgments of the discourse (sloth, purposelessness, decadence, etc). In this sense, this discourse concerns the control in realizing the self not only from the power to do so, but ultimately from the responsibility to do so too. What at first seems like a set of highly individualizing traits – purpose, ambition, direction, self-confidence, etc., need not be so much an individualizing opting out of society but a complex form of cultivating individual worth within and in relation to that society; part of an ordering process and an ordered state, a framework for social practice, which like ostensibly moral action is again founded on reciprocal exchange (a thoroughly Confucian notion, incidentally). In these respects, as with the discourse of moral character, it is that which is sacrificed that most counts, a transactional logic that makes this cultivation quite different from a simple investment. As with the credit earned for enduring hardship, this can sometimes seem to be quite the opposite of self-cultivation, though nevertheless self-induced.

Consider Li Na, a 19-year-old Anshan high-school student, who admires "good students, who are excellent (*youxiu*), with extreme talent (*shifen youcai*), who have been through a really hard time to be this excellent". "For example", says Li, "if they play the piano and *guzheng* (a Chinese musical instrument), they need to study from theory first, then the music second. They often practice four or five hours a day. This is really bitter" (*ku*). I nudge her by asking what it is about this "hard time" that makes these students so excellent, to which Li replies: "Normal people just play for one or two hours a day, just for a hobby. But these people, if they want to be excellent, they must practice for four five hours a day without food or drink." She goes on: "When they do the *guzheng* for many hours their nails become black; some people wrap up their fingers, but the most excellent don't wrap up their fingers because they want the real feeling." Further: "Their teachers say that when they play sad music they must also have an accompanying really sad and powerful feeling, so they don't wrap up their fingers." I ask Li, "Do their fingers bleed?", to which she replies, "No, it's not that bad!" Now, despite my thinking that it can't be that "bloody" excellent then, it is clear that Li alludes to a different, or rather further kind of distinction than the separation made between the learning of socially valued skills and the distinction of paying for violin lessons in Chapter 3, a distinction that begins and ends with the *guzheng* player herself.

The distinction Li invokes is less about the acquisition of socially esteemed forms of ability, or their demonstration, than about the pursuit of and indulgence in "excellence" for its own sake: there is nothing obviously social about it, and there is no explicit competition in her imagery. The "hard time" she depicts is as much against the "self" as others, and in a way evidently related to the Authenticity discourse examined in Chapter 2 – "the real feeling", she says. The *guzheng* player's (almost) bleeding fingers are talked about as if they were a kind of sublimation, a kind of spiritual transcendence or perfection drawn near through the intensity of material discomfort, much like the self-flagellation Christian monks practiced in medieval times. The making-present of control here is a qualitative refinement of a purely artistic persuasion intended precisely to break out past the limits of the form and rigor required to learn the instrument, strictures that can ultimately stifle and choke creativity.

Li goes on to mention Langlang, perhaps the greatest of China's pianists, balancing her admiration with an acknowledgement of the life-sapping sacrifice made, a sacrifice that has somehow taken something fundamental from him in exchange for some supposedly higher plane of being called "excellence". "His father beat him until he played. He doesn't do anything save play, so he's like a withered date" (*kuza*). It is interesting that Li seems to romanticize the *guzheng* experience, since this seemingly transcendent element to the Personality discourse, with its element of exaggeration, ardor, the pushing on through the pain barrier, and so on, lends itself well to myth-making. On the "other side", of course, as in the case of the road out into the original countryside discussed in Authenticity (Chapter 2), lies purity, truth, and so on, but in an entirely sub-jective sense – a metaphysic of (almost Buddhist) enlightenment that necessitates the process of walking the metaphorical road less-travelled alone (Propp 1985).

Thus, in many respects, this discourse begins where the Authenticity dis-course left off: with the agent who with relentless focus strives to find foun-dational truth in himself, just as do those daring middle-class Chinese individuals who now pioneer the road out into the mountains in order to explore the original natural, hoping to find themselves masters of their own fate (see Chapter 2). Alternatively, the relevant point of reference could be how rural migrant narratives emphasize self-development and the improvements to their "personality quality" through suffering and hard work (see also Chapter 8). In any case, the highly individualized nature to this discourse, the immense personal resources invested and indeed the cost exacted in the process, make entrepreneurship a very useful metaphor for our purposes here.

Bittersweet

Consider Lin Wei here, owner of the restaurant in which I washed up dishes in Anshan, whose retrospective narrative about overcoming humble beginnings and bitter trials is highly relevant. From a base of "extreme bitterness" (*tebie ku*), as he tells it, Lin built himself up bit by bit, starting out as a painter-decorator, where he was frequently ripped-off, before opening his first restaurant six years ago. Lin claims that his father dying early in life gave him "a good foundation", teaching him that whatever the situation, he "must tackle it independently and with purposeful application" (*nuli*). He goes on:

Success is something that everyone must achieve for themselves. Everyone must eat the bitterness of their own struggle. Hardworking, you must be hardworking. Whatever it is, you must do it yourself; you must not be idle; you must be hardworking and fond of physical labor.

Now that Lin has become rich, however, he is in fact extremely idle and rarely lifts a finger to do anything except smoke, eat or drink; he is certainly not fond of physical labor. Though he appears to only ever hang around with his friends, chat, and go touring to shop, he denies that his life is leisurely (*xiuxian*), preferring the term "relaxed" (*qingsong*). He perhaps senses that he is to be judged decadent, a distinct negative in terms of this discourse, and shifts suspiciously around behind his cigarettes as if he has something to hide. Now that he has lots of money and all the spare time in the world, does Lin study? "No, I'm too old; it won't go in", he replies, "I don't read; I watch television and 'fry' shares" (*chao gupiao*). Nevertheless, it is clear from Lin's narrative that self-cultivation of the kind he imagines is actually very close in the discourse to the self-denial and self-deprivation which was explicitly a major theme of the previous chapter on the discourse of moral character; very close, that is, even though it seems that projects of self-refinement should be diametrically opposed to the demand for selflessness in the Chinese construction of good moral character. In both discourses, a particular kind of performance requires that something be exchanged for it: the greater the sacrifice made, the greater the reward gained; exactly the same ascetic logic, except that here the referential dimension of action and judgment is inverted from others first to the self.

Highly successful Anshan entrepreneur, Liu Zong, lives by a principle:

> By eating the bitterness of bitterness you can become a person above persons (*chide ku zhong ku, fang wei ren shang ren*). The reason for my success is mainly that I can eat bitterness. How can I say? It's all the effort (*xinku*) I have expended. I took my entire essence and put it into managing my business: enterprise culture, enterprise management, enterprise decoration, etc. I definitely can't say that it was physical bitterness-eating on my body; rather it was my entire spirit and energy (*jingshen*) that I invested. Perhaps other people would have used this time to play mahjong, eating, dancing, etc. But my time was entirely invested in work. Several years ago, when I was setting up the business, my days of work every day were extremely long; I only ever slept for several hours.

Liu Zong is clear: her success directly reflects the effort she has put in. However, she alludes to more than the simple return on investment. There is also that which her effort has taken from her in the meantime. The point is made by comparing similarly causal constructions operated by other Anshan people, such as, "If you don't eat the bitterness of bitterness, you can't eat the sweetness of sweetness" (*buchi kuzhongku, nande tianshangtian*), with the broadly equivalent Western version, "No pain, no gain". In the Chinese construction it is not simply the gain that is important, which is the point of the pain in the Western construction – that is, where the pain merely accumulates to a somehow prior point of exertion, but rather the interrelationality of social practice per se: the Western construction lacks the reciprocation of the social referent to the same extent, hence the juxtaposition of individualism versus collectivism in positivist-inflected management literatures, which cannot possibly hope to capture this relationalism.

This is what entrepreneur Zhang Xiuzhen means when she volunteers the following statement:

> You have to first give something up before you can get something back. Just now I talked about being willing to expend (*shede*). First you must expend (*she*), only then can you reap rewards (*de*). Some people say to me: "Is it the case that you set up this business, made lots of money, and now want to give some away?" Obviously, you'll never have any profit if you're like this, and will never get rich. Rather, everything you have now, you must be willing to part with. You must be in accordance with causality. Only where there is fruit can there be a cause. So you reap what you sow.

It is thus, in fact, equally as acceptable to sacrifice the self for the single-minded pursuit of personal achievement in China as it is to sacrifice the self for others, because just as moral action is also legitimately cultivation of the self, self-cultivation is also manifestly moral in its referent. Whether it is acts of demonstrable altruism, on the one hand, or the refining fires of sacrificial bitterness, on the other, the logic is ultimately the same: agency transcends the divide, no less, between the subjective and objective worlds, uniting itself with that which is shared about all experience. Or at least that is the social construction! Indeed, it is only the sensation of resistance that discourse puts up as it is displaced by this reflexive "pushing out" (to borrow a term from Chinese sociologist Fei Xiaotong and put it to a different use) that leads individuals to think that that which is in fact constitutive of the subject-object relation is somehow lost. For that effort almost Munchausen in its conviction, captured in the expression about students in imperial China tying their hair to the ceiling and placing an awl against their backsides to spur them to greater efforts whilst studying for the imperial exams (*touxuanliang, zhuicigu*), is also what joins individuals in communion with others.

The Personality discourse is thus ultimately about both the power and powerlessness of discourse. First, the power of discourse, where you must be an upright sound revolutionary, an honest child of the people; able to "eat bitterness"; able to undergo something that takes something from you in order to achieve something greater; able to endure evil to arrive at the good, and so on (Jacka 2006: 53). This is a discourse that goes beyond the Chinese State's efforts to inculcate a particular morality in the populous that impinges on the credibility of the Communist Party – abstinence, frugality, the "Yan'an

Way" – to an almost universal statement of human purpose and meaning – Bunyan's *Pilgrim's Progress*, the self-flagellation of Franciscan monks, the Buddhist path to Nirvana, a discourse that speaks of something fundamental to human life per se (Propp 1985). Second, Personality is about the powerlessness of this discourse when it is turned around and made into a human condition by individual agency, since this road can only be travelled alone as it is lived out in the narratives with which individuals synthesize their own identities. Thus is the Chinese construction of moral character, and in particular the "proximity law" which demands that a "good" action serve your own people first and strangers last, provided with a stabilizing counterpoint where self-exertion lends an individual, and therefore pan-Chinese, imperative to a morality that would otherwise be given to warring tribalism.[2]

Cultivating technologies

Consider now the different ways this discourse is made to work by Zhang Xiuzhen, as she interprets her rise from the fields of nearby Xiuyan, a small town with a jade mining industry, where she was born in 1970:

> I used to ask my mother and father what life was life outside the mountains, and they would say to me: "You study well now, and after you've got into university you will change the fate of your life."

Zhang never made it to university. She had two younger sisters and two older brothers at a time when women were severely underprivileged, especially in rural areas, which meant that when her father fell into a coma for five years at the age of 42, as she tells the story, she had to single-handedly care for her mother, her siblings, and her elderly grandmother:

> While my brother had to study a craft, and was allowed to leave home to study driving, and mechanics, I stayed at home and worked the fields, burnt the coal, cooked, worked manure into the land, and planted trees. As the heavy responsibility of life fell on my body, I worked in factories doing heavy work suitable only for men, and suffered horrific injuries.

In 1992 Zhang decided that learning about computers would give her a competitive advantage. When she finally came out of Xiuyan to gain work experience at a hotel in Dalian, she was one of 35 selected from 400, and then one of five selected from these. When Zhang studied English, she says, she would "get up at 3am even if she did not have to get up till 7am". Eventually Zhang found herself working as a waitress in an entertainment facility owned by the son of the one of the most powerful industry magnates in Anshan, eventually marrying this boss and becoming a full partner in the business. Zhang interprets her extraordinary success in terms of migration: "By moving you can live" (*rennuo nenghuo*). Now, she can speak as if she has arrived.

"And so how did I get to where I am now? It was all because of my own struggling (*fendou*) that my life changed". Though Zhang has paid dearly for her success with blood, sweat and tears, the perception is that the exchange adds value, a personal realization that could not have been realized in any other way, or by anybody else; one that was broadly guided throughout its genesis by her force of intent.

Today, Zhang puts this same existential control to use in the cause of developing her network-marketing company. She tells me at length how she cultivates her business in systematic fashion:

> Look at my condition. I have my target, I have my plans. Giving yourself a little pressure is correct. But you don't want too much pressure. You must go pace by pace. You can't miss a step; missing a step is no good. You have to leave your trail of two footprints on the ground. You can't just set yourself a target too far from you. For example, if it was a step, if I wanted to step up all of them in one go this would be impossible; you can only do it step by step. First you must have plan, a target plan. I must think, "How to complete", and every day repeat this action. And secondly, you must do things accordingly to the plan. When you come across a difficulty, you must think of a way to get over it. You need to have a position to orient you when you're anxious. I think I'm this kind of person, I rely on my own perseverance and striving; there is nothing I can't do. But only if you're willing to do things in the proper sequence, gradually, with perseverance, can you do it; with the right attitude you can do anything. It cannot be the case that you will always get results every time you expend; sometimes you will expend and not get any payback, no results at all. But if you don't expend, it'll be even more the case that you'll never get anything back. Life is fair; we all have 24 hours per day. But how long we live is up to us. Life is in the palm of our hands. Just see if you treasure it. Especially fate, it's really not easy to get. You must always think: now that my parents have given me a life, they have given me this environment, I must strengthen myself. There is nothing difficult in front of me. I always say "when the car is at the bottom of the mountain, there must be a road"; you don't need to think about it too much.

In the first instance, Zhang's narrative shows how the process of self-refinement, though essentially qualitative, and for all the sheer intensity of will that she exerts, might nevertheless be a very disciplined, precise, exacting and graduated process, systematic and methodical in its rationality, so that there is ultimately no difference between forms of "existential" control that are explicitly qualitative, such as that which Li Na invokes in the *guzheng* player's reveries (above), and the more technical, formulaic forms of control Zhang invokes here: insofar as both are existential, both achieve fundamentally the same result, and both somewhat presuppose each other. Some Chinese may of course see more value in impulsive, ostensibly unstructured expressions of will: we saw in Chapter 5 on "Sociability" how an excess of control, perhaps as planning, calculation, or formalism, can be judged negatively where impulse and flair are desirable. Further, indeed, control might perhaps sometimes only be achieved by acting largely on instinct – "going with your gut", as it were – so that any amount of planning and meticulous deliberation is actually insufficient on its own. This even though an element of grit, determination and a particular resistance to the impulse to give up when the going gets tough is no doubt required for social distinction, even if the ultimate goal is personal liberation. Even the most disciplined of efforts can be insufficient for achieving control: mere effort just makes you headstrong.

For distinction, ultimately, the uncertainty of the "game" must be embraced. For it doesn't matter how hard you try, you can never be sure whether it is your effort and control or something else that does the trick, something like faith, luck, or that element of imagination which roams free of the will. Willing, indeed, may sometimes by itself trigger "miraculous" results, or at least that is the social construction (think of cancer sufferers who "fight it off" against all the odds). On the other hand, the miraculous breakthrough can sometimes only come when you entirely let go of control, when you browse an unrelated source or meet with an unexpected encounter, such that discipline is highly valuable and useful in a way that disciplines ultimately are not. Effort, that is to say, must always be complemented by an "external" element beyond agency itself – "fate", as Zhang puts it – so that the actual engagement in such projects does not prevent an advance that can only come when, in the worldly imperfection that all humans share, individuals cannot but help but relax their control and see the way forward – the "car at the bottom of the mountain" (as Zhang puts it).

Exercising the "self" in this way therefore requires something of an "authentic" (Heidegger 1962) realization of individual agency's possibilities for being, including its inevitable finitude. Control requires that you be resolute in the face of your being, including an always imminent death (that which lies outside your capacity for "final coherence"), thus making coherent narrative sense of your present from all possible futures and from interpretations of the past (cf. Heidegger's notion of "Authentic Dasein"). As Zhang puts it (above), we must objectify our lives in the "palm of our hands". That is to say, that in this sense of individuals taking control, they do so ultimately from no one else, because what they find is what they, and they alone, already had. However, this need not be conscious as a process and certainly not rational as such. "You don't need to think about it too much", as Zhang explains. Indeed, only the likes of the positivists and other methodological individualists think this active disinvestment of self can be consciously grasped for anything more than the vaguest promise of a moment. As well as being close to myth-making in the discourse, therefore, we are close also to mysticism, but resignation to fate remains entirely insufficient for social distinction. Positive affirmation is still very much required; the gods help only those who help themselves. "Fate", as Zhang puts it, is "really not easy to get ... we must strive with all our might".[3]

All Zhang's other constructions are thus made subordinate to an intensely vital energy. As she continues elsewhere, "Every time my mood is bad, I'll go to the top of a mountain and shout to the North, South, East and West, shouting out my wishes, that my business will be good, and my dreams will be good; all my dreams from near and far, no matter if it's a big target or a small target (*mubiao*), they're all within my grasp". Vitality, indeed, is very much expressive of Zhang's innate personality (cf. the relevant discussion in Chapter 5), and indeed vitality is where this discourse tessellates most closely with a sense of self-confidence (*zixinxin*), self-respect and esteem, enthusiasm (*reqing*) and optimism (*leguan*), creativity (*chuangzao*), courage (*yonggan*), exploration (*tansuo*), an expansive, pioneering, enterprising spirit, as opposed to small-mindedness, pettiness, and intolerance, all of which are also negatives of the central importance of magnanimity in the Sociability discourse (Chapter 5). The vital person positively welcomes and actively consumes whatever he/she encounters, but an "open" willingness should not be mistaken for unasser-tiveness, or self-denial: "internally referential" control is highly assertive, a kind of assertion maybe less understood in the West, perhaps, but an assertion that orders the world even as it orders the self.

Control, indeed, need not even be conceptualized in terms of positive assertion at all in order to be an acceptable form of social competition, for in some situations control can be quite indirect. If your actions fill the gap of indeterminism with drive and direction, as in most of the purposeful exam-ples about Olympic training and so on (above), this is of course unacceptable, and perhaps more obviously called control. However, if your control is used in a stabilizing or entropic way (*wenzhong*), that can also be acceptable. Self-cultivation can be apparently quite static, just never entirely stagnant; indeed the tension between the imperative to be earnest, engaged and assertive, and the distastefulness of being overtly ostentatious, is resolved by moderation, simplicity, acting in a "naturally" fitting way, and so on, all of which are highly self-disciplined forms of assertion, and not at all passive. The case of conspicuous consumption is similar: ostentation shows loss of control. People in control don't need this. If your ostentation is expected in your role or position, though, this is necessary, and shows you are in control. This is as true of consumers in Anshan, China, as it is of consumers in other places.

For some people in Anshan, moreover, the embodiment of taste must be played down, almost denied, in a highly controlled way, so that praise and compliments are deflected as if unwanted, though nevertheless yet reaped as such. Indeed, knowing when to document these forms of control is itself prudence. Further still, much of the time social actors are engaged in an entirely pre-reflective or largely unconscious form of control, the "done thing" that maintains social order and which is most obviously disclosed only when it is broken down by becoming explicitly out of control. This kind of control was most obvious when a woman threw a fit of hysterical anger about "self-ishness" and "the pressure of the crowd" on the train from Beijing to Anshan, for example, standing on her seat, shrieking and wailing at the carriage full of bemused passengers for several minutes until eventually realizing her embarrassment, her wrath turning away from the perceived offence to society at large, then the entire human condition, before she eventually settled down again, finding a ladder to climb down on by blaming an almost unidentified other for "swearing" (*ma*) at her.[4]

In any case, and most importantly, all these different types of control, technical versus qualitative, dynamic versus stabilizing, impulsive versus deliberate, conscious versus unconscious, fated versus free, selfish versus selfless, and so on, can never be really separated anyway. All forms of control become existential for exactly the same reason that all the discourses of this analysis are only separate as the result of their abstraction and iteration, and hastily collapse into one another again in their actual practice. Witness that many of the examples of self-cultivation discussed above had a distinctly collective referent: China's glory-reaping Olympians and the young girl swimming the Yangtze to please her father to name just two. Those everyday heroes willing to "eat bitterness" in their daily labor – moreover, do it for themselves, of course, not for their bosses; and the only reason that entrepreneurs' profiteering is legitimized in contemporary China is because their level-headed, skillful and self-controlled self-seeking instrumentalism is now seen as good for the economy as a whole.

We might also consider once again the sense in which your good moral character must be shown to such a degree in China (see Chapter 6); that is, that certain types of morally correct control that in the West would perhaps only be enacted in response to emotional stimuli, such as that arising from the immediacy of the necessity to help someone, in China become a traditional or habitual action, a rational rule by which you have to abide: you have to be proactive; you have to show consideration in certain ways; you have to send that text wishing your relative a happy mid-autumn day; you have to cry at your wedding if you are a young woman; you have to be a good host; and you have to profess your loyalty over and over in order to generate good will that will be reciprocated as favors, ultimately benefitting yourself. Just as the affective behavior becomes a rational imperative, the controlling, rational behavior also becomes an emotional reflex, so that there is little distinction between the senses in which you have to take the initiative to act.

All rationalizations are forms of rationality, which is intentional, and existential, and must be exerted against something other than itself. Thus, competitiveness remains the essence of self-cultivation, and this need not be of the "I've got the biggest car" type, but rather "I am in control of myself and my behavior, so that I control the rest", so that your competition is a comparator, a shared reference around which distinction is indirectly contested. Indeed, provided an opponent in this sense is present, social control may be commanded even through controlled bursts of being explicitly out of control. Yes, the power of discourse and its consumption extends even to this.

Control freak

Consider this final field note where a disordering of the self at once disordered the social world and exerted control over it. I was having dinner with my girlfriend, her parents, an aunt and an uncle at a hotpot restaurant. The uncle and I hadn't seen each other for over a year and he was very happy to see me. He controlled most of the ordering of dishes, and having done so motioned to the waitress to let the restaurant owner know that he was there; apparently the owner would know who he was. The waitress asked who she should say it was, to which the uncle replied that all she need do is tell her boss that the "big boss" (*da laoban*) was here. Shortly afterwards, the owner of the restaurant entered the room to greet him. Unexpectedly, however, he sat down to join us for dinner, changing the mood immediately. The rest of us had never met "Lin Wei" before, and were looking forward to a family meal without the somehow competitive dynamic.

Predictably, the discourse became very much centered on me, the foreigner. Unaware of my role in the family and assuming I was an "outsider", Lin said to me: "Do you know, this is the big boss?", whilst patting the uncle admiringly on the shoulder and sloshing our glasses full of beer. Everyone except the uncle and Lin were quiet except for the odd polite laugh. These two then asserted that I was "good" because I was "a foreigner", and that I was "formidable" (*lihai*). Then there followed a general agreement that I was "good" because I "study hard". Then another theme emerged as we became further engrossed in our hotpot and beer: I was also good, apparently, because I liked to eat a lot of meat; or more precisely, that these men liked eating with me because they could eat lots of meat and be out of control. Normally the uncle must control his diet, but just once or twice a year, he can go wild and indulge himself to excess.

Thus, we proceeded to eat hideous amounts of meat, making messy splashes as we ate, the uncle somehow orchestrating all proceedings by performing a very random kind of swishing and swashing of the chopsticks in the hotpot, a behaviorism my wife (then girlfriend) had previously told me she was taught was "bad manners" as a child. Red-faced and virtually drooling, the uncle said to me, but also for the whole group: "It's best when you pick up a load of meat in one go so your whole mouth is full of meat!" This same uncle usually refuses alcohol on account of needing to project the control appropriate to his position, but on this occasion drank many bottles of beer with Lin and I. The uncle directed proceedings and Lin facilitated, ushering plate after plate of lamb to our table. By the end of the meal, I had eaten about half a lamb or thereabouts. Lin then splashed out books of vouchers on us for his restaurant amounting to 10,000 yuan, enough for around 40 large group meals, half of which were refused because his generosity, it was felt, was just too excessive – out of control; but that was the whole point.

It has already been discussed how excess behaviors like these can help forge communal relations and masculine identities at the exposition of the Sociability discourse (Chapter 5). Here, however, eating as if out of control had a role in projecting a more overt form of social power. The uncle would possibly have been overexcited to see me anyway, but we have eaten together many times to excess, and many other times in an uncompetitive fashion too. In particular, there was something about these men finding a worthy opponent in me – a young, carnivorous Western guy, to arrange their competition around and test each other with the social domination stakes. The women present were the backdrop upon which the "game" was played. The uncle's wife was especially quiet at the other end of the table opposite him. My girlfriend's mother was also quiet and self-controlled, sitting straight and not interrupting. Similarly, my girlfriend's usual attempts to wrest control from me at times like this were completely silenced on this occasion. With the uncle calling the shots, the women knew better than to make a fuss about stopping us in public, especially in front of Lin, who was not family. Rather, the barrage followed later when we were home: "You should control yourselves; you shouldn't overdo it; you should say no", etc., the price to pay or sacrifice in this case accompanied by sweats, dizziness, and a disturbed digestive system.

Control and self-cultivation, then, though an existential logic, is always a question of balance worked out against the social world and its structures. "Power is nothing without control", conjectured the long-running Pirelli tires advert, implying that control requires traction. Whether rationalized as ordering or disordering, the will must be channeled, focused, tempered and disciplined for distinction, yet never entirely tamed. The pianist Langlang (above) achieves greatness only by internalizing prior codes upon which he improvises, invents, and innovates: his self-cultivation is informed by the world. No doubt Farrer's dancers dancing "individualistically" into the mirrors of Shanghai's dance clubs (Farrer 2002) – that is, rather than dancing together in a "collectivist" fashion – are engaged projects of intense self-control, worshipping at the altar of the god within, at the site of the internalization of externality as it were, imposing form on the formlessness of agency and ordering the self in a way that is no doubt called "individuality" but that need not necessarily be any more narcissistic than the *guzheng* player's painful ecstasies. The dancers dance thus because doing so accrues a particular kind of socially constructed value in that context: it would certainly not be the same if the dancers took off their clothes and defecated on the dance floor just to be different. Only avant-garde artists can get away with that sort of statement, and their point is precisely this one: the dancers are no more different than the respect accrued to a qigong master or ascetic priest for his efforts to transcend the subject-object divide.

Art, like all forms of composure, such as the juggler who creates the illusion of manipulating many balls at once, or the disc-jockey who blends together two or more simultaneously playing records into a single soundtrack, is what individual agency makes of all the various conflicting elements that life presents to it, which is ultimately to speak of what individual agency makes of itself. Individual mastery requires consistency and innovation; discipline and imagination. Only in this way is it possible to project a style defined not by reference to any others but that can be called your own, and by which the complex, disparate and apparently unconnected elements of human life can be subjected to a single authorial thread that identifies you in a way that satisfies both yourself and other individuals. This thread, a "trajectory" (de Certeau 1984: xviii), is of course a metaphor for the operations in practice right now.

Materialism

The remaining chapters of this book will demonstrate that certain people, and certain "types" of people in China, are writing the trajectories of their lives more than others. By way of setting up what follows, I briefly introduce the two remaining discourses abstracted from my analysis, "Materialism" and "Status", both of which are less irreducible categories of judgment and practice like those discourses elucidated thus far, than that in which these other discourses are crystallized.

Materialism is a massive concept which I will not try to define here. For our purposes, let it simply be noted that "Materialism" concerns the self that projects itself onto and over material objects as consumption, which need not be necessarily understood as consumerism, which is a pattern of practice that borrows meaning from the conflation of Materialism and Status (see discussion below). Materialism is an objective projection of the whole discourse, all the other discursive rules already elucidated bearing on a material projection. It is that actual physical place where the metaphorical relation that first emerged where the "self" which was recognized as having the agency to contribute to discourse in principle (see Chapter 2) now opens up onto the totality of the material world, all the previous analyses having progressively hollowed out the discourse, leaving only the material thing in itself. This is not at all to say that material is "outside" the discourse unaccompanied by the subject, or that the self asserted through the other discourses is somehow not engaged with material. Quite the contrary, Materialism is that necessary condition of all the other discourses where individual agency re-cognizes itself in discourse, intelligent self-awareness and the senses appropriate to an embodied agency of course being given together.

Materialism is thus even more "existential" than the discourse of control and self-cultivation articulated here, and to this very real extent completes the epistemological perspectivism sustained throughout; insofar as it traces a sort of oblique fit with the formal structures of subjectivity iterated at Authenticity, Materialism turns this relational theoretic backwards upon itself towards an almost Cartesian objectivity. When seen from an analytical perspective, however, and indeed somewhat by virtue of these latent spatial and visual metaphors (see Chapter 2), a discursive "space" that might seem to concern the "visual" topography of the entire "objective" sphere is actually quite narrow, so much of this scope having already been mapped in the previous chapters. That is to say, that with Materialism, the entire analysis can now be seen to take a particular form actually presupposed by the authorial agency undertaking it. Put another way, though we now demarcate a place we call "Materialism", a place that should "logically" be "filled" by analysis, this space has become increasingly redundant having already been handled in conjunction with the other issues from which this space is inseparable. More figuratively put still, individual agency cannot apprehend itself as a material thing in itself since all objects are by definition apprehended only perspectively, which is to say within always still social discourses: through, as it were, the eyes of the Other (Ci 1994).

Status

If the elements of a system have no positive content (as maintained by the Post-structuralist approach) but are rather defined by their differentiated relation to everything they are not, any analysis could continue to identify ever-increasingly small elements of the whole before a "discourse" was introduced about which there would be nothing left to say, the capacity to impose structure having collapsed into the instantiation itself. For this same reason, Materialism is brought together with "Status", which concerns the judgment of the individual as a socialized category, a discourse which is also, though in another sense, that in which the entire language is crystallized.

Status may be thought of in two ways: first, as an objective grid, like a hierarchical ladder of statuses where individuals are identified by and/or identify with a label ("rural", "urban", "worker", "cadre", and so on); and second, in terms of the immediate situational relation to others, where speaking and action will change according to whom is being addressed and so on, the rules determining how exactly being highly conventional. Status is therefore less a mode of judgment in which individuals can transgress as such, than a synonym for the distinguished individual per se; it is that final structural principle of this analysis where although there will always be some outlying points in instances of judgment that remain distinctive for their apparent randomness and lack of fit with social structure, every boundary judgment distinguishing validity from invalidity must necessarily be seen in terms of its duality: as the judgment "in itself' (as part of a continuum of judgments), and as the measure of the judgment's social credibility, contingent on its fit with similar judgments and with the "status" of its maker (Lamont 1992). Quite the opposite of the agency first granted the autonomy to make classificatory judgments in Chapter 2, Status is therefore where individual agency is "consumed" by the categories of social structure even as it consumes these in judgment.

This means that materialism and status need not be fully explicated in terms of their conceptual genesis as has been done with the other discourses, but can be much better understood when examined in conjunction with those other discourses. Since materialism and status both come so close to the actual practice of distinction, that is to say, there is proportionately greater analytical value in pursuing the "grammar" of how individuals consume these discourses differently in articulation. It may as well be explicit here, however, that materialism and status are perhaps most relevant where they are made to converge: at that point in discourse where the judgment of the individual in itself (as it were) and the judgment of the social classification of the person are arrived at each through the prism of the other; where horizontal expressions of individual difference have been colonized by vertical references to forms of subjectivity that can only be paid for with money. The following analysis thus allows this conflation of materialism and status to be drawn out in conjunction with the other discourses of this analysis as the research moves to understand how judgment is configured within social categories; to understand, indeed, how social categories are configured by judgment.

The following analysis does not pretend to be an exhaustive account of Chinese or even Anshan society, but is rather intended to best reflect the wide range of individuals who informed this study. The following chapter examines the rural migrants with whom I worked at Lamb Buddha, a large hotpot restaurant. Most of the data come from young men, meaning that the analysis complements extant studies of Chinese female migrant workers by allowing male-gendered inflections of discourse prominence (e.g. Chang 2009; Pun 2005; Zhang 2001). Chapter 9 brings together a swath of broadly "working-class", middle-aged urban adults, drawing out the grammar of social distinction along the vectors of age and gender. Finally, Chapter 10 analyses a range of middle-aged adult individuals all of whom are distinguished from those analyzed in Chapter 9 by a rough composite of occupation and professional status, discretionary income, educational level, and family background. Each analysis similarly shows how discourse is consumed by different individuals in different ways, but in ways nevertheless approximate to individuals of similar objective positions in society, thus charting a third way between individual agency and social structure.

8   Migrants

The internalization of externality

Lamb Buddha is a privately owned hotpot restaurant in Anshan with approximately 20 kitchen staff, 20 serving staff and a further ten management and administrative personnel. My employment here followed from eating a meal at the restaurant with some relatives shortly after the restaurant opened. The owner, named Lin Wei, was eager to please, and humored me when I said that I wanted to work in a service industry business. He genuinely thought I was joking when I replied "Wash dishes" to his asking me what I could do, but this changed to comments about "foreigners being very interesting" (*hen youyisi*) and "foreigners being formidable" (*lihai*) when he saw I was serious about the idea. Some days later, I reported for duty, and the staff manager explained to the kitchen staff that I would juggle the demands of washing dishes with observing and conversing, "thus learning about Chinese culture and society". After several weeks in the kitchen, I found that I was able to gather personal data in my colleagues' dormitories, or squatting on the roof of the restaurant, away from the structures of authority that defined our initial relationship.

My approach to my colleagues was open-ended and aimed to elicit spontaneous thoughts and reactions. Driven only by my focus on the deictic markers by which informants position themselves in relation to discourse, I did not pursue an interview schedule as such; rather, my role was to develop quality information by earning trust through dialogue, to listen and be informed, to react impartially but sensitively, taking every conversation as a valuable example of self-assertion (Heimer and Thøgersen 2006).

All but one of my kitchen colleagues was a rural migrant. They performed menial and monotonous tasks 12 hours a day, seven days a week. One or two female migrants of reproductive age joined women from poor urban families on the restaurant floor; notably the entire serving staff comprised young women (Hanser 2005). Clerical and administrative workers, and those involved in the purchasing and transportation of goods, were of urban-registered household status without exception; the former were middle-aged women; the latter were middle-aged men. These urban staff would gravitate together towards the office end of the premises, avoiding the hot and sweaty kitchen, and joke that the difference between them and the migrants was the same as the distinction between cadre and worker from the State-owned enterprise era. Some lower-ranking urban men would occasionally come by the kitchen to hang out, but perhaps only as a foil for cheating some leisure time on the job out of their employers (de Certeau 1984: 24–28). This limited interaction was entirely harmonious, though the urban men would notably be louder, confident and laughing, and the migrants always quieter and more careful. Even those urban staff working at the same wage level as the migrants would occasionally make statements belittling the "farmers". Correspondingly, many of the migrants volunteered that they were of the "lowest level" (*zuidiceng*) in this urban context. China's categorical urban-versus-rural household registration divide (Cheng and Selden 1994), as well as inequalities of age and gender (Jacka 2006), were therefore highly significant dimensions of status here.

Most of the young men analyzed here, named Zhang Jiali, Lin Chuan, Xue Liang and Wang Cuihua, characterize their rural familial origins as a source of authenticity, moral purity, and social belonging, positives that they felt the urban environment either was devoid of or actively denied to them (Halskov-Hansen and Pang 2008). Consider Zhang Jiali, 20 years old, who had moved with his family "out from" countryside climes elsewhere in Liaoning Province three years ago, where he "had a simple life, close to nature, working as the sun rose, and resting as it fell": whereas Zhang finds the people from his home "sincere, plain, simple, and true" (*shizai, pushi*), he finds people in Anshan city "fake" and "two-faced" (*xuwei*) (see Chapter 2 on Authenticity). "The city is competitive", Zhang explained, "It follows the laws of the jungle: whereas the countryside is relaxed, the city is extremely tense; I must work hard or be eliminated through competition".

Other migrants made constructions almost identical to Zhang's. Lin Chuan, aged 22, similarly finds the city ambiguously moral, preferring the countryside and the friendly people there too:

> In the countryside, we set up a table in a big yard, start the barbeque, drink, take our clothes off, get bare-chested, and drink. Oh my, it's really good, enough to make people really envious! Our neighbors are all extremely exuberant (*reqing*). We get everything together from around the village to eat, and everybody sits in the same place; it's extremely lively, buzzing with excitement and exhilaration, not like in the city. People in the city are complicated (*za*). It's like we can't make head or tail of what they're thinking. What are they thinking in their hearts? Sometimes we're scared of losing things; if we put our things down, they'll take them and use them. We need to be really guarded against this; not like in the countryside, where we don't even lock our doors when we go out. Here, in the city, we fear robbers at the door and thieves coming in; we have security bars. We've got to be really careful. In the countryside you don't need to be careful. If you want to go to someone else's house you just go

in; if you want to watch television you just switch it on; and when you've finished you go; it's really relaxed like that. Not like the city where it's really tense and everyone is different.

Thus, Anshan's urban sphere was constructed as a place of uncertainty and mistrust vis-à-vis opposing virtues that these migrants believed were embodied in themselves (see Chapter 2, and Chapter 5 on Sociability).

Xue Liang, the youngest migrant at 16, responded to my asking whether his family was from the city or the countryside, by stating "countryside" with a bold yet naïve-sounding assertion. Xue left for the city because his family was "comparatively poor". He didn't want to leave, but wanted to take responsibility for alleviating the burden on his overworked and aging parents. With Zhang and Lin (above), Xue maintained:

> Generally speaking, city people are not as good as people in the countryside. I like the countryside. I don't like the city, because I can play when I'm at home, and pick vegetables, kick a ball around and do as I please. I can go to the mountains and catch a chicken, catch a fish, fish with crude nets (*laoyu*), and go fishing (*diaoyu*) in the reservoir!

Xue thus conjures a life of simple pleasures and simple gradations connected with nature and feeding the family: he was probably telling me that as well as fishing with nets he has also fished with rods!

> In the countryside, you can play as and where you like. But you can't do this in the city. You can play, but if you make the city dirty or break something, people will tell you off.

In this way, Xue spoke of Anshan as if it were an object that bites with only limited provocation: urban consumers had "sworn" at him before, for preparing the wrong vegetables, as it is the trend to bully serving staff into paying for mistakes or breakages from their own meager salaries (Lei 2003).

The externalization of internality

Despite their underprivileged status, however, not one of these migrants apologized for the urban disdain for the countryside. Both Zhang and Lin volunteered that the countryside is a place of natural tranquility, quiet and with clean air, and contrasted this with the pollution and noise of the city. Zhang believes people live longer in the countryside, too, and in defense of his roots, Lin was eager to stress that the countryside is developing now, "with mobile phones, roads, and city people visiting in their cars", thus walking a fine line between different and competing constructions of the countryside (see Chapter 2, pp.37–39). That is to say, that although these migrants want the countryside to be pure, unspoiled, and sustaining in contrast to the "inauthenticity" and "unnatural" façade of the city, they also want to project an image of a countryside that somehow conjoined the best of all possible worlds. Essentially, they take what little they have and find a way to put a positive spin on it in order to compete socially.

Indeed, though all these migrants were similarly loyal to their local roots and, thrown together, formed a temporary unity of identity around this shared basis (see below), not all expressed an anti-urban configuration. Wang Cuihua, the fourth migrant, the oldest of the four and the longest "out" of the countryside, rather likes Anshan and seeks to establish himself here:

> How can I say? In every respect, the environment is cleaner; the city is cleaner than the countryside. The conditions in the village are not good, and the city has parks. There are no karaoke and discos in the village.

Lin Chuan, too, though he did not side with the city over the countryside, drew several distinctions between himself and members of his family who have never left the countryside, intending to elevate himself in my perception. Lin has grown accustomed to the city, I was to understand, and finds that there's "nothing to do when he goes home except sit around and watch television". He is aware of having been changed by his exposure to the urban sphere, an experience that has come with the need to acquire a taste for economic and symbolic intricacies:

> In the beginning, I couldn't understand why the clothes I wore in the countryside could be worn for many years, but here I needed to change clothes every quarter. And why I had to buy bottled mineral water when the water in the countryside I could drink straight from the well. Everything in the city required money.

All these young migrants originate from the countryside, but their identities are characterized by a fundamental ambiguity arising from increasing integration into urban ways of life. Lin Chuan, indeed, already five years out of the countryside, has learnt to handle the complexity of consumption and become fluent in the fluid dynamics of individual identity; he is adept at making the best use he can of the range of goods and cultural products around him to compete socially and is in many respects indistinguishable from urban-registered men of his age.

The fact that Lin buys "fake" branded products is more a source of pride than shame. Of course he is aware that his Nike training shoes are not the "real thing" – everyone knows that only people with money buy the "real" product (see Chapter 2). What is more important to Lin, and the people around him, is that he has shown sufficient control of his environment to know what the top brands are, to have surveyed his available options, and to have had the ability to find himself a counterfeit without getting ridiculously out of pocket (see Chapter 3 on Knowledge). When Lin showcases his skill in the kitchen, his friends laugh openly along with him, admitting, boasting even, that their trainers and clothes are counterfeit too, positively reveling in a mutually recognized craftiness as the unspoken rules of the game are spelled out: in the city, *you must be competitive*, and so long as you do so in order to survive as a player, to remain on top, the arts of the inauthentic are entirely acceptable. Indeed, it was precisely through the confessional acknowledgement of "inauthentic" tactics that a sense of authentic identity and belonging was evoked and shared (de Certeau 1984: 24–28).

In exactly this way, too, the migrants were happy to gather to watch me do *taiji* in the kitchen, forging solidarity from our mutual insubordination of the system. These situations were about "us" in the kitchen versus the urban staff "out there" in the restaurant: while one or two serving staff would occasionally join in the fun, others would skirt away to ensure their participation was not seen by the manager. All such jollities were immediately suspended at the slightest hint of her presence. In the end, it was of course only the manager who represented the system. Some of the urbanites would have happily joined in had they not been so afraid of her. If she were to betray even an inkling of delight in symbolic insubordination herself, the entire system would be lost. Her role was essentially to keep up the appearance of an "objective" system that existed only insofar as she had to respect the owner. Indeed, this might be a poignant (if somewhat exaggerated) metaphor for all of Chinese politics, with its transcendental signifier somehow beyond all accountability – currently called "Hu" – and over 1.3 billion individual subjects accountable to the system only insofar as they report to the "level" above.

Experience is everything

Lin Chuan, Wang Cuihua and Xue Liang all failed to complete China's mandatory nine years of middle school education. All offered a combination of failing to study well and the costs of further education as reasons for dropping out (see Chapter 3). Zhang Jiali began the first year of high school before dropping out, he says, for similar reasons: "My father really didn't want me to continue studying because he could see I was so tired." Zhang nevertheless attempts to claw back some of the social capital an education would have granted him, a reflection of the deep regret he later admits to me: when he quit, he makes sure to add, his teacher and all the other students came over to his home to try to persuade him to stay on, "because at that time I was the one in the family with the brightest hopes of going to university". Xue, the youngest, explicitly states that the decision to drop out was a sacrifice made for his family, against their wishes: he knew his parents needed him to earn a wage (see Chapter 6 on Morality). Wang explains that he was "kicked out for fighting", which is probably as much a glamorization of his failure as it is true. I ask him straight, "You weren't good at study?", to which he replies affirmatively whilst trying to avoid being explicit. He later admits that he "couldn't memorize the words" and "couldn't handle physics and geometry

Figure 8.1 Kitchen staff. Photography by Kunal Sinha

class". Zhang says exactly the same, indicating that these young men have worked out how to justify their predicaments through close negotiation with each other.

Since coming to Lamb Buddha, however, Lin and Xue have developed skills that distinguish them from many of the other kitchen workers. Whereas most of the others merely sort and chop vegetables, or wash dishes, Lin has been trained to prepare herbs and Xue to operate the meat cutter. However, neither of these is really an "ability" (*nengli*), they say, "Anyone can do it if they've been shown". Zhang Jiali, too, knows enough Chinese *gongfu* (martial arts) to win him the doorman's job, but his skills are only rudimentary. Even so, he clearly feels that his brief stint at a youth military training academy is a valuable form of symbolic capital: he wears military clothes with his jeans, consciously identifying himself with a particular sector of the lower reaches of society (see Chapter 7, the sections on Materialism and Status). Rather less consciously, Lin chides urban people for not knowing about the "local products" (*tutechan*) that have recently begun to be sold around the city, quite missing the point that urbanites now reappraise these products as desirable precisely because these products are considered backward – that is, *tu* (see Chapter 2, p.34).

Acknowledging this lack of formal education, the migrants emphasize the value of practical knowledge and the experiences they have gained through travelling to many different places to work: the process of self-transformation undergone is asserted as socially competitive in a way that provides an interesting counterpoint to scholarly types and those who invest everything in their children's education (see Chapter 3). Zhang Jiali, for example, at 20, has an age "suitable for accumulating experiences":

> From the north to the south, from Shenzhen to Liaoning, the restaurants are often very different; the style of management is different. From the north to the south all the things I have seen are different.

It emerges, however, that Zhang has never in fact been to the "south" himself; indeed, he has never left Liaoning. When Zhang speaks of collecting experiences, therefore, he speaks for the migrant workers as a group, as if this is their capital, as if this is the kind of person he is becoming:

> Our ways of doing things are all different. I just diversify (*duoyuanhua*) more and more. For example, take a problem: normally speaking, there's only one way to solve it. But after you've travelled extensively, you've seen the same problem dealt with in different ways in different places, there are many ways to solve the problem.

Telling it how it is, but with laudable optimism about the transferability of different kinds of capital assets, Zhang further wagers:

> Urban people compete using a different kind of competition: they rely on their brains. But we only have the ability to work. They develop their knowledge to get from "white collar" to "gold collar" to "CEO". We must hoard experiences. Only by collecting enough experiences can I finally do some business I like. These are the only choices I have: this or return to the countryside. We just do our work well; the "white collars" develop their minds after they've done their work. We very seldom use our minds. I'd really like to use my mind, but it's not yet the time.

Of course, competing socially through strategic experience accumulation is a necessity, and these migrants admit they cannot compete on the same grounds as educated urbanites. And yet, this admission marks the beginning of the counter-tactics they surreptitiously hatch, for without this these young men have only their young bodies to offer in service to those who profit from their labor. Coming to the city is expressed in terms of a highly individualizing emphasis on self-cultivation. Once again, Zhang Jiali is especially strong in these respects:

> Because the city is so competitive, I must incessantly strengthen myself. I'll prove to them that I was right; I'll start up a business, and that's why I'm travelling around now collecting life experience. When I've

accumulated enough experiences, I'll go and do what I want to do. Because everyone has a dream in life and I'm running along in accordance with my dream, waiting for the day when I grab hold of and realize this dream, and then I'll be really satisfied, and will have a rich life. I'm just not like some other people. In China, because of the depression over where their names are listed in the high school entrance exam results tables, great numbers of students commit suicide every year. In fact, if you add them all together, there are loads like this. The pressure is too great. And nowadays, there's no guarantee they'll be able to find a good job even when they do graduate.

The "depression" and "pressure" from which Zhang says graduates suffer probably says as much about the dark undercurrent of his "dream" as it does about the overstretching to which Chinese students are widely supposed to be subjected. Zhang's pride in making his own path in life stands in tension with the gnawing certainty that having chosen to drop out of high school all he can do now is graft it out as a laborer and cultivate the hope of one day starting a business. In just this way, all these men except Xue, the youngest, articulated entrepreneurship as the paradigm of success. Lin Chuan aims to be able to arrive at work on a motorbike. He must "rely on himself [and] hard work" to get there. He aims "to have the things that other people have" and is "developing towards this target now". He will soon leave his job and help his sister sell fruit in the city markets, a move that many farmers and migrants see as a step-up possibly within their reach. In the future, he will "do a little business, exercise the brain, and buy a car".

Self-made makers

This entrepreneurial streak and all-round excellent grasp of the internal dynamics of self-cultivation (see Chapter 7 on Personality) makes these young migrants quite distinct from the older migrants in the kitchen who grew up in the centrally planned economy. Whereas the younger migrants are "incessantly striving to develop" (*buduande zhengqu*), and "learning from going to many different places" (*zounan chuangbei*) to work and so on, the older migrants at the restaurant see themselves as resigned to work hard in the city, but remain still essentially rural first and foremost. The younger migrants are highly competitive, in a sense a force to be reckoned with in the city, drawing strength from their youth, their mobility, and the strategic community of other migrants: factors which equally distinguish them from Anshan's many laid-off urban workers who scarcely evince positives of the self-cultivation imperative, and who offer instead a discourse characterized by, among other things, a distinct malaise (see Chapter 9).

The older migrants in the kitchen, mostly women a full generation older than the young men analyzed here, encourage the younger migrants to learn some English from me, and emphasize the value of having a character that will "push on and up" (*shangjinxin*) and never be satisfied; but these women nevertheless all say that they themselves are generally "satisfied" (*manyi*) with the way things are now, and are glad that things are no longer like the past, a vague gloss that masks the acceptance that they will never now transcend their lower working-class status, the promise of enterprising projects of individuality applying only to bright, young, productive migrants (Jacka 2006). Indeed, insofar as these younger migrants' narratives are characterized by this very strong dual emphasis on gathering experiential knowledge and on the importance of incessant striving as the means to success, these men trace a trajectory through the "discourse of distinction" (Hanser 2008) remarkably similar to many of Anshan's private entrepreneurs, who likewise defined themselves against people with formal, cultural knowledge, and tended to emphasize the value of their own enterprising initiatives vis-à-vis this perceived deficit (see Chapter 3, p.52; see Chapter 7 on Personality).

There are further similarities, too, between the younger migrants' discourse and that of Anshan's entrepreneurs. In much the same way as his own boss, Lin Wei, likes to tell the story of how he made his fortune "from nothing" on account of his own effort (see Chapter 7, p.120), Zhang Jiali defines himself against the "laziness" of those born to and spoiled by privileged parents:

> In fact, the opportunities a person has are not fixed from birth. I can strive for my opportunities. If I'd been born into a family with lots of property, I reckon I'd be really spoilt by their indulgences; little by little I'd become lazy, because I could rely on my family, because they had a lot of money. But we have to rely on our own strivings. We strive for ourselves. And through this unceasing striving we can gain more experiences for ourselves, gain more strength, and understand another aspect of this society. But they do not understand this aspect; they are unable to go and compete: they only know that when their food is ready, they can come and eat, that they can just buy clothes whenever they like. They haven't a lot of social experience.

In this way, these migrants are considerably more independent than the pampered offspring of the new urban elites, who tend to be heavily reliant on their parents, and are often comparatively lacking in competitive edge: these migrants' lives may be bitter, but their narratives are their own. Zhang Jiali sets this independent trajectory strongly against those who exercise power through personal political connections, believing that if he relies on his own efforts he'll "always be stronger than those who rely on dodgy networks". Lin Chuan likewise connects a strong narrative about social inequality with scorn for corrupt officials; he more generally links "laziness" and "avarice" with a lack of success, dislikes those who "loaf about", and believes people should always "strive onwards and upwards". Notably, wealth and luxury consumption are entirely validated for these young migrants if the wealth has been earned through individual skill as opposed to corrupt means: "If someone has earned their wealth", Zhang explains, "I will emulate his successes and aim to over-take him" (see Chapter 2).

Emulation, indeed, probably explains much of the similarity these migrants share with entrepreneur discourse: they know that this is the right tune to be singing in the contemporary era. More than that, though, these migrants cast themselves as actually extracting from their urbanite entrepreneur employers the means to become successful and to supersede them one day (cf. Hsu 2005). Even as they give themselves over to the extraction of surplus value, which is alone what legitimates them in the eyes of those who "see like a State" (Scott 1999), these migrants aim to usurp the alliance of State and capital interests that presently exploits them, but from the inside, a stealth tactic of "poaching" (de Certeau 1984) upon this discourse without being seen. Lin Chuan, for example, talks of "borrowing strength" (*jieli*) from people he most admires, "people with knowledge", but nevertheless concedes that he only rarely actually meets anyone like this.

The play of difference

Accordingly, the essentially improvisational nature of how these migrants insinuate themselves into the constraints of apparatus defined for them largely by others is also reflected in the balancing of this strong and rather serious emphasis on self-cultivation with an equally strong playful and leisurely dimension; and this in a way that seems quite genuine – that is, not as a ploy to mask the reality of their exploitation, but a highly self-realizing and self-actualizing inflection of discourse quite unusual in China, and not at all dissimilar to the way in which students in Europe "go travelling". The term that Zhang Jiali and Lin Chuan most use to refer to their incursion into the urban sphere is *chuangdang*, meaning "to charge about and loaf around", a word which casts the experience as at once imminently purposeful but also as random, carefree and fun. Zhang explicitly talks about coming out to work as "play", making the point in his explanation that "We come from afar, walk around, go everywhere and turn around". Though he must work hard for the privilege of this frivolousness, Zhang delights in his project of individuality-making, evidently believing that a unique value accrues in the process – a value quite distinct from the capital he generates for his boss.

Xue Liang, the youngest and a newcomer to the city, explicitly does not share this latter inflection: though he responds to my asking if he likes his job by saying he is "incessantly improving [his] abilities" every month, he also stresses that the experience of coming to the city is not about enjoying charging around and loafing about like it is for the others. Rather, this is a harsh exile he has imposed upon himself to contribute to supporting his family, an expressed function of his strong filial piety (see Chapter 6). It might be reasonably surmised from the fact that the other migrants also demonstrate a strong link back to the family (but to a much lesser extent than Xue) that Xue will become adjusted to enjoying charging around and loafing about with his colleagues, and become more independent from his family as his labor forces him to find his freedom within it. A young lad new to the kitchen from Shaanxi Province tells me how he ran away from home to come to Anshan against his parents' wishes, quite contrary to the filial demands by which all "good" Chinese are supposed to abide: his coming out from the countryside was entirely to play. Thus, although these young migrants know the rules for proper practice, they aspire to redefine these as they take control of their lives, changing established orders as expressions of their individuality.

Once again, the individual most different in all of these respects is Wang Cuihua, the eldest of the "young" migrants and the longest out of the city. Wang is not only sad that he dropped out of school, but angry: "If I was a university graduate, maybe with a masters or PhD, I wouldn't be in this kitchen today; I'd be working for a firm, in management." Wang's narratives, indeed, are characterized by an overwhelmingly fierce sense of self-cultivation to which all his other constructions are subordinated, and this in much the same intensely vital way as was the case with some of Anshan's entrepreneurs interviewed (see Chapter 7). Had the gods rolled the dice differently for Wang, he no doubt would be in a very competitive position; and indeed the Gods yet might, for Wang seems to recognize that his fate is not written in stone. Wang will fight to get back into contention, and no amount of loafing about with his colleagues is going to get in the way.

In this respect Wang is sharply distinguished from Zhang Jiali and Lin Chuan, both of whom make very strong narratives of self-cultivation too, but both of whom allow this to be subordinated to competing socially by having good social rapport with people of a similar social position (see Chapter 5). Zhang, for example, reads a bit to "improve himself", but nowhere near so much as he invests in loafing about with his colleagues after work. Lin, too, seems to talk more about self-cultivation than he actually acts to cultivate himself, and what positive narratives of self-cultivation he does make, though strong in themselves, are matched by an equally powerful sense of being resigned to a life of being poor and underprivileged expressed in narratives of inequality of resources and opportunities. It is as if Zhang and Lin are just showing that they know what is required for them to succeed (indeed, one wonders if they have Wang in mind as a role model for their ideas), but do not or cannot practice what they preach: "It's not yet the time", said Zhang about wanting to "use his mind" (above). Thus, the aims and dreams of starting a business and taking narrative control over their lives that these young migrants share remain in most cases somewhat ethereal. This may, of course, also be what binds them so closely together (Pun 2003: 486).

In it together, for themselves

As well as individual striving, these migrants also consciously lever the feeling of good social rapport and community shared between them as strategic asset (see Chapter 5). No doubt this is brought on by necessity and consciousness of the lack of being able to succeed independently. Zhang Jiali's investment in this form of competition is huge, his exuberance of character somewhat accounting for the strength of his instantiations of other discourses. His discourse is littered with inclusive gestures and exclamations that "we" (i.e. me, him and our other colleagues) are "brothers", a "team", and a "family"; and terms such as "harmony", "peace" and "happiness" proliferate in his repertoire:

> We're all working together. After work we play games, you know, computer games. We formed a team (*tuandui*), and this team is just like a big family. We're like brothers. We're all together; in fact you could say that he is me, and I am him. We are all like this, so we all wear the same clothes. When we go out we're all the same. We set up this team (*zujian zhege duiwu*) and we all really like it. We've all come together from every place to Lamb Buddha. Now, after we've got along with each other for a while, we really understand each other. And after we understood one another, we set up a team, and became brothers; really good brothers, just as if we were family. We, this band of buddies (*gemenr*), so-called 'brothers' (*xiongdi*), we're all single children, and we've all left home, you know? China has a saying: "Having one more friend is to have one more road" (*duo yige pengyou, duo yitiao lu*). So we like to make good friends. We go out and drink together; we're happy and open-hearted (*kaixin*). Then we go singing, or playing. We also chat, and when we're together it's "freedom of speech" (*yanlun ziyou*): whatever you want to say, you can just say it; if you don't want to talk about a particular problem, and I ask you, there's no need to answer it. Everyone's really happy together; it's really good. If today we want to drink some wine, we'll go out drinking together, and everyone will play until late at night: drinking, happy, and free of constraint. These waitresses, we've got pretty good relations. For example, if we want to drink today, we'll go out and drink, and they'll come with us. But they only drink a little bit – we men drink loads – after all drinking's not too good for the body. As long as everyone's really happy together at that time, that's fine.

Note how Zhang's enthusiasm makes his talk of "work" immediately turn into talk of the "game" and the "team", spilling on from there into talk about the other kinds of "play" in which he and his band of brothers indulge: work and play, fiction and reality, are all blurred by the metaphoric of sociability based on supposedly innately exuberant character (see Chapter 5). Note, too, that drinking is a huge part of Zhang's construction of good social rapport: he mentions alcohol 25 times during a two-hour interview and nearly always in the context of friendship and belonging. Note also that the importance of social rapport is not just about being friendly or liked: there is a highly strategic nature to Zhang's competition that he does not attempt to disguise. The *duiwu* he uses for "team" can also mean "rank and file" as opposed to leaders (again reflecting his self-identification with the lower strata of the military).

As with the conflation of experiential accumulation and incessant self-cultivation discussed above, Zhang sees it as necessary for him to compete through social rapport: this is the only way he can avoid being "bullied" (*qifu*) by those more powerful than him, he says, and if he has more friends he'll be happier and won't be eliminated by the competition:

> Although I have no money, I've got lots of friends, and they are true friends. If I'm in real trouble, they'll help me out, but he [the hypothetical privileged urbanite against whom he is defining himself] won't. And when the day comes when he's got no money, all his friends will leave him.

Xue Liang, the youngest, shares with Zhang the view that his colleagues are "like a family, brothers and sisters", who protect him from being bullied and help him get over his intense homesickness. Lin Chuan, too, frequently uses "we" as if speaking for a community of migrant workers, and likewise complains of urbanite bullying. Quite distinct from middle-class students in a university dormitory, who form hierarchies almost immediately based on all manner of variables and dimensions (class background, social popularity, fashionability, etc.), these migrants would not allow hierarchy to form between them (see Chapter 7, section on Status), but the sense of belonging they articulate is not at all altruistic (Halskov-Hansen and Pang 2008); there is little thought for the self-sacrifice and the "good of the people" common to the older, pre-reform morality (see Chapter 6). Though the "collectivity" (Pun 2003: 486) remains the source of moral integrity, the belonging asserted is a proximity bond defined against the urban sphere that surrounds them and ultimately a means of self-promotion. This is how solidarity is formed, and individuality is articulated as the free choice to identify with similar others.

Consuming themselves

Material consumption plays an important role in binding these migrants together (see Chapter 7, section on Materialism). In the large excerpt above, Zhang Jiali makes reference to the fact that all the young migrants from Lamb Buddha have bought the same T-shirt, a printed design from a store that trades without shame on the name of the successful Hollywood movie *Pirates of the Caribbean* (see Chapter 2). Every month, on the evening of the day they get paid, the kitchen and waiting staff go out eating and drinking together wearing these T-shirts. Some blow their entire salary in a single night. Some, Zhang says, borrow and blow so much that they have to hand over their wages to their creditor the day they get them. Lin Chuan, whose sociable rapport construction is strong, but not as strong as Zhang Jiali's, doesn't always want to go: he would like to save some money, but fears that if he doesn't go all the others will think him "stingy and ungenerous" (*linse*) (see Chapter 5). When these migrants consume together they share the costs precisely between them, a practice they call "AA zhi" (see Chapter 5, p.91);

there is no concern to outdo each other in generosity because of face issues. The exception, for Lin Chuan, is when he consumes with his girlfriend, in which case it is expected that he will pay for everything, an expectation thrust upon him by the demands of "responsibility" (*zeren*) (see Chapter 6). As with all these four migrants, finding a girlfriend and his poor home condition are expressed as the two imperatives that drew Lin Chuan into the city to work in the first place. These two themes are importantly linked: Lin couldn't find a girlfriend in the countryside because he "hadn't developed", had "no future" and "no money" – "marriage and all that requires money". Yet the reason he can't save much money is because he has recently found a girlfriend and must spend so much of his income to impress and woo her.

It is significant that these young men have consumer behavior concomitant with their symbolic boundary management. Zhang Jiali, single, describes his consumer behavior as "carefree" and "easy-going"; "I'm not like those who calculate what to do with their salary every month, whether to save or spend." Then, as if Zhang is aware of how these statements elevate his primary competitive element, sociable character, over his also strongly espoused self-cultivation, he adds that although he can be impulsive, he will save for things he really likes. He may have Wang Cuihua in mind as a comparator here again, who earns more and saves more (see below). This is also where Zhang and Lin most differ from the majority of the entrepreneurs analyzed elsewhere in my research (see Chapter 7): Wang Cuihua has a sense of control and cultivation to his consumer behavior that, without exception, my businessperson informants all say they had in their youth. Wang will only keep a little money in his pocket, but plan to buy larger purchases. From Zhang's strong sociable rapport perspective this is considered "tight" (*kou*). Zhang concedes that age may be a factor, now referring to Wang Cuihua explicitly, who at 24 must "find a girl and buy a house". Indeed, whereas Lin Chuan is motivated to earn and spend primarily because of his girlfriend (see above), Wang is single, more focused on developing himself and realizing long-term gratification, on the lookout for a girl with whom he can grow (see also below).

Almost needless to say, however, alongside the excesses of affable comradeship and "playful" self-actualization that bind these migrants closely together, another major part of how these persons strategically compete is a firmly frugal inflection of discourse (see Chapter 7, section on Materialism). Though an excess of exuberant consumption between friends is important to Zhang, he also thinks that designer brands and luxury consumption are wasteful. I am to understand a reference to Zhang's boss, here, who is known to have spent several thousand Chinese yuan renminbi (CNY), "even as much as 10,000", on T-shirts (about ten times as much as Zhang earns per month). Zhang professes to prefer substance to form: "In fact, I may have a shirt just the same, but with a brand that is not inferior, and mine will be longer lasting, more durable." Defining himself against the excesses of the rich he asserts:

They haven't learned how to manage the money, but we've learned how to fully bring the money into play, so that it's not dead but alive, and will become a lot from a little, and enable me to live on – only then can I say I have the ability to create my own road. If you give them 100 yuan and give me 100 yuan, I may be able to live for a month on this 100 yuan, but they can only live for a day.

However, Zhang will not be pitied by any narrative of inequality, contending that his own competitive configuration levels the playing field. Indeed, it is not merely the value of economy that Zhang is keen to impress, but the moral purity and fiber that attends a frugal life, defined against the superficial emptiness of wealth:

There are some people with money who will despise (*qishi*) you for not having money. He thinks he can use his money to make you do anything. But he doesn't know that money can't do everything. There are some things that money can't buy. He doesn't understand these things. He's always thinking: this money of mine can do anything; I can buy anything; I can have a woman, a car, a house; and everyone is embracing me.

Both Zhang and Lin seem to settle for a life of second best in material terms, and find a kind of nobility in that: "If everyone else had a house worth several million yuan I'd be satisfied with a house worth several hundred thousand, and I wouldn't draw invidious comparisons with them." They draw comparisons, too, against another new kitchen-hand from Jiangsu province whose parents supplement his income, allowing him to spend "every fen" he earns on fancy haircuts, clothes and arcade games. Zhang says the new arrival's parents are also poor, ordinary workers, but don't discipline their son like his own parents do.

Predictably, the most frugal of the group, Xue Liang, is also the one who invests most in the competing through constructions of "good moral character" (see Chapter 6). This theme is not especially strong in any of the other young migrant workers, except where it is employed to derogate the city at the expense of the countryside (as above), or to document filial piety by dutifully remitting part of their income to their families. However, moral character does not form a major organizing principle in the narratives of any of these migrants except Xue. Xue's mother is old; he cannot allow her to go out earning all the time (*lao zhengqian*), so he has left the familial countryside home to work for her. As soon as Xue saw the "bitter work" (*xinku*) his family were putting in to help him through school, he dropped out and worked the land with them for a year before coming to the city. Of the 850 CNY Xue earns per month, he lives on 150 CNY and saves the rest for his parents. Xue says his parents save all their money for his future anyway, so he gives everything he can to them now. Thus, "moral" sacrifice repays "moral" sacrifice. Xue misses them terribly and is only very rarely in contact with them because they're always at work in a factory "where there are no phones". Like Zhang and Lin, Xue says he's not bothered by inequalities of wealth so long as he is cheerful, and so long as his parents have money to spend and are not worried about food and clothes.

Making it: distinction within the group

As maintained, the fourth migrant, Wang Cuihua, is different on nearly every account from his colleagues. A closer examination of his trajectory through discourse sheds further light on those from whom he is so different. Having ardently worked his way up, acquiring new skills at restaurants around the city since first arriving from the countryside seven years ago, Wang is now the kitchen staff supervisor. At nearly 2,000 CNY per month, he earns more than twice what Zhang, Lin and Xue do, enough to launch him, as a single man, into more "middle-class" levels of discretionary expenditure. Wang articulates his difference from the other migrants very keenly, drawing upon his relations with his colleagues only in order to distance himself from them:

> I have no way to talk with the others about the things I think about; they are mindless, playing and gaming. I am thinking about work, and moral things: how to be a person (*zenme zuoren*); how to earn people's respect; how to improve my quality of life; how to give more significance to my life; and how to bring my own ideals closer and closer every day. They only think about playing, eating and drinking.

The main difference between him and the others, Wang says, is that whereas they waste time and talk about useless things, play on the internet, play cards and go drinking in their spare time, he cultivates himself. When he was younger, Wang used his spare time to research things online that would improve his abilities, "never telling others about it", strategically avoiding competitors who would trip him up (see Chapter 3 and Chapter 7). "I read and apply what I learn to my life", he explains. His favorite book is the biography of Li Jiacheng, Asia's richest man, whom he admires for his self-cultivation and control. Concomitantly with this emphasis, and quite the contrast of Zhang Jiali, Wang drinks when he goes out but only one or two bottles: it's "sickening" to drink lots, and "bad for health". Of course, this saves him money too. Though Wang lives in the same dim dormitory as the others, this is by no means a necessity for him, but a choice. Besides, Wang has been in the dormitory long enough to commandeer the best space, a room that he shares with his junior "apprentice" (*tudi*), a recent migrant. The other migrants have to share at least four to a room. Wang "keeps" (*yang*) a fish and a plant in his room. He likes to come from work and see the results of his cultivation swimming to and fro, and the plant sprouting leaves (see Chapter 7).

Wang says that doing this greatly improves his environment and shapes his character and taste (*taoye*), instilling in him a great sense of achievement. He is the only one of these migrants who uses any such lifestyle concept; in the others' narratives, constructions of self-cultivation are limited to hard work, perseverance, and vague economic ambition. Wang also tries to improve his "personal quality" (*suzhi*), a term that the others don't use at all.

> I don't want to be mediocre; I don't want an ordinary life. If this year I don't have enough money to realize my dreams I'll just keep working on for another half year, a full year.

Wang's future is just to "work, marry, and save money for this", but spending money is also an important part of this, because Wang must find a girlfriend. Clothes are the only thing on which he spends. Despite his earnest self-cultivation, he buys "leisurely" clothes, "like the Kappa brand", as if to make it appear that social distinction comes easily to him. However, particular brands are not so important as a "novel and original style" and whether or not the product suits his "outfit". Again, this form of consideration is entirely absent from the other migrants; Lin Chuan may be proud of getting his knock-off Nikes for 45 CNY, but this is only about the logo itself rather than any sense of expressing his own style.

Wang admits that the sense of expressing his individuality through clothing has been an acquired taste:

> My thinking has changed since I came out of the Shandong countryside. I used to only require that clothing was warm in the cold, but now I also want it to look good. Perhaps in another few years my requirements will change again, so that not only is it good-looking but that I also pursue the latest trends. That'd be even better.

When Wang goes to discos, he goes with other people, not his colleagues from Lamb Buddha. Wang has had these other friends for years, he says, before eventually admitting that they are migrant workers in other restaurants also. He didn't want to make this explicit at first; he wanted me to think he was entirely integrated into the urban sphere. Realizing I was aware of this, Wang added that he has urban mates from Anshan also: apparently, he goes to the nightclubs because these friends invite him there. Wang also gives the impression that these friends are older than him, and that he can learn from them. However, the consumption (*xiaofei*) level is too high for Wang in the clubs, he says. I ask him if he goes to the clubs to find a girlfriend. He says "no" in a way that suggests that the girls there wouldn't be interested in him because of his rural migrant status (see Chapter 7, section on Status). He describes this situation as "chaotic" (*luan*), possibly to disguise this implicit admission. Somewhat contradicting himself, he then says that he doesn't often go to the clubs anyway, as if he has just been telling me he goes there only because doing so would cast him as of a higher status. He then betrays himself further, trying to "save face" as he ducks away from the charge I have drawn: the high level of consumption in the club has nothing to do with his not looking for a girlfriend there; it's just that he prefers to save his wages. None of the female waiting staff at Lamb Buddha have taken Wang's fancy; he has higher aspirations. He eventually volunteers that wealth and status are directly related to your chances of finding a girlfriend in China (see Chapter 7, sections on Materialism and Status): "Players look for someone at approximately the same level; only the very rich can afford to take someone without thinking about whether they have money or not."

However, Wang is confident about his chances of finding a bride to match his self-perception; he has proved to himself that he can hit self-imposed targets. He once promised himself he would buy himself a chunky gold necklace when he first earned 2,000 CNY a month (see Chapter 7, section on Materialism). He saw others wearing them and envied them. At that time he only earned 600 to 700 CNY per month, so he saved. In fact, he had enough money saved years ago to buy one, he says, but he had set himself this target and wouldn't buy it until he earned 2,000 CNY per month. In this way, Wang describes how he climbed steadily up the ladder, target by target, constantly applying himself to learn new skills. "What exactly is it that you have and the others don't?" I ask him directly. "They lack a heart for striving on and up", he answers. Wang must "lead them by example", "by not eating and smoking on duty", he says, thus documenting the awareness that personal development comes with social responsibilities. Thus, in Wang alone among these migrants are constructions of self-cultivation narrated retrospectively; the others, Zhang Jiali and Lin Chuan, still speak as if they have yet to achieve (see Chapter 7).

Wang's emphasis on the importance of civil behavior also sets him apart from his colleagues. Civility is not high among most of these men; Zhang Jiali always has filthy hands and fingernails, for example. However, all these young migrants are much more cognizant of civility than many of the older migrants and indeed many urbanites. Working in an industrial kitchen that must be meticulously cleaned once a week for inspection no doubt raises civil consciousness; and Zhang, after all, works on the door. The fear of urban customers who will complain if anything is found dirty is also no doubt a factor here. Wang is the only one who draws on civility as a major competitive discourse. Again he confesses:

> I'm not scared of you laughing. When I first came out from the countryside I didn't even know that I should wash my feet before I slept; I only washed them once a week. Later, slowly, after a year, I realized that other people washed them every day, and so I tried it a couple of times. Ah! My feet felt so comfortable! After this I slowly began to change in other ways too.

Wang, apparently, also only infrequently washed his clothes before, and his skin would itch because they were dirty; later he began to change them every day or so. He also began to wash his socks and change his underwear every day. At this point, it seemed like Wang was going through a mental list of all the hygienic things he does, unprompted by me, as if these behaviors were perhaps not quite as second-nature to him as he intended to make out. Feeling the need to justify himself in this way had no doubt come from the exposure to his urbanite friends. Sure enough, in due course Wang began to moan about people throwing things out the windows without caring whether other people were below or not, a typical urbanite civil grievance in Anshan. Of further relevance here, however, was that Wang was the only one of these four migrants who evinced awareness of the difference between the spatial sense of civility and the more aesthetic aspects of this discourse (see Chapter 4 on Civility, p.72), testifying to the extent of his appreciation of and allegiance with the gloss of urbanization:

> Not only is this a kind of respect to other people, but also a kind of respect to yourself. If you go out with your friends when you're dirty, and see a friend, and your body is dirty, and your clothes are worn out and shabby, this is disrespectful to others.

While Zhang Jiali, by contrast, expressed a concern to keep the restaurant peaceful, this was more about his duty, and ultimately masculinity, than it was about civility. Though Zhang was quite considerate in civil terms, and polite, he made no judgments of this civil form in his boundary management. Xue Liang mentioned in passing that he washes feet and body before sleeping, but otherwise, like Zhang and Lin Chuan, mentioned civility hardly at all.

Diachronic discussion

Looking at the patterns of discourse and behavior revealed across and between these young migrants, it might be supposed that there is a certain typical trajectory that migrants take through discourse over time. Those very young, naïve, and still strongly attached to the countryside home, like Xue Liang, in whom the familial inflection of discourses of good moral character was by far the most dominant, may likely become more like Zhang Jiali and Lin Chuan as their distance grows from their families in spatial, temporal, and discursive terms and they enter their early twenties. For those of Zhang and Lin's age, for whom such constructions were notably less significant, however, girlfriends evidently become a demanding reality, and the pressure of having to compete socially means that earnest application (see Chapter 7) and experience accumulation (see Chapter 3), and the conflation of these asserted vis-à-vis urbanite persons with a formal education, emerge to take a significant place in these migrants' narratives. Even so, insecurity and youth-fulness mean that this conflation is subordinated to the importance of achieving good social rapport between colleagues and the other similar persons with whom they have been thrust together through the experience of migration, who effectively become the surrogate family. At this stage, material resources still prevent these migrants from breaking into competition in the urban sphere, though they do mix with lower-ranking urbanites and similarly youthful urbanites, blurring boundaries.

Wang Cuihua may be exemplary of a further stage of evolution where, several years on, and with several more years of maturity under the belt, the tension between the imperative to cultivate and maintain inter-collegial social rapport (see Chapter 5), on the one hand, and personal achievement (see Chapter 7), on the other, has been resolved to the benefit of the latter, and these young migrant workers become single-mindedly focused on their futures. Those who are unable to make this transition are faced with return to the countryside or perpetuity in the kitchens, often alongside eventual sons and daughters as was often the case at Lamb Buddha. Many, if not most, migrants, eventually return to the countryside. For those who sense the promise of avoiding this fate, the preference for the countryside as the locus of morality, authenticity, and hope for the future evidently shifts towards the city too, as discourse and reality inform one another.

At this stage, finding a mate, securing a higher income, saving money, thinking about owning your own house, caring for your material presentation, image and style, and so on, all become much more important in inverse proportion to the fading importance placed on collegial and even family relationships, though this latter inflection cannot be openly professed in the China context for fear of the charge of "selfishness" (see Chapter 6): Wang Cuihua says he will help his family if they need him, but strongly emphasizes that he must achieve his own success first before he can really be in a position to help others, a distinctly modern discourse (Beck 1992; Beck *et al.* 1994) that only other competitive, middle-class, urban Chinese seem to share (see Chapter 10). By now, cultural codes of civility are highly invested in as a marker of increasing urban belonging, acquired perhaps through alternative, inspirational, and openly strategic friendships sought with possibly older, wealthier and more powerful persons from whom these migrants can learn and with whom they can grow (Bourdieu 1984). While leaps and bounds on the social ladder remain prevented by social stigma and familial pressure to marry at approximately the same "level", it is not entirely inconceivable to see that at this stage the fate of rural migrants may blend with those urban families heavily affected by lay-offs from State-owned enterprises, through intermarriage and so on, as was the emerging case with Lin Chuan and his girlfriend, incidentally.

In every case, these migrants will have undertaken an epic journey rich with raw material to consume as projects of individuality. As rural migrant-turned-entrepreneur Zhang Xiuzhen put it in Chapter 7, "By moving you can live" (*rennuo nenghuo*). This may likely be the way of things to come in an "individualizing" China, for it is highly significant that for all the intensity of feeling and belonging shared by the young migrants, this was all to change almost overnight as they found their individual destinies. Within just a few months of the data for this analysis being collected, Wang Cuihua never returned from what was supposed to be a brief trip home to see his family in Shandong: he found his girl and stayed to get married. No-one in Anshan knows what he is doing now. Zhang Jiali moved on from Lamb Buddha even before I did: when the young urbanite man who had previously held his job on the door returned and took over again, it was understood that stepping down was the proper thing for Zhang to do. In time, Xue Liang and Lin Chuan had moved to different restaurants, too, cashing in on their mobility and networking skills for a tiny raise in pay at jobs scouted for them by other migrants. Almost all of the older migrant kitchen staff, on the other hand, remains at Lamb Buddha to this very day, washing up dishes and peeling vegetables, with little hope of moving anywhere. Individuality, after all, requires that you differentiate yourself in relation to your environment, and it is so much easier to differentiate yourself against your own future than your own past.

9 Workers

This chapter analyzes a range of men and women who were once "workers" at Angang Steel or one of Anshan's other, affiliated, State-owned enterprises. "Worker" (*gongren*), the State-ascribed category of the Maoist era into which all the informants examined in this chapter were born, was a privilege very much reserved for the class supposedly "leading" in Socialism, the "masters of the house" (*dangjia zuozhu*) epitomized in the State-owned enterprises and federation of trade unions. In the wake of State-owned enterprise restructuring and the rise of the private sector in reform-era China, however, "worker" status has become somewhat the mark of a curse (Solinger 2002). Official references to "worker" (*gongren*) have accordingly been replaced with less politicized forms (such as *laodongzhe*, etc.), but many working people still identify with the category for its association with a particular set of moral qualities – very similar to the authenticity alluded to in propaganda posters of the Daqing oil field – and for the urban household registration that comes with the territory. My use of the term "worker" in this analysis therefore reflects these informants' use of the term in self-reference.

Nearly all the informants analyzed here know each other. All the men are skilled manual workers at a steel machine-roller repair factory owned by a Mr Zhao. All the women, bar one, are either cooking staff at this factory or otherwise wives of these steel workers. Many of the men were in fact Mr Zhao's workmates at Angang until he "took the plunge" (*xiahai*) into private enterprise just a few years before the first wave of mass industrial lay-offs (*xiagang*) swept through Anshan in the late 1990s (Giles *et al.* 2006; Hung and Chiu 2003; Won 2005). Those of Zhao's workmates too old to compete in the ensuing scramble for jobs sent their sons to him while they eked it out on meager compensation until they could claim their pensions. Some of Zhao's workers still receive various State subsidies themselves; indeed, some still have full-time jobs in the State sector and work with Zhao in the evenings and at weekends. Since Angang is by far Zhao's biggest client, moreover, his entire business is still highly dependent on the State. These workers are therefore State-market (in)transients, who still have one foot stuck in the planned economy, yet work out the micro-political ramifications of Anshan's reforming "rust-belt" infrastructure in the private sector.

Limbo

In important respects, many of these workers trace a similar trajectory through discourse as deployed by the migrants examined in the previous chapter. None are particularly secure in their place in the urban economy, and none, they themselves tell me, are any more than a generation or two away from life in the fields themselves. Nearly all spin narratives characterized by a profound sense of social inferiority, a complex matched only by strong differentiations from the countryside which they construct as inferior in ways that reflect their insecurity. It is as if these workers are caught between town and country on a journey of "migration" that has begun, been interrupted, reversed and started all over again over a period of several decades thanks to State projects of social engineering. In particular, the formational experiences of being "sent down" (*xiaxiang*) to work in the fields as youths during the Cultural Revolution that nearly all these workers share means that even those with no immediate familial links to the countryside exist in limbo between there and the city. This period is spoken of as if hanging like a millstone around these workers' necks, occupying a large place in their discursive apparatus, loading them with a particularly acute consciousness of being unable to compete in terms of knowledgeability (see Chapter 3). None of these workers read much; some have difficulty writing. Those who have only mandatory education work side by side with those with some tertiary education, a situation very distinct from current high-school leavers, who are virtually guaranteed better possibilities for employment if only their families can afford the privilege.

By way of introducing some characters, consider Fan, for example, a welder of 52 years of age who was laid-off from Angang very early on, and has worked at Mr Zhao's factory for the last decade. Fan and his wife bring in a total of 7,000 CNY per month, which is quite good in Anshan, but Fan must work six days and complete six shifts of sleep-in night duty before he can return to his wife. Unlike those still working in State-sector jobs, who receive substantial subsidies on housing, medicine, and children's schooling, this income has to cover everything. Fan is in fact a distant relative of Mr Zhao's, but remains acutely aware of the distance between them:

> Zhao is a boss; I'm just a worker. Our status is different; I'm just a pauper, a wretch. The contrast between us is too big. We have different positions; it's unequal. The difference is massive. Everyone has different positions.

Born in the countryside himself, Fan doesn't feel the need to condescend to the countryside. When he happens to mention thieves coming around the factory from rural climes he calls them "outsiders" in a manner that simply indicates that they are not from around here. Fan's wife, however, a recently retired high school-educated English teacher of urban origin, refers to these same people as "farmers", sneering visibly (see Chapter 7, section on Status). Fan only had primary schooling, and despite her profession, his wife can only say a few words of English with me. Her reading is limited to fashion magazines and she watches television a lot.

Fan's colleague, Xu Dongbin, a welder of approximately the same age, professes "emotions" towards the countryside: his father "came out" of the countryside in the 1950s. Xu feels that "farmers are more honest than urban people" and that "city life is too quick". "The countryside follows the Confucian ethical code", Xu explains, "It's plain and boring". Indeed, this is what Xu is like too (see Chapter 5 on Sociability). However, Xu wouldn't like to go and live in the country: "Some conditions are not so good; the city environment is better; information and shopping are more convenient." Xu took high school but says he's "got no culture"; his knowledge has "only reached a certain level". He's "very ordinary", he says. Xu reads newspapers and magazines, but no other literature.

Chen Qian, one of two female cooks at Mr Zhao's factory, was born "in the suburbs". "Yes, near the countryside", she reluctantly admits. Chen came to the city to marry an urban worker who worked with her father at the age of 23. She is concerned to come across as urban, but betrays her roots by coming down on the "wrong" side of a discussion about coarse grain cereals:

> When we were young we all ate coarse grain. We only ate fine grains when guests came. When we got ill we could have better food. But I really liked coarse grains. Occasionally I still eat them now. But back then it was tough, I had no choice, whereas now it's because I like it, just occasionally. Most of the time I eat fine grains now, but I also mix them together. Now that people have a better standard of life they can eat whatever they like. In any case, coarse grains are no cheaper than fine grains these days.

Despite an adult life in the city, Chen still thinks in "coarse grain" ways: she still eats mostly "fine" grains and believes she should align herself symbolically with the latter. Therefore, although some of these workers lever their urban status as a social advantage over their countryside cousins, none have the sufficient mastery of the discourse that would allow them to consume as if "disowning" their urban status in favor of "rediscovering" the virtues of the countryside, as some more "middle-class" people have recently begun to do (see Chapter 2 on Authenticity, p.41).

Xu Xiaoyan is the other cook at the factory (no relative of Xu Dongbin). She was born in Anshan in 1959. Her husband is a middle-level worker in the security department at Angang. Their total family income is approximately 6,000 CNY, but her husband is entitled to benefits that many of these workers forfeited when they took up jobs in the private sector. Xu says that her middle school attendance during the Cultural Revolution "wasn't real education". Like many of these workers, she put all her energies into being a Red Guard.

Knowledge was not respected then. The best thing was to take part in social movements. So many were sent down; their culture is lacking and they went through great hardship. I finished middle school but didn't learn much.

Xu feels the crucial factor in her fate is her age:

China's national leaders are either all older than me, or younger, and graduated from university with new skills. People of my generation are stuck between elderly parents in their seventies with pensions but without a lot of money, and children who must study very hard; we can't find jobs or earn much money because we've no education. Many of us are unemployed and without skills. Only a few can use their skills to fix cars or do electrical jobs for others; most have become housemaids, cleaners, cooks or babysitters. We can't get pensions from the State-owned enterprises. People born between 1955 to approximately 1979 were all born quite poor. So many people suddenly came back from the country in 1976. The oldest ones went to jobs in State-owned enterprises, but the younger ones were assigned to whichever work unit their parents were working at, but without any rights, pensions, sick pay, or minimum wage. Many 1980s children, by contrast, have gone to university, and have lots of money.

Xu creates a narrative highly apologetic and confessional in form, as if wanting to show that she is aware that acknowledging her "ignorance" is a first step towards distinction. Though she has no "high academic record", and "no career", she most admires people with "cultivation" and "culture", but it is very important to Xu that this academic record isn't shown off in front of others. Xu doesn't like to have her ignorance pointed out: she likes people with "very civilized manners, who are very modest, easy to get along with, polite to younger people and people of lower classes, and treat everyone the same". Apparently Xu finds these values in me:

When these people talk with younger people no matter if they are an MA or a PhD, they won't make others feel uncomfortable, it's the same as meeting normal people. But after a while when they get on with each other, they'll show many unusual and surprising things about themselves that others can learn from. These people have ability.

The ability Xu applauds here is not only that of "cultural capital", but of demonstrating knowledge in a manner compatible with creating social rapport, of generating a particular kind of "social capital" (Bourdieu 1984), or of knowing how to appear knowledgeable whilst saving others "face" (see Chapter 5).

A similar positioning is drawn by Zhang Jie, the only person in this group not connected to Zhao's factory, but whose retired father was a "worker" at an Anshan State-owned electricity company and whose husband remains a worker at Angang today. Zhang "likes people of culture, but not too high; because I can't communicate with them". Zhang had a high school education but still "feels ignorant", she says: she was once disgraced at a job interview when she was told she had "no education". These constructions indicate that these essentially "working-class" individuals find it a bonus that a foreigner whom they perceive as being of higher status – a concept closely linked with my "academic record" in the Chinese popular understanding – is prepared to speak with them as equals. Of course, the fact that I am an overseas researcher probably makes these informants feel especially conscious of their comparatively limited education no matter how hard I might try to avoid this. Yet this positioning nevertheless indicates a highly significant dimension of difference from other more "middle-class" persons (as analyzed in Chapter 10), who notably do not so willingly defer to me in the same way.

Stuck

Being "stuck" (see Xu Xiaoyan above) is a major negative of control (see Chapter 7 on Personality), but although these workers develop narratives that highlight their lack of control over their circumstances, the acknowledged source of their mutual disadvantage is also given a competitive edge in an attempt to get ahead. In defense of their lack of knowledge and education, the practicability of the Cultural Revolution experience is drawn upon as an asset. After valorizing farmers as "plain, honest and hardworking, and able to eat bitterness", Xu Xiaoyan identifies herself with these virtues: "Managers", she says, "appreciate staff of my age because we can eat bitterness (*chiku*); we can get things done" (*nenggan*).

In this respect, though urban, these workers draw on the countryside as a platform for self-assertion even more than do the young rural migrants analyzed in the previous chapter. This is because while rural migrants stress the familial countryside home as the source of their moral integrity, they are too optimistic, and too vital to reproduce the urban disdain which denies their competitive edge over these dilapidating workers. Notably, not one of my migrant informants used the term "eating bitterness" (*chiku*) to describe their experiences, or indeed stressed any other kind of "bitterness" in their lives. Some did, however, use the term "hardship" (*xinku*) to describe the fate of their relatives back in the countryside; that is, precisely the fate Xu Xiaoyan seeks to manipulate to her advantage. Sadly for Xu, as the State increasingly emphasizes bitterness-eating capacities to reconfigure the boundary between its allies and non-allies in terms of marketable productivity and raw effort, many of these older workers find themselves over the hill and more bitter than bitterness-eating, sharing an apathetic, pessimistic, and fatalistic inflection of discourse quite far removed from the enterprising dynamism evinced in rural migrants' discourse (cf. Griffiths and Zeuthen 2012). Even where the self-cultivation and self-control discourse is manifested as actively working in these workers' narratives, it is primarily the sense of working for others that is expressed, a stifled sense of self-control that rings to the moralistic tune of the socialist planned economy rather than of entrepreneurial self-cultivation as such.

Take Mrs Zhou, the long-term unemployed wife of the "senior driver" at Zhao's steel-roller machine repair factory. Mrs Zhou spends her "spare time" cleaning and playing mahjong with friends; she evidently watches television a lot, too. Zhou doesn't really have much to do, she says. At one point, she says that "people with money rely on their own effort to succeed; if you're lazy you'll never succeed", but she adds that you also need "good fortune" in the Chinese market – fortune she believes has been denied to her:

> Society has changed. When everything was run by the State-owned enterprises it was easy to slack off. But now, at the private firms, it's 100% effort. Most people who've been laid-off are now doing ad hoc work and get a base salary of 500 to 600 renminbi per month. Those who are aged 20 to 30 can easily find work, but for us older people it's really difficult. The work unit doesn't want us; society doesn't want us. We are the laid-off, the really laid-off (*zhen xiagangde*). The young people don't want to go to State-owned enterprises. They go directly to recruiting agents to be placed in private firms. If you've got a specialism, it's easy to find a job; if you haven't, it's very difficult.

Like Mrs Zhou, Fan's wife also hangs around the house all day, watching her daughter play computer games. Her daughter is home from studying "metal" (*jinshu*) at university in nearby steel-capital Shenyang. Fan's wife brings up a recent television program, demonstrating that she is most motivated by an especially frugal kind of self-control (see Chapter 7, section on Materialism):

> There was a young girl who arrived in the city straight from the countryside. Her parents were unlucky with no money. The girl never spent any money, never bought any food, ate the minimum possible, only drank water she boiled herself, and so managed to live on less than 200 yuan per month. She made a list of everything she spent for a year. To earn a little extra money the girl looked after suitcases for other students when they went home, earning 20 yuan per day this way. The journalist asked her if there was any money she shouldn't have spent that year, and the girl replied that she once made the superfluous purchase of some bananas. This was really eating bitterness (*ke chiku*). I was so moved by this. I think more programs should be made like this to show students that their lives are so comfortable and teach them to cherish their lives.

The girl in the television program endures such a sparse life as a form of "self-sacrifice" for her family, endured in recognition of the sacrifices they have made for her (see Chapter 6 on Morality). Fan's wife clearly admires the technology and thrift with which the girl controls her expenditure (the lists, etc.), as well as her resourcefulness (the tending of the suitcases, etc.), but it is primarily the girl's resilience, indomitability, and capacity to withstand that most earns her esteem (see Chapter 7). The suggestion that narratives such as these are useful for teaching the "comfortable students" of today about the value of life only further furnishes Fan's wife with the semblance of a pre-reform era mentality. In these ways, these workers' projects of individuality are somewhat static, inhibited by the insecurity that comes with poverty, and are characterized by a typically "working-class" respect for hardship, a virtue made of necessity – a distinctly ethical discourse that consolidates their consumption of the discourses of this analysis.

This morality, moreover, is tinged with a defensiveness that fails to disguise the resentment these workers feel for privileged people born to more affluent times. Within minutes of the above statements, for example, Fan's wife was documented moralizing with a harsher edge:

> Those young people about 20 years old, who hang around on the streets in cars. They don't study; they don't work. They have bad habits. When they're small they get whatever they want. They've learned bad habits from the internet. These people have never learnt anything, so they're terrible. They come from families with comparatively good economic conditions; they're not poor. It's not money that decides they turn out this way; it's their family upbringing. The parents spoil them. All the children have mutated; their thinking is sick (*bujiankang; youbing*).

The judged here lack a typical "working-class" work ethic: they neither work hard (see Chapter 7), contribute to society (see Chapter 6), nor understand the value of money (see Chapter 7, section on Materialism). This, on account of an upbringing contrasted with these workers' backgrounds. Thus, in the absence of so much that Anshan's emerging middle class are acquiring, these workers seek an anchor in the familiar root of socialist morality, and those powerful enough to affirm themselves in their own virtue are damned.

Bitter

The distinctly moralistic tone of these workers' judgments is perhaps the strongest theme to emerge from their analysis; the frequency with which they speak as if they define morality absolutely, without reflection or irony, is remarkable (see Chapter 6). Even as they make harsh moral judgments, moral supremacy is asserted explicitly, without disguise or sophistication, as part of a strategic positioning within the broader discursive shifts of China's reforming economy and society. Fan explicitly links reform with moral decline: "There were no bad things before: no prostitution, no gambling, and so on. But now we have lots of bad things everywhere. This is all connected to economic development." Fan is adamant that he won't drink wine and play around. He shuns high-level cheer and unrestrained mirth: he needs money.

He doesn't go to pubs, dancing halls, or singing halls. I ask him if the people who do so are good. "Only if they have a reason to go", Fan replies, "like business where they have to treat people". No doubt the fact that I also know Fan's boss, who supports Fan's family, shapes his judgment here, but the moral position is clear. "If you've no reason to consume like this, it's a waste: pleasure just for the sake of it." Business, though, is interestingly shown to legitimize practices that would otherwise be considered immoral.

Fan then brings up two much younger men from the factory and tells me they go gambling and whoring: "Everyone's got their own lifestyle, but if you've got a wife you shouldn't go out." I ask him if he ever did these "bad things" when he was young. He replies not: "No, because I'm from the countryside where the economic conditions are extremely hard" (Fan's parents were farmers – see also above). When Fan got married, he and his wife had a total of only 500 CNY to their names; he understands the value of money because he's "eaten bitterness", he says. It is significant that Fan's colleague, Xu Dongbin, also makes powerful constructions of moral character and links this with self-seeking consumption in just the same way. Fan and Xu identify with each other through their narratives, each staking a strong morals-versus-money position, distancing themselves from the activities of younger men with more profligate and hedonistic spending. Suspecting this, I try a question on Xu that I rarely used precisely because of its explicitly "moral" implication in the Chinese context: "How do you live like a decent person?" (*ni ziji zenme zuoren*), to which Xu replies:

> You must be wholeheartedly sincere, just and righteous. Not do things in dishonest and twisted ways. We have a tradition in China: you shouldn't just buy whatever and everything you like; you must have responsibility to your family and to society. I look down on those who don't care about their kids and family, but eat, drink, play and entertain.

I enquire as to what kind of "play" Xu was thinking of exactly; his reply confirms that he is probably thinking of the same people as Fan:

> Drinking, dancing and playing around with other girls. They've got good clothes and good food but don't give a damn about their family, wife and kids. But these people are not necessarily young, and they do not necessarily have money: they borrow money to play. Money and moral quality (*renpin*) are not necessarily related. Earning money is not the most important in life. Fair competition is also important in earning money. Some people don't give a damn if their money is good money or bad money.

Since Dongbin's investment in constructions of moral character was clear here, I tried a reverse tack by asking him directly if anyone "looked down on him", to which he confirmed that some people say he is "too conservative" (*tai baoshou*), and that, "yes", this was often these other people who drink and play. Dongbin was reluctant to accept the idea that he is a "really moral person" (*hen you daode de yige ren*), recognizing that to inflate himself in this way would be somewhat contrary to the good moral character for which he evidently wants to be known. Instead, Dongbin would rather be thought of as "traditional", an attribute he explains by reference to the way he tends to his family, as well as by reference to his "innate" personality (see Chapter 5), which amounts to saying the same thing: he is good, whereas those who are not "traditional" are bad.

Xu Xiaoyan is similar in these moral respects. She romanticizes her nostalgia for an innocent Socialist paradise: a purity beyond judgment spoilt in the reform era. She contends of her youth:

> Back then, there was no invidious judgment in people's hearts because everyone was of the same level. We were carefree, and happy, because we just lounged around without anyone to learn from, and played with the household waste or a box. We had no toys. There were no well-built houses. There were no pretences because everyone was poor. There was never any comparing between us. The older children brought up the younger children. There was no pressure to make invidious comparisons because everyone was the same.

Xu says the pressure to make invidious comparisons has come from the fact that she struggles to satisfy monthly [economic] requirements, "while others have cars, motorbikes and nice homes". When invited to describe these "others", Xu breaks into a sweeping judgment against people who: "Get a certain position, but not on account of their own ability and still think themselves great; who have money and power but don't know how to use it." Suspecting a personal grievance, I ask Xu if she is thinking of anyone in particular. A friend, she explains, "has a small business; they have slightly more money than me [and] think they are great". Explicitly, it is the lack of moral character Xu levers: "Some people with power are scared that people will ask them for help: they don't want people to call. But people with power should be willing to help those who call for their help."

Thus, true to this form, Xu makes her judgment center on altruism (see Chapter 6). Xu is of good moral character herself, I am to understand: "I want a good family and do my work well. No matter who I'm working for, I need to do good work. People like me can't make much money, so we try to serve others well." Thus, Xu is aware that she must use what she has, and altruistic service features alongside "work" as a last resort. Her creeping use of the plural "we" reflects her attempts to draw strength by self-identification with a social category from which she would actually like to distance herself.

Xu then proceeds to develop this inclusion-versus-exclusion dynamic from the explicitly moral to the less abstractly social, still speaking as if money has hollowed out a past borne of collective hardship and that has caused particular problems in terms of the reciprocity demanded in Chinese society:

If someone with memories of the past, who now has money, invites a poor person to eat, it means they're good, moral. I have no money to invite others to eat so I must choose an inferior place to eat, or struggle to pay. Courtesy demands reciprocity. In the end I stopped accepting others' offers to eat out, making excuses not to go. The others talk about things over dinner I don't even know about. When I invite my old friends to dinner they make excuses not to come: they don't like it because it's not up to their standards. It's all to do with money and power. I don't want to hang out with them; I like to be with people of approximately the same level. After going once I wouldn't dare go again, and didn't sleep for many nights.

Xu extends this same line of discussion into courtship and marital relations, linking China's reforms with moral ineptitude in ways broadly comparable to Fan and Xu Dongbin's judgments of whoring (above).

Most people of my age were still introduced by their parents to get married; we did not freely choose. Nowadays you look for someone with money. Before, finding a partner, I was concerned to look for someone sincere, someone straight and honest, with working ability and a job. I didn't think about money. Divorce was very rare. But many married people from my generation have divorced now. Now there is a difference between the rich and the poor and it shows in emotional and love respects. If you've no money, no one's interested. You need money, a car, a home, and some power. In my era, the maximum age gap between partners was four years, but now large age gaps are quite permissible. Lifestyles have changed; young girls take money from old men and then break up.

It is perhaps significant that the way in which constructions of moral character are made to consolidate these workers' narratives is notably different in both Zhang Jie and Chen Qian, both of whom, born in 1966, were too young to be steeped in Cultural Revolutionary fervor. The difference is most clearly seen in these workers' attitudes towards child-rearing. None of these workers' children are doing especially well academically, which somewhat distinguishes them from children of more "middle-class" parents, who generally achieve well, school for longer, and sometimes abroad. Where Xu Dongbin wants his daughter to "have a good income and to grow up to make a good contribution to society", and where Xu Xiaoyan wants her daughter to "do good things, find a job and make steps that fit into China's development", the younger Chen Qian only emphasizes the importance of her child's development and her role as mother: she makes no emphasis on altruism beyond the remit of her immediate family. The younger Zhang Jie, too, wants her son to "go to university and have a stable family", but makes no mention of wider "contribution", "responsibility" and so on.

I ask Zhang about how she raises her son. "We don't have too high demands", she replies, "As long as he can find a job and a basic salary to have a family". Struggling to get her to open up, I ask her for an example of something that happened recently that she really didn't like. After a delay, she begins to talk about her son as if she can think of nothing else. She doesn't like it when he's "naughty"; she wants him to be "hard-working" but has "no specific target" for him. It is only after she says that she wants her son to have good "moral quality" (*pinzhi*) that she has significantly more to say: she reminisces about once meeting a desperately poor boy whose father had disappeared and whose mother had been left penniless, stressing the importance of being "responsible" as a parent.

Thus, not only are Zhang and Chen the least discursively competitive of all the women interviewed here, but they are also less bitter than either the elder Xu Xiaoyan or Fan's wife from the "sent down" generation. Though constructions of moral character play an integral role in their narratives, an aspiring invidiousness might be necessary for older workers with few alternative resources.

Aspiring moves

Despite Xu Xiaoyan's identification with a past socialist moral paradise, indeed, she elsewhere makes equally strong statements about how awful the "sent down" experience was, and how ugly was her rivalry with the local farmers: she looked down on them as "country bumpkins" while the farmers called her a "rich princess, unable to eat bitterness". This discourse resurfaces when Xu is casually invited to comment on rural migrants to the city:

> They're extremely disorderly, lacking in education and personal quality. If speaking on the phone, they're too loud. They don't pay attention to hygiene. Their clothes aren't tidy, so as soon as you see them you know they are farmers. Their appearance, their clothes, their skin is black from exposure to the elements. Basically they're not used to decorating themselves and they can be distinguished by their behavior.

Xu thus seeks to splice the best of the revolutionary morality with her "distinguished" urban status, but the privilege of mastering discourse in this way comes only with a certain level of urban security Xu does not have. This privilege, moreover, somewhat requires that you do not so openly make the strong invidious comparisons Xu says she overtly opposes, but cannot help but do so when she is offered the chance. Although Xu makes upwardly aspiring moves in her narratives that necessarily entail the acquisition of a certain discursive fluency, therefore, correct judgment, which includes how to judge and indeed judging without seeming like you are judging, is a further distinction denied to her. Though it is not in the interest of my research to prove a single causality, let it be noted that the disposition to make judgments of others' moral character makes these workers quite different from more "middle-class" informants, who themselves tended to speak as if aware that such a nakedness of judgment was uncivil in exactly the same way as is not wearing clothes in public (see Chapter 10). For now, let it be noted that Xu's aspiring invidiousness has nevertheless managed to convince the comparatively simple Mr Fan that she received a high school education, when in fact she had only middle school and did not complete that because of the "learn from industry; learn from the countryside" movement.

Fan and his wife have made an aspiring move of their own, too, however, having recently spent their life's savings on a sweltering hot sixth-floor flat surrounded by gardened houses, where old party cadres have long been allocated privileged residence. This move up in the world, however, is only a superficial make-over, and cannot in itself resolve Fan's inferiority:

> I'm not like the cadre neighbors. Their cultivation and education is higher. I never come into contact with them. Their life patterns are completely different. I'm just a proletariat, an ordinary proletariat (*putong baixing*). Cadres have knowledge. Our status is different. We never come into contact. They don't really understand me and I don't really understand them. These other guys relied on their parents to bring them on – they have no experience of real poverty. I only had my mother; my father died early of illness when I was three years old leaving four children. In Anhui, in the 1950s, that is, in approximately '58, '59, and '60 when there was nothing to eat, me and my family would eat grass and tree bark to stay alive. It was very good to eat; we liked the kernels in the grass best.

It is highly significant that the cadre category is seen as the clincher in this neighborhood: none of these workers can be described as cadres and none are Party members. The discourse here is therefore as much about division in terms of allegiance versus non-allegiance to the State – that is, despite these workers' urban status – as it is about age, education or anything else. Fan's wife never comes into contact with her neighbors either: "I don't understand them; they are a different level, I evade them." My wife (then girlfriend) puts it to her that the place they now live is very good, which isn't taken at all condescendingly. Rather, Fan's wife agrees and adds of her own accord, "even when we lived in a noisy place we just got on with it", and then further, "I don't like to harm other people; I don't want to look down on others", that is, an assertion of her "good moral character" that nevertheless reflects the perception that moving to this more distinguished area is somehow attended by the need to condescend to others.

By contrast, Fan, who of all these workers is the closest to the countryside, seeks to compete socially only in terms of moral character. Unlike his wife he seems to see things only in somewhat naïve terms of "good" and "bad", and in this respect shares a trajectory through discourse similar to some of my younger rural migrant informants. "Innocence", therefore, accompanies proximity to the land. We might also make the observation explicit here, that invidiousness of judgment is much more the province of the women in this group than the men, who tend only to make explicitly moral judgments when encouraged to do so, and then only impersonally. Whereas Fan and Xu Dongbin are quite accepting of their social position, and offer moral judgments only of more or less hypothetical others to illustrate that they are themselves good husbands and fathers, the more aspiring women, and Xu Xiaoyan and Fan's wife in particular, actively volunteer moral judgments intended to "socially climb" (*panbi*) whenever they can.

True players

Yet, some of these male workers are more competitive at bending the discourse to their advantage in the first place, though they do so in ways very distinct from their female counterparts. Though both are in their fifties, Mr Huang and Mr Zhou, thus far not discussed, both juggle full-time jobs in the State sector whilst working for Mr Zhao every spare minute. Huang describes himself as "a high worker, not a cadre", an emphasis quite distinct from his colleagues who describe themselves as "wretches", "ordinary", "stuck" and so on. Both Huang and Zhou strongly emphasize their practical value, not in a wistful, desperate hark back to the Cultural Revolution, but in current projects. Huang compares the State-owned enterprise system "where people moved slowly", with the private system "where people move quickly", marking himself as someone who has been successful at changing with those changes. He drops references to the USA, the UK and Germany where "one man can do any job", showing that he knows about these places (see Chapter 3). Huang has "no time" to drink water whilst working, he says, as a mark of his earnestness: he wants to be seen as industrious and hyper-productive. He has no time for exercise, "Of course", but he's "very strong nevertheless". Thus, constructions of control and self-cultivation take a much more expansive form in his discourse (see Chapter 7).

Related, and quite unlike the less competitive workers and their families discussed here, Huang "hasn't got the time" to make judgments about others who pursue entertainment. Besides, he doesn't "have the inclination"; he just wants to "earn money". Huang paints a picture of his worldview for me:

> There are two types of boss-to-worker relations. The first just makes it perfectly clear what he wants you to do, and then pays you precisely according to the task or the hours you put in. But the second kind of boss, like Mr Zhao, will let you do two days work in six hours and still get paid for two days. We don't talk money before the job. We just do it as quickly as possible even when we know we would get paid less. But I can't do it all for no money, so Mr Zhao still gives me the full price. Mr Zhao has a big heart.

Underscoring the reciprocity element in Huang's narrative is the awareness of the malleability of the discourse, the tactical guile shared by the rural migrants analyzed elsewhere and the bending of rules (see Chapter 3). As if deflecting the implicitly attendant charge of moral bendiness, Huang lays ultimate responsibility for this reciprocity with fate: "If Mr Zhao tells me to be there at eight, I'll be there at six. I love Mr Zhao. Love doesn't come without a reason" (*ai bushi suibian lai*). Huang's affection is explained by the loss of a finger at the factory ten years ago: "It was my own fault", he admits, "but Mr Zhao bought me some painkillers which I refused because he shouldn't have to pay when it was my own fault". Huang could not have afforded these extra-special painkillers himself, but by suffering this pain, and making the self-sacrifice of not taking advantage of Mr Zhao's generosity, he institutes himself as of excellent moral character and ensures that Mr Zhao will reward him accordingly in the future; indeed, there was extra money to pay, and hospital fees, but Mr Zhao covered it all even though he was under no formal obligation to do so. "This brought us close together, emotionally, so whatever Mr Zhao asks me to do, I will do it without question." Thus it is clear how the affective element of behavior becomes explicit and rationalized as a kind of moral control, as explored in Chapter 7 of this book.

Strongly emphasized here, too, is Huang's service as a worker, a competitive stress quite different from some of the others discussed above: the less competitive informants only articulate a moral cause greater than that of serving their immediate families via their hopes for their children's future, hopes that have an air of hopelessness about them. Huang, on the other hand, knows for sure that his contribution makes a difference to something bigger than himself.

Huang then creates for me a three-tier model of how the world is segmented according to his point of view:

> First there is the management level, the cadres who don't work. Then there are the skilled workers who do high scientific research; some here can earn more than the managers. Then, the third level is like me: a worker, repairing equipment, maintaining, doing the things that the others cannot do.

The simple fact that Huang conceptualizes himself at the bottom in terms of three hierarchical levels makes it unlikely he chooses to be there (see Chapter 7, section on Status), but he nevertheless highlights his unique value: "doing the things that the others cannot do." It is further significant that he puts the official cadres at the top, even though the highly skilled and entrepreneurial may earn more: allegiance to the State is the real clincher in the distribution of power here – without this wealth makes you a liability. Huang's probable sleight that the official class does not contribute ("work") itself makes him more competitive than most of the other workers analyzed here who evince little such skill or ambiguity in their judgments. Huang also talks more, simply put, and excels at it, two factors that make him in these ways much more similar to the more middle-class figures analyzed in the following chapter. Indeed, there is further explicit acknowledgment in Huang's narrative that mastering the discourse requires being malleable with the rules: in a hushed voice, he tells me something that bonds him and Mr Zhao together: "Because I'm still in a State-owned company, I can still make stuff disappear. If I can get some materials for free from that company, I'll give them to Mr Zhao for free. Yes, basically I take them. Mr Zhao knows, but I don't tell him the details." Thus Huang is something of a player in a way that some of the other men analyzed here are not: he uses what he can, because he has to. Such is the way of making it in Anshan's reforming economy.

A further major part of what configures some of these workers as "true players", again related to being malleable with the rules, is their highly typical use of constructions of sociability. Though their constructions are nowhere near as potent as constructions made by younger male workers (see Chapter 5, p.84), Huang, Fan, and Xu Dongbin all invest in the typical "northeasterners versus southerners" discourse of regional authenticity in a big way. This construction is highly gendered, and centered on a highly individuated form of self-expression. Fan describes his personality as "speaking directly": he speaks whatever he thinks, he says: "Others can't judge me because I speak from the heart; I'm frank and honest." Fast-talking Huang (above) describes himself as "very proud and cool" (*haoshuang*); he has a big smile, and laughs a lot. His discourse is full of markers such as "don't be polite", and "chill out a bit".

Figure 9.1 Blast furnace. Photography by Gao Yingchuan

He also volunteers a contrast between introversion and extroversion, saying he himself is the latter.

Huang is as heavy on the smoking as he is on sociable character, but only drinks one bottle of beer a day, because there must be control "for work" (see Chapter 7). Nevertheless, he makes frequent hearty motions for me to "eat more", and, although it is only the first in-depth conversation we have had, he feels that we should "be at ease" with each other. "We have bonds", he expands: "When people get to a point, they can be very much at ease; if you haven't got to that point, you can't be at ease; being at ease means that whatever you want to eat, you eat, and whatever you want to say, you say, and you needn't ask permission to go to the toilet. We'll go out eating and drinking and I'll pay for everything." Friendship, comradeship, and trust are thus equally and especially important for Huang – his being is true. When offered the chance to define his personality, Xu Dongbin says he is: "An introvert, not an extrovert. I don't like to show myself off; I am steady, sedate. Extrovert people act differently; they have different deportment. Being more introverted is more traditional than modern." Yet Xu nevertheless thinks he should be considered "proud and cool" when I ask, underlining the inclusivity of the construction of "innate character" (see Chapter 5) in the northeast region.

Some of the women in this group draw on the same discourse too, even though the character of this construction is typically masculine in nature. Zhang Jie says she is "extrovert" and likes people she can "have a good talk with", which is of course a comment as much about her ability to maintain rapport with others as it is her personality. Zhang also encourages her 14-year-old son to study the guitar as a function of innate character: "The guitar is more suitable for a boy's personality than the piano. Boys who play the piano are like … elegant (*youya*). For boys it's better to be a bit wild (*ye*): men should be like men; women should be like women." Thus, this form of construction is highly heterosexual also (see Chapter 5, p.86).

True to this form, this highly gendered emphasis is inverted in these workers' constructions of civil behavior (see Chapter 4). Civil behavior does not feature as a priority amongst this group. Such constructions are almost entirely absent from Fan's narratives – that is, Fan who is closest amongst the group to the countryside, again highlighting the distinctly urban nature of the civil discourse – though Fan makes no notable transgressions in my presence. Xu Dongbin builds no constructions in civil terms, but is concerned to bring up his son in a way that makes "manners", "respecting elders", and various other constructions, fit well with discourses of good moral character. Huang has a curious habit of putting his hands on my shoulders and arms as he welcomes me into his home, and proceeds to touch my hand a lot during our conversations. Neither he nor any of the several other people present seem to think this strange; he does it for emphasis and sincerity. When a juicy mess from a watermelon Huang had excitedly bade me eat began to drip off the tabletop onto me and then over Huang's floor, he was not at all bothered to stop its flow, an observation that brought back memories of eating in peasant homes where the hosts would spit out unwanted pieces directly onto the earthen floor. These men spit at work, but not at home.

Material girls

Where constructions of civil behavior discourse are consumed for strategic purposes amongst these informants, it is only really the women, second-generation urban residents all of them, who obviously compete in this way. Zhang Jie hates "spitting, the throwing of rubbish, and the wearing of clothes in a disorderly way". The gender factor immediately emerges as explicit: "It is hot outside, but some men don't respect others and take their shirts off. People should choose the situation; it's not a swimming pool around here." Zhang Jie also doesn't like "people without manners, who don't say excuse me when asking the way: they just say a, or uh, and never say thank you". Zhang goes on, fusing constructions of civil behavior with the moral imperatives of being a good mother and altruistic regard for society:

> When I'm on my bicycle people in front just spit without looking behind them. Others just throw rubbish out of the window from high up without looking. When I brought up my son I needed to be really strict on their manners. If he had a lollipop he would have to carry the wrapper until he found a trash can; and then the stick, he couldn't just chuck it on the floor. You must be clean; people will think the people in the area have higher personal quality or civility. People are like this because of their parents; they weren't brought up well. I have a neighbor who cleans her house, but just brushes the rubbish outside onto the street; she has bad hygiene habits. Habits are very important. I taught my son to cut his nails into a bag, not to do it onto the floor. You need to protect the environment in these small ways; you must pay attention to controlling your behavior beforehand, not just clean up after. Anyway, my son's not a messy person in the first place. If you protect the environment every minute you won't need to have a massive clean-up. Take the people in the street cleaning up; they have to always clean up because people keep making it dirty.

Xu Xiaoyan similarly brings up "uncivilized manners", explaining that this refers to people who "sit incorrectly in a public place", who "speak loudly because they think they have money", and who "gesticulate excessively and think they are the center of everything". True to the strength of exclusive judgments emergent from women throughout this analysis therefore, constructions of civil behavior also play a much bigger part in these women's narratives than the men's.

We might also observe that these latter two iterations are congruent with Zhang Jie's younger-than-average age for the group (civil behavior being a discourse generally stronger in younger, more modern persons in the China

context), and Xu Xiaoyan's generally aspiring profile (she wants to be identified with more knowledgeable and cultured types as shown above). Other
women here, however, aspire to be civil but make considerable transgressions
without knowing that they do so (see Chapter 3): Fan's wife offers me fruit,
speaks with her mouth full of food, and burps out loud without any disguise.
Mrs Zhou, likewise, burps twice without discretion and coughs three times into
my face during a conversation in which she nevertheless said things like this:

> Better, taller buildings; wider, better roads. People's personal quality and
> civility are also better than before. Before, people could just spit wher-
> ever. People put litter in the bins now. Before, they just randomly chucked
> it on the floor. The fighting is less now, too. Before, around about the
> eighties, there was a lot more fighting everywhere; but after the nineties it
> all changed. The people had no personal quality: whenever they spoke it
> was to swear at people.

I put it to Mrs Zhou, "Aren't people still like this?" But she was adamant:
"No, only a few; if you do this now, you're certainly immoral (*bu daode*)."

Thus, we might note that not only are constructions of civil behavior an
important part of the way that the women in this group compete, though they
do not entirely practice it, but moreover, these women do not separate constructions of civil behavior from their assessments of moral character (see
Chapter 4, p.74; Chapter 6). Ultimately this is a question of politics: the State,
of course, deliberately manipulates the explicitly moral, that is, altruistic,
angle to civil discourse, because this is to what the post-Socialist masses most
respond (see Chapter 6). Many of the more "middle-class" individuals I have
encountered, however, tend to compete much less urgently in terms of moral
character, and demonstrate a disposition to separate judgments of moral
character from their judgments of civil behavior as part of both consciously
and unconsciously defining themselves against people like these workers who
conflate these logics.

The gender divide in the consumption of discourse is also evident in the
way these workers approach materialism (see Chapter 7, section on Materialism):
essentially the women in the group compete much more in this way. This is a
divide that was not evinced by the younger people who informed my research,
be they migrants or urban registered, where both genders seem to care a lot,
though perhaps not equally, about their material image. Neither was this
gendering so immediately obvious in elderly people either, where it often
seemed that both males and females cared similarly less about their material
appearance than younger people generally. The men in this group of workers
only treat materialism as important in order to distance themselves from it as
a function of moral character, as shown above. Xu Dongbin dresses in a
scrubby white vest and pajama-type shorts, and is not at all concerned to
present himself differently when I visit his home; this is congruent with his
limited investment in discourses of civil behavior and with welcoming me as a

member of the intimate rather than of the public. Fan only wears shorts and sandals when he is out of his overalls, and happily sits with me, smoking in his stained white vest and boxer shorts. Fan professes respect for his boss, Zhao, because, "Although he has money, power and influence, and economic strength, he doesn't show it off; this is internality (*neihan*) as opposed to externality (*waibiao*), where internality comes from the heart and externality is just about boasting".

The more competitive men in this group have a slightly more enhanced sense of competing in material respects. Both Mr Zhou and Mr Huang are rarely seen without a collared shirt and a combination of black leather shoes, dark formal trousers, and thin white socks. Zhou sports a shiny leather belt with conspicuous buckle of the same symbolic order. This is how lower-level government cadres have typically dressed in recent decades, and these gestures towards formality, though now widely seen as unrefined by more "middle-class" types, nevertheless serve to distinguish these workers from Fan and Xu, who don't make the effort and subsequently share more in common with unskilled manual laborers or people on the peasant fringe, who will often be seen wearing at least one item of military camouflage clothing, identifying with a Socialist ideal where everyone dressed more or less alike.

The women analyzed here compete much more in terms of materialism. Zhang Jie, again true to her form, understands that competing in this way is linked to the aesthetic dimension of civil behavior; it is important to her that she is seen as presentable, even though she is quite poor:

> When men and women are on the street they should take care of their appearance. Even if you don't wear make-up, you must do your hair, wash your face, dress tidily, etc.; you must respect others and they will respect you. Fashion is extremely important to me. Fashion symbolizes that you have a young heart. If I wear a more beautiful necklace I feel like I'm not old. Some young people don't care about their appearance, and so they are already old. Some people wear clothes that look really beautiful; others look very backward.

Mrs Zhou, too, who evidently wants to talk about this, also has a strong sense of why a person's "external appearance" is important:

> It reflects personal quality and individuality very deeply. Dressing appropriately in public places is very important. I like to dress up so that when I go out in the evening my friends say to me: "You look very beautiful today." If this happens my heart will be really comfortable.

Mrs Zhou has a necklace made of blue cloth. I tell her I like it, and she tells me she has a gold one but prefers this one "because it is more out of the ordinary". Eager to develop this theme she produces a pair of trousers with handmade beads sewn into them:

See, it's very unique: it's important to express individuality through your appearance. Chinese society is very realistic now. If your family looks at you and thinks you look very ordinary, this is not good. If you look very modern, people are more inclined to want to get along with you.

Thus, contemporary realism, which we might well understand as competition, is implicitly contrasted with Maoist politics: though it is important for Mrs Zhou to be "out of the ordinary" as a function of individuality, it is also important to look good for her family, overlapping constructions of materialism and moral character, a facet of "face". Spotting the tension in her statements, I challenge Mrs Zhou by asking, "So it's important to be individual and to do what others like too?"

Mrs Zhou replies affirmatively to this, so I immediately follow up by asking whether there is a contradiction here. She laughs wryly, pauses, and says there is no contradiction. Thus, I choose a different tack, asking: "If this notion is so important to you, how do you judge others in terms of their external appearance (*waibiao*)?" At this point, Mrs Zhou brings up that word "internality" (*neihan*) again, the concept that Fan uses to oppose "externality" (see above). Sensing an insight into the formation of individuality that might help this research, an insight quite contrary to the received wisdom of the China-watchers in the business and management worlds, I inquire further after her precise meaning: "Does *neihan* mean liking different things to other people?" "No, this is not correct", Mrs Zhou replies, putting a simple individualism out of the picture. She immediately adds the following as if to confirm the relational value of the concept: "If you go to a public place looking bad, if they don't understand you, people won't respect you." "*Neihan*", Mrs Zhou ventures, "is an individual viewpoint" (*geren de guandian*).

Inspired, I check: "Is the meaning of *neihan* the same as what you said about uniqueness of individuality just now when discussing your necklace?" And further, "Is it about expressing something from the inside that is individual and personal through an appearance on the outside?" Mrs. Zhou affirms "yes" to both these questions, explaining, "Just like my necklace, I'm the only one who's got one like it". She then produces a ring from somewhere, saying, "Everyone else's rings of this style have only one decorative bead on it, but I thought it didn't look so good, so I put two on it; I like to do things differently to other people". Mrs Zhou has just told me that "*neihan*" is not to be simply understood as "liking different things to other people", so there seems to be something especially important about the externalization of an internality to her definition. She understands "*neihan*", a concept initially understood as "inner", as a metaphor for the subjective attribution of value to an "external" object – a necklace, a ring, a person – and this attribution is somehow constitutive of the perspective (the "individual viewpoint") that attributes it, the value invested in the object thus remaining imperfectly understood by alternative perspectives on discourse (see Chapter 2, p.27).

Thus, to paraphrase the opening passages of the ancient Taoist classic the *Tao Te Ching*, "From one there came two, and from two there came many", an observation that should support the perspectivism sustained throughout this research, as well as the gendered self emergent in this analysis.

10 Professionals

This final chapter analyzes a number of broadly middle-aged adults from households where the primary breadwinner is or until recently had been a professional at one of Anshan's major public enterprises, or at affiliated businesses. All of these individuals are distinguished from the "workers" analyzed in the previous chapter by a rough composite of occupation and professional status, discretionary income, educational level, family background and their consumption of the key discourses of this analysis. Some are senior-level engineers or technicians at the higher-end of the scale, with some sort of oversight for junior staff; others hold "white-collar" professional office jobs; and others are purely managers. None are official State functionaries, and none are to be thought of as having significant status as such, although the fact that these individuals hold professional positions situates them in discourse in a way denied to those individuals analyzed in the previous two chapters. Though some of these individuals know each other, they are much less intimately involved with each other than either the rural migrants and workers were; neither do they share the same sense of belonging within a group or identify so readily with a social category as those individuals.

This chapter is therefore structured somewhat differently to its predecessors: as a series of thematically connected portraits of individuals taking up different positions within a loosely defined "field" (Bourdieu 1992) of practice characterized first by a distinct diversity of individuality rather than as a comprehensive analysis of a "group". The chapter is structured to begin with individuals who are not so different to the workers in the previous chapter and ends with individuals who are very different indeed, thus showing how a more "middle-class" disposition emerges from the "working class" disposition just developed. This means that by the end of this chapter my analysis becomes almost tautological in form, iterating the ways in which, to greater or lesser extents, and in different ways, these individuals collapse the key discourses developed throughout my analysis into the form of their legitimate instantiation. Wherever possible, the data are allowed to remain close to the context in which they were collected, facilitating comparisons with family members across age, gender, political affiliation, and so on, further drawing out the "grammar" of the instantiation across these.

Party line

By way of introduction, consider Mr Zhou, a 49-year-old neighbor who can be interestingly compared with his wife, 48, and his mother, Grandma Liu, who lives in the same home. Zhou's State-owned enterprise salary is actually less than Mr Zhao's factory workers' (see Chapter 9), but Zhou enjoys substantial benefits on healthcare, rent, and so on. When Zhou introduces himself as a "high-level engineer" his mother immediately parrots the words "high-level!" (*gaoji*) for emphasis.[1] When I pose the matter for confirmation, Zhou cannot resist asserting that he is of "high knowledgeability" (*hen you zhishi; hen you banfa*), no doubt further intending that I notice his explicit linking of knowledge with practicability, the implication being that he can "work anything out". Grandma Liu immediately butts in again to reiterate this emphasis – "My son can fix anything" – with an unguarded nakedness of assertion that seems to place her closer to some of the less educated workers analyzed in the previous chapter than to her son. Rather than boast, indeed, and as if to demonstrate he has more to offer in discursive contention than the average handy-man, Zhou prefers to let his knowledge speak for itself: though I have only asked a few banal questions to begin with, he launches into a highly strategic narrative, referring to political history, theories of population growth and of economic stratification, and making all manner of comparisons with other countries, sustaining this for quite some time.

Notably, both women present seem to assume that this is the kind of knowledge I have come to hear. Evidently they are very proud of Zhou. However, while Grandma Liu constantly interjects with chatty and opinioned commentary, Zhou's wife seems to have very little to say for herself, a somewhat subservient gendering pattern repeated in every household where the male spouse was the primary breadwinner here (see below). Of significance, perhaps, is that while Zhou managed to make up on lost schooling part-time after the Cultural Revolution, a factor of the cushioning effect provided by the relative comfort his family enjoyed at the time, Zhou's wife did not supplement her limited basic education, which perhaps accounts for her relative "in-articulation" now (see Chapter 3, on Knowledge). It is necessary for me to interview her alone on other occasions, where she reveals a "habitus" (i.e. a trajectory through the constructs of this analysis) not unlike some of the less competitive women analyzed in the previous chapter.

Despite the enhanced knowledge and skills that distinguish Zhou from his wife and mother, however, Zhou is nevertheless in many respects very similar to some of my worker informants too. Particularly similar are his constructions of moral character and his contrast of these with the logic of money and materialism (see Chapter 6, on Morality; see Chapter 7, section on Materialism). Zhou is not at all poor; his family lives comfortably enough in one of the better parts of the city, in a flat granted to his mother on account of the fact that his long-dead father was a military General (see Chapter 7, section on Status). However, Zhou nevertheless scorns people he knows who have "divorced their wives, left the kids, and shot off to the south to earn money" in just the same way as those divorced wives do themselves. "We're not like that", says Zhou in sum. Zhou explains that he just doesn't have the urge to earn enormous amounts of money like some do because he doesn't care much for "specially" dressing his appearance. His son, at university, absorbs much of the household expenditure, but he doesn't care for the latest trends either, Zhou explains, perhaps reinforcing the impression that they are unable to afford him anything above basic consumption anyway.

Unlike the workers' very similar money-versus-morals moralities, however, Zhou's morality takes a much more explicitly partisan form quite absent from the discourse of the workers, none of whom were self-professed allies of the State in any sense other than that in which their working was a contribution. Zhou is "very proud" of being a Communist Party member, believing that it's "good for society, like Christianity". "No commerce, no evil", he maintains (*wushang bujian*). He cannot be provoked to express any ill of the Party or government at all, even though his father died in Mao's purges. Zhou and his mother speak almost as if with one voice in these respects, as if uniting to provide a record of what they stand for: Grandma Liu has an excellent moral reputation, I am to understand; though she is not the party representative in our community she makes up for this perceived deficit by volunteering harder and longer than anyone else. She would like to be thought of by others as of excellent "moral quality" (*daode pinzhi*), to which she adds "comprehensive quality" (*zhengti suzhi*), explaining that this may also be understood as "political cultivation" (*zhengzhi xiuyang*).

While Zhou works, Grandma Liu spends her days scouring the six different newspapers delivered daily to their home for instructions from the government, which she cuts out and displays around the neighborhood as posters. These include: "love your country; build up Anshan", "arduously struggle; be hardworking and thrifty", "don't throw rubbish or dirty things about", "don't make a lot of noise in public places", and so on. Cut out too are those sections on "family health" and "health knowledge" (*baojian zhishi*), which are sewn together in little books for safe-keeping; the remaining paper is recycled once every three months "for five-and-a-half mao per jin" in a fashion perfectly congruent with this distinctly Socialist blend of altruistic service, rule-governed technocracy, and material frugality. "Health is important so I won't be a burden on my family", says Grandma Liu, naming the exact times and places of everything she does throughout the day. "I have a strict routine, a particular time for doing exercise and for eating every meal. Being a little bit more casual wouldn't do at all". I ask her if she ever does anything for herself, and not for others, to which she replies: "Not much, not really, I'm all about serving the people because I'm a member of the Communist Party."

Though Liu and Zhou's politics are similarly partisan, however, it is significant that civil behavior emerges as a factor of Mr Zhou's morality in a way that it does not for his mother: where Zhou identifies people who spit on the streets with a "lack of knowledge" and scorns drivers who blast their car horns at pedestrians as an indicator of their status (Zhou does not own a car), Grandma Liu makes no constructions of civil behavior in her boundary management at all. Zhou thus demonstrates the ability to separate judgments of civil behavior from judgments of moral character in ways that his mother does not, whereas his mother prefers instead only to judge in explicitly altruistic terms as many of the workers in the previous chapter were apt to do.

Although Zhou agrees with his mother that the "good" officials of bygone times are different from those "bad" officials and businessmen of the contemporary era, the importance of "not carelessly spitting phlegm or urinating" is not necessarily equivalent to other, overtly altruistic imperatives such as "serve the people" and "contribute to society", as it evidently is for Grandma Liu. If civility, a much more modern discursive paradigm than China's proximity altruism morality is carving out space for individuality amongst even the most die-hard of Communist Party supporters, then it certainly is for other individuals of this approximate social class, as this analysis will show.

High-tech, low-cash

At 71 and 68, Mr Bin and his wife are not so much younger than Zhou's mother (above). A retired "high-grade engineer", Bin likes to compete through "learning" (*xuewen*), just like Zhou (see Chapter 3). Repeatedly using the word "calculation" (*suan*) to describe his work and skills, Bin evidently likes to recall working alongside foreign engineers, reminiscing for me how they would try to compete with one another in terms of knowing about this or that technical aspect. Bin seems to feel that this gives him an element of international credence: he wants to make sure I know he went to Japan on work in 1990. Bin then wants to document that he knows about the UK, about Gordon Brown succeeding Tony Blair, the "War on Terror" and the corresponding tensions in the USA: he goes on to broach all sorts of strategic comparisons between China and the West in ways comparable to Zhou (above), though I am happy just to listen. Bin's wife, however, who used to work in a non-managerial capacity for the City Administration, the same place as Zhou's wife and at a similar level, does not engage in this kind of discourse at all. She does, however, tell me that she's been to Beijing, and then later that she's been to Shanghai, as if she wants to document the fact that she has first-hand experience of central and advanced places too.

In this case, Bin and his wife feel the need to signify that they are capable of communicating with me, whereas others, it is implicit, would not necessarily be able to: their greatest problem is that their wealth doesn't live up to their perceptions of Bin's technical expertise. As soon as I arrive, Bin mixes apologies for his home not being more luxurious – "It's a little bit lacking" – with demonstrations of knowledge as if he is trying to show me that he knows he has an intellectual capital more than his means suggest. Being an engineer has not earned him enough money, he says, both he and his wife making numerous similar admissions throughout the interview (see Chapter 7, section on Materialism). Bin and his wife have three children, reflecting their age, since younger urban people usually only have one. Their son, they are keen to tell me, "has a 180 sq meters home in Green Intelligence City", an up-market, newly built, out-of-town housing estate. Their own flat, they tell me, is "only 70 sq meters" (see Chapter 7, section on Materialism). Their front room is small but cozy in appearance, with a welcoming-looking but aged and not especially well-built sofa.

Bin and his wife have little option but to pursue reflected glory through the success of their children, a function of showing that they have excelled in their role as "good" parents (see Chapter 6). They bring up their son again, telling me that he works for the Bank of China and has recently been to France, the UK and Sweden on work, elements impressed upon me quite early in our encounter. As with some of the less competitive female workers examined in the previous chapter, the success of their children is a source of pride invested in more by Bin's wife than Bin, for she does not have the option of competing in terms of technical or intellectual expertise as he does. Again pursuing reflected glory, both Bin and his wife talk a lot about other people whom they think have lots of money, apparently assuming that I will think this worth talking about. Bin mentions various celebrities and foreign expats; his wife mentions Da Shan, the Canadian man famously adopted by the Chinese nation, and Da Niu, his younger and much more recent British equivalent. Thus, they betray a knowledge base informed primarily by television. Like Zhou (above), Bin does not have a car but both he and his wife talk of others who have one as if they think that having one is a symbol of wealth and status; the pride is evident when they tell me their daughter drives one (see Chapter 7, section on Materialism).

Thus, having evidently figured out why I am interested in them, both Bin and his wife seem to want to talk about ways to make money too, putting it on record that they are fluent in the language of business, but always with an apologetic tone for their own lack of success. Bin's wife tells me of her younger sister who "has a business; they have money and their child is in the UK studying", once again as if she wants it to go on record that their family has overall garnered an above-average level of success, though the evidence to support this claim is in fact elsewhere. Beyond this systematic refrain, but again perhaps because they cannot afford much by way of material pretension, Bin and his wife evidently want to project a message of "simple and friendly" to me, a function of competing through the Sociability discourse (see Chapter 5). Bin's wife claims that they are "relaxed" (*suibian*) vis-à-vis the formalistic and wealthier Japanese, thus excusing any sense I might have had that they are too relaxed. Although very kind and generous, however, neither Bin nor his wife are especially strong in terms of sociable character, a form of competition that tends to be the preserve of more vital men and women (see Chapter 5, p.84; Chapter 7, p.126).

As with Grandma Liu (above), age is probably an important factor structuring the fact that neither Bin nor his wife seems especially concerned to compete in terms of civil behavior either: neither makes any boundary judgments in these terms at all. Though significantly older than all of the workers in the previous chapter, however, neither makes any obvious transgressions in these respects while with me either. Notably, however, whereas Grandma Liu feels the need to condescend to China's farmers in order to feel secure in her urban status, Bin and his wife do not: they emphasize instead a quite antithetical focus on the modernizing and international sphere, only mentioning the countryside in order to demonstrate awareness of living standards and the evolving situation there; that is, primarily as a function of competing through knowledge.

Attitudes towards the countryside are a significant factor of difference between nearly all the individuals analyzed in this chapter and the workers analyzed in the previous chapter. Though the countryside features no more than two or three generations ago in the lives of most of the individuals described here, these more self-affirmed individuals are much less inward-looking than Grandma Liu, who for all her aspirations of urban status has an ideology and world view still very much rooted at the time at which her husband passed away, at the tail end of the Cultural Revolution. Also unlike Grandma Liu, neither Bin or his wife make any strong moral judgments in front of me, evincing a certain control in judgment more familiar to Zhou (above), though without his partisan Communistic politics. True to the gendered form that emerged in the last chapter, however, Bin's wife was slightly harsher in her moral judgments than Bin, occasionally showing visible disdain on her face in relation to various topics in a way that Grandma Liu and Zhou's wife demonstrated too, but that Zhou did not. Lower levels of education and proximity to the countryside thus have greater impact on uncivil behavior and overtly moralistic judgments than has age alone.

Café control

Consider next, Mr Cao, another "high-level engineer" at Angang, whose rank is somewhat higher than Zhou and Bin at "section-chief" (see Chapter 7, section on Status). Both 54 years old, Cao and his wife, Zheng, were amongst the first back to university after the Cultural Revolution in 1974, and were classmates there with Mr Zhao, the boss of the workshop staff analyzed in the previous chapter; their educational level is thus distinct from those individuals described thus far. Cao's father died as a result of criticism in Mao's purges, as did Zhou's (above) and Mr Zhao's too. It is curious that having a parent who suffered for political reasons under Mao is socially distinctive: a sign of some noteworthy family background that none of the workers in the previous chapter inherited (see Chapter 7, section on Status).

Cao and Zheng both read history, foreign affairs, English-language fiction, and so on, literatures quite distinct from the technical and partisan readings that fill Zhou's house and in which Bin is also versed. They have several hundred books on display in a smart but not overstated cabinet and frequently make off-hand references and gestures towards them, intending for me to notice and comment. Zheng cackles that they've "got high culture!", mocking what she probably sees as the vulgarity of others who might say they have as such. Cao chuckles a bit at this but visibly maintains self-control as if aware that even this is bad taste. Their passion for reading was not so much inherited from their parents, they say, because there were no books around then; rather they just "gradually acquired the taste of reading in the comfort of our own home".

Every time I visit, Cao positions his massive frame in the same grand, black armchair across the coffee table from Zheng's, so that he looks upon his impressive array of literature every time he looks up from reading. Zheng, on the other hand, looks up from her reading at him alone, framed by the blank white wall, her teenage sweetheart. They interface by means of the coffee station between them, which serves to stimulate discussion. They drink "real, fresh, Brazilian coffee" (see Chapter 2, on Authenticity), given to them by a "friend in Brazil", but they have "many other kinds of coffee too", just as they "have other friends abroad also". Thus Cao and Zheng make knowledge take on a very different guise, crystallizing it with a highly controlled lifestyle concept (see Chapter 7, on Personality). Significant, perhaps, is that they never had children, and have therefore had lots of time for themselves; they did, however, adopt a son, a relatively uncommon thing to do at the time.

Cao percolates the coffee, every maneuver made with an accuracy truly striking for such a large man. Zheng places biscuits and other niceties on the table. It is unclear whether the biscuits are placed before us or before Cao as such, an uncertainty that seems to momentarily puncture the aura of exquisite control. As if by explanation, Cao proceeds to eat nearly all of the biscuits, consuming far more than both Zheng and I put together whilst somehow maintaining the same precision. They do this all the time, they say, as if a British guy popping around for coffee is not at all unusual, though it certainly is. Both readily admit to loving the effects of coffee on the reading mind. I mention that my girlfriend's parents, much more typical of middle-aged Anshan people in this respect, believe coffee is bad for health, to which Cao contends that a little coffee is no problem, and actually good for health. Both add two sugar cubes to every cup. These little habitual treats are evidently far more important to them than the rigorous self-controlled diet and health-monitoring that many adults in Anshan pursue (see Grandma Liu above, for example). Exercise is not on the agenda for Cao or Zheng either, again something to which few Anshan people of middle-age in non-manual jobs would openly admit. Cao and his wife prefer a different kind of control and cultivation, a cozy home hedonism centered on sugar, caffeine, and intellectual tidbits, itself fuelled by a level of material comfort that exceeds by some measure Bin's similarly cozy home (above).

Importantly, there is no shame in desire here (see Chapter 6); their pleasure is no less sensual for being so reified (see Chapter 7, section on Materialism). This especially civil style of consumption is a function of Cao and Zheng's Sociability too (see Chapter 5): they do not wish to appear stuck-up about manners, but as smooth as the coffee they drink. However, theirs is a cultivated ease devoid of the coarseness and tactile intimacy common in many other homes in Anshan: there is no interruption or obtrusiveness in any sense bar the occasional sharp peak of laughter from Zheng. The three of us seem to share a mutual awareness of knowing when to speak, where to sit or stand and how to move. Indeed, Cao and Zheng successfully produce the feeling in me that out of all my Anshan informants, their home is where I feel most at home as a visitor. Every question and response is taken with discretion, tact, delay and measure. Hands are placed one on the saucer and one on the handle of the bone-china cup. Any movement from this position is made slowly and deliberately, cup and saucer touching down noiselessly, every time. Even a little mess in the kitchen cannot upset Cao and Zheng's control: they are not the type to get agitated about someone coming over; they do not sterilize everything and arrange everything just so. I even find myself wondering if it would not have been beyond them to have left a little mess in the kitchen thinking it would reinforce the easy-going impression they like to give. At any rate, they do not rush around to do the washing-up while I wait on the couch, preferring to get right down to the important business of leisure.

Of the two, Cao is more composed than Zheng, leading in all matters of discourse. Zheng is for the most part happy to listen, asking questions less often, commenting on our discourse, but never interrupting her husband. I find I have to make the occasional glance over at her as I listen to Cao to ensure that I am not excluding her. Well-educated herself, however, Zheng leaves an impression quite different to the other women described here: less a case of lacking the equivalent right to represent, as seemed to be the case with Zhou's and Bin's wives (above), Zheng leaves the impression that her discursive potency would probably be quite the match of her husband's were it not for the fact that a younger, foreign male was in their home; she probably feels that too much assertiveness for a woman in this context would be uncivil, or defers to her husband's lead for reasons of face. It is significant that Zheng wishes to be known by her own name, whereas Zhou's and Bin's wives are content that I know them only as such.

Of further significance is that neither Cao nor Zheng make any explicitly moral judgments: they do not doubt that they are good; they are positive and self-affirmed in their worth; and they do not feel the need to judge others as bad. Though both share a healthy respect for tradition, the morality they proffer is forwards-looking, modern and international, characterized by the consciousness of a responsibility to society that is not found in most of my informants' familial-centered moralities. Both Cao and Zheng, that is to say, consistently demonstrate the ability to transcend their own predicament as the problem in discourse, making morality subordinate to self-control and cultivation, which in their case emerges as the almost exclusive driver of individuation. Related, their politics are anti-Mao, full of praise for the reforms and current leadership, and pro-democratic, though neither is especially strident in their advocacy, perhaps regarding expressed passion in these matters as itself somewhat uncivil.

Rightful resistance

The explicitly political dimension of discourse, however, emerges as a major factor attending the increased discursive capacity the professionals analyzed here possess vis-à-vis the factory workers in the previous chapter. Individuals of dispositions otherwise highly approximate to those workers demonstrate a much more public inflection of Cao and Zheng's conflation of knowledge, civility and individualized control. Consider Du Bin, for example, where the critical politics many of these professionals broadly share (see also below) is much more clearly articulated than by either Cao or Zheng, but where it is also equally clear that a position critical of the State can only be legitimately articulated from within the comfort of position essentially allied to that State.

Du is another mid-level State-owned enterprise manager, of about the same level as Cao. Du's wife, however, earns far more as general manager of a major State-owned enterprise in the region, meaning that Du's household should be considered "upper-middle class" (*zhongshang*), he says. His wife's job is powerful enough to make it problematic for me to visit them at home, but this does not interfere with Du's down-to-earth, sociable, and assertive character; indeed he is quite typical of the character type supposedly innate to the region, and in this manly respect quite similar to some of the male workers analyzed in Chapter 9 (see also Chapter 5, p.86). However, although Du likes to emphasize that he can eat "four whole bowls of congee", and "freely expresses" his opinions on almost any subject no matter whether we are in the park or in front of his colleagues at work, he is nevertheless always in control: he only likes to drink "to make friends" and doesn't "get drunk or shout a lot".

Indeed, Du is very civil and modern in his masculinity, cooking daily for his wife, for example, a gendering scarce in the families analyzed thus far (though Cao and Zheng, above, cook together). Du says he likes to "keep a distance" from people in public spaces because for the most part they're just interested in excess drinking. By contrast, Du is "really concerned about rights" (*quanli*), by which I am to infer that he thinks in civil terms most broadly (see Chapter 4). This kind of excess drinking "comes from the government", Du explains, "from those officials who believe that everyone must come to see their sons get married and pay their respects". "The waste; the noise!" he laments. "What's more, the pressure to do the same in reciprocation is immense. Others accept the pressure to do it, but I've got my independence: I won't do it if I don't want to."

Thus, Du articulates a strong sense of individual agency, making constructions of civility directly opposed to the corruption fostered by China's "proximity"-style morality (see Chapter 6): his "independence" is more important to him than the political binds that sustain so many other people's notions of the good and the right. Of further relevance here is that Du likes to talk to his buddies in the park about "social contribution" (*shehui gongyi*) and "sticking up for your individual rights", the former of which is not at all to be understood as altruism, the latter of which is politically problematic. His friends, though, are not interested; they only like talking with him about things like fitness, doing the shares, earning money, foreign education, the climate and the urban environment, he says. Du likes talking about all of this too, but if he talks about "sticking up for your rights", they say he's "too over the top", and ask "Why would you talk about the government?"

Let us examine an example of what Du means by "sticking up for his rights" in his own words, so that the internal dynamics of how these rights emerge as a function of discursive competency can be understood. Following a long and full-frontal attack on single-party rule, the lack of law enforcement, and corruption, which I will not append here, Du ventures the following:

> Essentially, we must have harmonious development. There is a need to construct a spiritual civilization. There are no morals anymore. Since the 1990s people don't know the difference between good and bad; they don't care about others; they know about commerce but not about society. People's essence is basically good. But some leaders' essence is bad. They tell everyone they'll do good things and then they become corrupt. Basically, the system is fundamentally flawed. It's not just the kids who are influenced by this but their parents and the government officials too. In [the] past people had traditional education – Confucius, Mengzi, Mao Zedong thought, etc. – but this is broken now. There is a church in Anshan, you know, people can't fit in. The USA relies on religion and belief. What does China rely on? Nothing! Material life is better these days, it's true, but spiritual life is much worse. Children are unhappy; they're always over-studying. Farmers don't know how to educate their kids, and don't even know how to show them the difference between good and bad. They need to read books, but they don't know how, can't afford them, and have no interest in cultivating themselves. But there is hope because we are in the digital age where people can use the internet. There will be enough people who understand to help China reform peacefully. But even at university, the students have too much freedom: they don't have to go to class; when they're online they just waste all their time playing games. They don't know about society, they think society has no relationship to them. They think this is a matter for the Communist Party. The government is aware of this now and is trying to rectify it. Governance has changed from Mao's stress on the "essence of the people" (*mincui*), the "grass roots", productivity and quantity, to a stress on the "elite" (*jingying*) introduced by Deng Xiaoping, and Jiang Zemin's "three represents" and so on. The two are not contradictory. Fusing the elite with the masses is China's future. The masses are the body, the elite is the spirit.

There is no doubt whom Du holds to account for the problems he articulates. He comes close to directly threatening the State – calling peace into question, for example. Where he says there is "hope because we are in the digital age where people can use the internet", he can surely only mean that he hopes that Chinese will increasingly think outside of the "proximity" box imposed upon them by their government. Although some of his comments are enough to set alarms ringing in the nearest Public Security Bureau, Du cleverly couches his criticisms in terms of official State discourse, enabling him to move in and out of subversion. Du is careful to cast a positive light on Mao's thought, and on "traditional education", thus marking his allegiance to his roots, putting it beyond question that he is a man of "the people". He also makes sure to mention the theories of Deng, Jiang, and Hu, and to apportion credit where it is widely acknowledged as due, for the way the government has addressed pollution and improved "material life", and so on. Indeed, Du cannot help but implicitly align himself with the "elite": he needs it to be clear that he is speaking from a position allied to the status quo, shouldering himself with part-responsibility for resolving the problems he describes. Less enemy of the State than deeply concerned stakeholder, therefore, Du is able to probe the boundaries of legitimacy in ways that would quite likely get lesser-ranked people in serious trouble.

However, there can be no doubt that Du takes up the altruism and proximity of the moral character discourse in which the State is so invested ("the system"), and turns this against itself, taking from the discourse he opposes exactly what he needs to subvert it. He frames his criticisms in moral terms – "There are no morals anymore", and so on – but makes this subordinate to a different kind of "responsibility", an individualizing agency that demands a certain civil concern for society and the voices of individuals speaking "the truth" as he puts it. This lends his discourse power, making his position more rightful than the ethically inflected righteous resentment expressed by some of the workers in the previous chapter. Essentially Du writes (rights?) himself into a discourse which, as he portrays it, pertains to deny him this agency, and in a very skilful way.

Elsewhere, and with equal significance, Du makes similar narrative turns which resolve the tension between self-sacrifice and self-assertion so that it is much more legitimate to express individuality in self-referential terms: he is openly explicit that "individuals must take responsibility for themselves before they can take responsibility for anyone else", an attestation that is positively antisocial in China's mainstream moral climate. In a discussion of child-rearing, he says that "the traditional way of Confucian thinking is holding us back", thus further replacing the altruistic and proximity considerations of the "moral character" discourse with more modern views of the subject. Yet for all the skill from which his legitimacy derives, it cannot be overlooked that much of Du's legitimacy derives from his wife's senior position in the State apparatus. Indeed, his identification with the elite serves to justify his exemption and social elevation from the problems he describes, even as it also shields him from official sanction.

Self-conscious

Freedom, indeed, might not be free. Legitimate agency comes at the price of surrendering to that which is greater than the individual in order to get something back. The point is best made by further considering Chen Xueyuan, an active promoter of "humanism" in whom the call for politics with an explicitly universal social referent is perhaps clearest, but in whom the mix of formal education and civil disposition seen in some of the other professionals analyzed here is matched by the absence of any affiliation to State resources at all:

> I believe all persons are equal. Whatever situation people are in, whether you are a beggar, or whether you are the Chairman of the country, in respect of your individual personality you are all equal, and should all be respected by others. We cannot say that just because he is a beggar he is not a person; it might just be that he has no education. As a person he must be afforded respect by everyone. I am like this: if I see a person begging, I'll give them some money, give them 1 kuai, 5 kuai or 10 kuai. If you want to be someone of high personal quality (*suzhi*), you can help them temporarily resolve their hardship, which can also help them relieve their long-term hardship. Because they are beggars, they may not have any ability to work; they have to rely on these practices [begging] to survive. If you help him a little, he can buy bread, or a sausage, and make himself warm for a while. These are things I really think people should do. When I'm with my daughter and we see a beggar on the street, I often tell her, "When you're grown up like Dad, you must give the beggars a little money; don't just look at them having nothing to eat without doing something, you must help him a little". There are many people who do this kind of thing in China, but they still do not understand universal consciousness (*pubian de yishi*): people are equal; all people are equal; no matter whether you've money or not, everyone is equal.

Chen's universalism explicitly addresses the "proximity" law structuring Chinese moral discourse (see Chapter 6). It is surely also significant that Chen frames his criticism not only in terms of the "simple" proximity law but also in terms of status: it is not just the stranger for whom he feels empathy, but the beggar, a person of the lowest status possible in the contemporary era of capitalism. The contrast of the beggar's inherent moral worth with that of "the Chairman of the country" is a direct attack on the government's manipulation of proximity altruism as a means to sustain economic growth – where the State promotes, if even tacitly, a corrupt and nepotistic economy beyond the reach of the law and positions the Party as sole guarantors of the nation's security against foreign foes. Chen's strong emphasis on charity and compassion for the weak and downtrodden speaks to all those who are unable to see beyond their immediate proximity obligations to their family, employer, and (where it suits) country, and so on, towards an independent and political consciousness that begins with the individual (see Chapter 6).

Unlike Du Bin (above), however, Chen has been made to pay a most unfortunate price for his individuality. Like every one of the breadwinners in this group (except Bin) who were either born or married into Communist Party power, Chen's father was an official, a "national, high-level cadre", meaning that Chen had a good start in life (see Chapter 7, section on Status). Chen himself trained at a college for government officials prior to joining Anshan's Environmental Protection Department; he has always been well-cultured and has a genuine passion for the environment, so had ample opportunity to succeed in his career. However, Chen did not join the Party, and neither did his university-educated wife. Not only did this stop Chen progressing, he feels, but (as he says elsewhere) the "philistines" at work forced him into early retirement at the age of 50:

> I was looked on in a bad light, and they took their revenge on me. I wasn't willing to work in this corrupt institution because this corruption ran counter to my ideology. When I was working I was extremely unhappy. There were many unfair things, and many unreasonable things. They began to look at me in a bad way, and took their revenge on me.

As a direct result, Chen's material predicament is no more comfortable than the workers analyzed at the previous chapter, perhaps even less so. Certainly he is worse off than Bin and his wife (above), who were also strapped for cash. Chen lives on a low pension and what his wife earns from her middle school teaching job; their combined monthly income is less than 4,000 CNY, just above the statistical average for an Anshan household. Chen's material situation provides an interesting example of what happens when this politically active "middle-class" disposition meets with a tighter set of economic constraints than most of the individuals and households analyzed here enjoy. An education and an intellectualization of individuality is apparently a necessary but not in itself sufficient condition to divorce Chen from the sort of morality the workers in the previous chapter espouse; a certain degree of discretionary income, if not other "objective" factors such as political affiliation, is very necessary too:

> We don't really consume much. We pursue a high quality of life, but not that kind of luxury life. By a high quality of life I mean just buying a few things; comparatively safe foods, comparatively safe clothes, etc. All the clothes I wear are cotton, just like yours, cotton, without any chemicals; this is advantageous to our health. We spend most of our money on food, and some high-quality health products; not luxury products, but high-quality health products, the sort that can be accepted, like Amway. We spend about two-thirds of our money and save about one-third or one-quarter. We really pay attention, extreme attention. The foods are all chosen very attentively. But paying attention is no use: in China everything is chaotic; paying attention is no use. In this kind of situation you have to try to find the very safest of foods, the very safest. Take vegetables for example: you've got to choose the vegetables in season, and choose

some produced not far from here. If you choose ones from far away, they may have been polluted in transit; it's only food, this can happen very easily. Even in the foods that are supposed to be safe, the actual level of pollution is uncertain; there's no way to examine this. Even the government only very rarely announces the extent of pollutants in food. We ordinary people depend on a kind of awareness, a kind of feeling; but we can't be absolutely safe; there's nothing absolutely safe. Green foods: we don't know whether we can eat them either.

Chen frequently repeats his stress on "paying attention" throughout our conversations, as if this is an indicator of his mindfulness most generally, a function of control as well as knowledge (see Chapter 7). However, at this income level, after Chen and his wife have provided for their daughter, and without the spring of youth that advantages many migrant workers, self-cultivation apart from knowledge takes the same insecure, defensive and stunted form as it did in the workers' discourse. Chen is probably aware that he is revealing cracks in the wall of the social identity he feels is rightly his, and makes such repetition on paying attention as over-compensation, as if he really is in control. Hence, although the juxtaposition of health and safety against luxury is still quite different to the workers' essentially ethical judgments, all Chen can rely on is "a kind of feeling", an "awareness" that amounts to little more than a glorification of mistrust and skepticism, the most resourceful and practical of logics common to even the most savvy of the socially low. Chen cannot set himself above the discourse as Du Bin does (above), so must lower himself to the level of a similar tactical disposition honed in marginalized peoples in order to make do (see Chapter 2).

The new woman

This analysis has concentrated on men because the males in each household examined have tended to express a trajectory through discourse more relevant to this chapter than their wives on account of their education and professional positions. By way of emphasizing the argument that China's proximity altruism morality is eclipsed here by a crystallization of formal education and knowledge, constructions of civility, and individualizing discourses of control and self-cultivation, consider now Yuan Liwen, a female journalist and managing editor of a magazine, who not only complicates this analysis in terms of gender but also age or generation.

At 39, Yuan did not experience the traumas of the Maoist era and would have been too young to remember Deng's clampdowns; ten years younger than the next youngest person examined here, she has grown up in an age of reform. However, Yuan is old enough to remember real poverty, and is thus quite different from the "youth" of today. Yuan takes a strong position in discourse from the very first moment we meet. I approach her with "So, you're a journalist?", to which she replies not: if she were a journalist she would be able to write whatever she likes; as it is, she's "the voice of the government".

Yuan's assertion of knowledge and culture emerges very early on in our meetings too. Her university-educated father was a journalist for the Party, then an editor; her brother is an internationally trained scientist. She has hundreds of books around the house: economics, history, classics. When asked what kinds of people she likes, she responds "people with knowledge", to which she adds, as if by definition, "people who have pursuits" (*you zhuiqiu*), "people relatively with taste" (*you pinwei*). Noticing Yuan's conflation of knowledge with self-cultivation (see Chapter 7), I check with her which version of "pinwei" she means for "taste": the one that has a character meaning "flavor", and which is usually used to express a "horizontal" dimension of individual taste, or the one with a character meaning "position", which is most often used to refer to forms of material consumption coded for status that can only be paid for with money – a particular "vertical" dimension. Yuan is adamant that she refers to an individuating horizontal sense of "pinwei", though clearly she values this in a vertical way too.

I then follow up with: "And, what pursuit is that exactly?" to which Yuan replies with the individualizing emphasis I expect her to give:

> Everyone's taste is different, everyone's likes are different; I prefer that kind of intelligent woman, with knowledge, the sort of knowledge you get from everything you normally come into contact with; for example, from the influence of some works of literature that you like, from the influence of some works of art that you like, from fashion magazines, from your friends around you, these kinds of formations.

I give Yuan the opportunity to further position herself: "Do works of art have an influence on you?" "Of course they do", she replies. "Of Western painters: Dalí, Raphael. Raphael's 'Virgin Mary' is my favorite painting." The difference between merely saying that you like art, and naming particular paintings, one of which is your favorite, is self-explanatory, but Yuan then volunteers that she likes painting herself: her father, apparently, was an excellent ink painter. She acquired watercolor skills from him at an early age. Yuan also likes music – "classical" – and reading. Noting Yuan's trajectory through discourse, I am unsurprised that she positions herself as civil when I ask her what kinds of people she considers superior and inferior:

> I think that amongst those around me in my life, amongst those I come into contact with, their public morals, the extent of their standards of public morals, is severely lacking. Sometimes it can be those people with a comparatively high material foundation and social status. These should be those who have a comparatively high standard of social public morals. I often regret other individuals' public morals. Some people, if you look at their success, at their social status, they can be rich, really rich, but in

actual fact their level of public morals is not equivalent to the status they possess. I feel that amongst my whole social circle I am a very self-disciplined person, someone with a comparatively strong self-control, someone with high moral awareness. My public morals are comparatively high. In these respects my awareness and reactions are comparatively high. In fact you can see this even from looking at children: the most basic is that they should cross over the road at the zebra crossing. Sometimes when I'm driving, he can see that the traffic lights are red, that it's forbidden to cross; but they will self-assuredly and self-servingly step straight out, giving not a thought for whether you are in a car or not. And in public places they'll just chuck rubbish around as they please; as far as they're concerned this is quite normal. But me, when I go out, I will take a plastic bag and bag up my litter and take it with me.

It is clear here that Yuan proffers a morality very much informed by civility, and by personal responsibility. Essentially she makes a huge investment in the unique value of the individual, also articulating this position against moneyed but uncivil types. Though she does make explicitly moral judgments elsewhere, these all have a similarly aesthetic flavor to them too. I ask her why some people are like this and others not, to which she offers all sorts of spiritual assertions integrated by constructions of self-control and cultivation:

This is complicated; I think it's related to family upbringing. I think this is really important, and it's up to your internal self-control. I think that often people with religious beliefs, they will often have a comprehensive formation and cultivation of this kind of self-control. I've always thought about Western people's religious beliefs and Eastern people's beliefs; although there are so many differences and so many differences in matters of culture, but jointly this kind of yearning for religion reflects the demands of the human self. People must have this kind of control, it is a spiritual control. I feel that as long as this person or this group is actively pressing upwards, and strives to perfect the self, then this religion is truly great.

I test Yuan's boundary management for acquiescence to the "Morality" discourse, asking: "So your moral level (*daode shuiping*) is comparatively high?" As expected, Yuan refuses this bait, replying: "I'd say I was comparatively self-controlled." Even when she raises the explicitly moral subject herself, it is perhaps not so much the social referent of morality that she values as the cultivation of individuality through it:

I think my family origin is comparatively high, so the upbringing I had from an early age was comparatively good. And in addition, I feel that in the process of developing as an intelligent individual, I was someone who made comparatively strict demands of myself. For example, it seems that

Western religion also says this: Jesus is watching you, so you can't do anything bad. I feel I am someone who really believes deeply in religion, someone who's always thinking people must do kind things. People must have a kind heart facing the world, facing life around them and their friends. Believing in religion is very important to me.

Yuan is a divorcee. When we first met I allowed myself to deliberately trip into assuming that she was married, just to see what reaction I got, voicing this assumption in just the way that most Chinese do. Yuan was proud to say that she is a single parent: "I'm an independent woman; I'm in control." She has a great many books on being a single woman, being strong and achieving as such. Although Yuan draws lots of moral boundaries regarding her ex-husband, judgments that include his not being responsible, these judgments are always explicitly underscored by the judgment that he was not responsible to himself. Yuan divorced primarily because her ex-husband did not share her ambitions and motivation for self-improvement. He was always loafing about, playing computer games, smoking and drinking, and so on (see Chapter 7). On the occasion I raise the issue of responsibility in the abstract, Yuan is adamant: "You must be responsible to yourself, and always develop yourself." Related, she is elsewhere explicitly disdainful for the notion of unmitigated self-sacrifice shaping China's proximity altruism: only by first helping herself can she help anyone else.

    This same "habitus" is further evinced in Yuan's expressed attitude to child-rearing. It is primarily the realization of individuality through her responsibilities as a mother that she finds most stimulating:

> This not only depends on my own extreme hard efforts but on the child's efforts too. I have brought her up well, I expect her to have the same emphasis on effort as me; only then will this be a success. The best thing about having a child is that it makes your life complete. First you are your parents' child. Then you are an independent individual, gradually maturing. Then you birth a new life, and you have a responsibility you cannot overlook, a responsibility that it is really not easy to give up. You must raise the child until grown, infuse them with a good upbringing, knowledge, opinions, make things convenient for them, provide them with a life environment where there is nothing to worry about, an environment to study in.

Congruent with her emphasis on the aesthetic dimension of discourse, Yuan is in some ways quite materialistic. I first met her at a top-tier gym club to which my wife and I had been offered limited access. She drives a Hyundai, the brand name of which is translated as "modern" (*xiandai*) in China. She has extremely white skin, obviously investing a great deal in skin care. Though she makes judgments intended to show that she has the ability to use grooming products appropriately, she thinks it is bad taste to be thought of as materialistic, repeatedly making efforts to avoid being documented in these terms:

> Natural is beautiful, and it feels comfortable. I really don't like that kind of magnificent stuff and people who get really painstakingly done up. I like comparatively natural. As long as it suits, and is natural and comfortable, then that's enough. Many women are done up like a flower, with make-up done really thickly. You can see through them on the street.

Yuan asserts a "nature" that would be spoilt by any form of affectation, but it is against the "thickness" of other people's make-up that Yuan positions herself, not the wearing of make-up per se. The nature she advocates is therefore not quite as natural as it first appears (see Chapter 2). Though she claims purity for herself, all she can actually refer to is a more acute ability to distinguish between proper and improper applications of make-up (see Chapter 3). Yuan probably feels the need to appeal to nature in order to promote misrecognition of her privileged perspective, because having a privileged perspective in the first place is somewhat contrary to the Universalist logic of civility in which she is so invested.

Of further significance here, is that Yuan avoids referring to herself with any explicitly vertical metaphors such as "high" or "high-taste", though that is what she of course implies throughout: though her every "horizontal" assertion of individuality is also always attended by an "upper-range" positioning on a "vertical" axis, too (see Chapter 7, section on Status, p.131), Yuan knows that to assert herself too explicitly in this regard would be distasteful. Her legitimate taste – that is to say, her individual capacity to judge correctly rather than an explicitly moralistic measure of her character – is deflected and deferred, accruing in direct proportion to her non-explicit self-depreciation, an artful and illusory device quite ironically the opposite of the rather more crude and egotistical boast informing China's proximity altruism climate: she is legitimately tasteful not simply because she says so (indeed she does not), but because everyone but her apparently says so.

Of final significance here is that Yuan evinces absolutely none of the sociable characteristics supposedly "innate" to people of the region: this is of course further congruent with her general distancing from Anshan, since she likes to stress she is from Shanghai even though she left there some 25 years ago. Though Yuan gives voluminously of her personal character in social interaction, she once more balances this with a large measure of civility and personal control. She doesn't play mahjong, although her mother plays all the time: "It's unsuitable for me." In these latter, most feminine of respects, Yuan shares much with Zheng (see above), who also has a professional job at an approximate level, but who is considerably older, born and bred in Anshan, and lacks the strength of independence that is somewhat the condition and point of Yuan's positioning in discourse.

Figure 10.1 New woman. Photography by Gao Yingchuan

With Yuan, then, the discourse of distinction is laid bare in the form of its legitimate instantiation. She takes from the entire discourse exactly what she needs to make it her own. Yet, even as she articulates a highly individualized and individualizing discourse, her narratives share a structural homology with many of the other professionals analyzed here. Without any obvious organizing intention, that is to say, and although these professionals assert themselves in very diverse ways, these individuals are shown to assert themselves in ways structurally shared with other individuals of approximate objective positions in society vis-à-vis ways shared by individuals from very different objective positions. Even then, amongst a relatively disparate range of individuals, who unlike the migrants and the workers already analyzed do not readily voice membership of a specific collective, the act of asserting individuality is shown to be structured by systematic recourse to the very same discursive axioms upon which individuals from very different objective positions in society draw, just in very different ways. Thus, where individual agency is most alive, social structure is most immanent, and where social structure is most immanent, individual agency is most alive.

Conclusion

My research has developed a partial "grammar" for understanding how individuality in contemporary China is structured and generated. Based on a critical discourse analysis of ethnographic data collected in Anshan City, Liaoning Province, between 2005 and 2009, I have disaggregated the most elementary structures of individuation in their situational inflections and pursued the further regularities and modes structuring their instantiation, effectively working out post-structuralism's inspiration to chart a methodological third way between individual agency and social structure in the assertion of identity. By drawing out the fallacy inherent in conceptualizing identities in terms of division rather than in terms of relations, and of individualities as things-in-themselves rather than as socio-historical processes, I have sought to expose the connections between the skeptical and reductionist roots of logical positivism and the crude Orientalist categories with which Chinese consumers are stereotyped in social psychology-inspired management literatures. My analysis made no assumptions about the nature of Chinese culture, but was rather based strictly on the analysis of real-life data and the reconstruction of the first discursive principles by which my informants negotiated their relationships with the world. What, then, do we now know about Chinese individuals and their consumption of discourse?

We now know that Chinese individuals make recourse to linguistic metaphors in order to claim various forms of ontological purity for themselves, but that such ideals are fundamentally flawed. While some Chinese more or less successfully monopolize the strategic discursive positions necessary to make others subject, the majority are especially skilful trespassers of established categorical boundaries. Whether expressed explicitly, through irony or cynicism, in the flaunting of counterfeit products and brands, or through the "tricks" by which people get ahead of their contemporaries without getting caught, the secret is out in China: purity is an ideal to be exploited only in the act of its assertion. Similarly understood by rural migrants as they attempt to integrate into cities characterized by claims to purity denied to them, by laid-off workers nostalgic for socialism's eroding institutions, or by entrepreneurs exorcising their attachment to China's agricultural past by consuming "coarse grain" cereals in the countryside, Chinese individuals are acutely aware of how different constructions of truth and reality can be manipulated for competing yet possibly even converging ends.

Chinese individuals contest the validity of subject positions by asserting the value of different kinds of knowledge and rules. Some Chinese emphasize formal education, but we have seen how objectively very different Chinese who do not enjoy access to formal schooling share an almost routine alternative emphasis on practicability and a distinctly entrepreneurial grain of striving. In exactly this way, Chinese individuals' consumption of discourse has a structuring effect in society. In exactly this way, too, Chinese individuals of all sorts intuitively grasp that where the imposition of law and governance stands in strained proportion to individual resourcefulness, as it does in China, the capacity to subvert dominant discourses can be indicative of legitimate individual agency, forming solidarity with others. Through symbolic insubordination to forms of surveillance and discipline, and through the personal risks and local transgressions by which gaps in insufficiently formed official institutions are created and plugged, China is a place where individuals' remarkable capacity to improvise on their objective circumstances represents the nation's greatest hope for a future of better governance.

Chinese individuals are divided by different understandings of where the boundary between intimacy and social distance lies. Where individuals "belong" in this matrix depends largely on their age, gender, and education level, but it also depends on context: the same Chinese individuals might at different times variously denigrate others for spitting in public, share a laugh over loose wind with their familial intimates, and treat new acquaintances to excesses of generosity primarily as a means of demonstrating magnanimity to existing buddies. Discourses of intimacy and individual privacy nevertheless function to structure Chinese society across these complex manifestations. Some Chinese appeal to constructions of "civility" as functions of their social aspirations yet betray an insufficient understanding of the individualizing nature to this discourse; others differently confuse the same prophylactic with private ownership and brute materialism. I have argued that civility and privacy are discourses that while excluding others equally offer Chinese individuals "universally accessible" opportunities for self-advancement, even though I recognize that this is also to support a particularly individualized form of social hierarchy in the here and now.

Chinese individuals' practices cannot easily be separated into "emotive" and "rational" expressions of individuality. Certainly Anshan is a place where people of the city define their community by reference to the sense in which, they imagine, an emotionally generous modality of social exchange obtains as the "natural" result of geographical proximity and personal familiarity. However, my analyses have shown that certain types of "emotional" stimuli become traditional or habitual actions in Anshan, "rules" that have to be followed, so that individuals can often be observed to attempt to take over responsibility for things beyond their actual influence or capacity in order to consolidate social ties; correspondingly, "beneficiaries" may acknowledge the "credit" offered by confirming that such "sacrifice" is unnecessary, in which case a mutual "debt" or pledge remains to be resolved through future exchanges. To the extent that the "rule" "governing" this mode of interaction is ultimately inexpressible, since the principle itself does not conform to any explicitly "rational" logic, individuals in Anshan intuitively understand that the correct action to take in any circumstance is the reaction that, at least superficially, maximizes potential for sentiment-based fellow-feeling.

Chinese individuals, indeed, accrue moral worth through reciprocal processes of exchange. While Chinese moral discourse is highly altruistic, individuals' consumption of this discourse is often highly self-assertive. The same obligations that bind Chinese closely together, moreover, also profoundly separate them except when stimulated to unite against foreign powers. In these ways, we have exposed the differences between moral discourse in China and the contemporary West. Indeed, if we already understand social interaction to be inherently political, we may now admit that where the contemporary West makes all-pervasive claims of democratic egalitarianism, often vis-à-vis China's "authoritarianism", and where the Chinese state foments a popular rejection of such "Western values", moral discourse in China is the result of particular political forces which actively conspire to deny Chinese individuals intrinsic worth. As a corollary, many Chinese individuals are deeply invested in reproducing this essentialist cultural discourse, thus effectively making themselves complicit in denying themselves the opportunity to enshrine individual agency in politics. Moral discourse is changing rapidly in China, however, and we have seen evidence of many individuals who are willing to express the yearning for a more universal basis for value judgment.

For at bottom, Chinese individuals are just like "us", just with situationally specific differences to how they go about things. The idea that Chinese individuals can be authors of their own fates is latent with the same provocative power that this idea has in all human contexts. Though it is ultimately impossible for Chinese individuals to escape their own perspectives on the world, the realization that discourse can be stretched to anywhere is latent with the same radical capacity to empower individuals in China as it is everywhere – freedom in constraint. In this way, my research has shown that Chinese individuals appreciate how various modalities of practice which might seem passive can be equally as valid as more obviously active modes of practice: discourses of self-determination which might seem quite separate from each other – dynamic versus stabilizing, deliberative versus impulsive, conscious versus unconscious, fated versus free, and so on, are all expressions of the same existential agency. These are all expressions of individual agency making sense of its projection within the world.

All these findings have ramifications for Orientalism, of course, as well as for the actual practice of doing research; indeed, it is not so much that there is something quintessentially "relational" about China that would dispose Chinese individuals to appreciate the flexibility of essentialist concepts. Quite the contrary: China is a place in such rapid and violent flux that individuals

have little choice but to become highly adept at subverting essentialist allusions; and this, despite the sense in which China, as a nation among nations,
is deeply invested in the myth of its own originating foundation, the extension
of this purity over time, and its unfortunately politicized consanguineous
manifestation. As researchers, academic or applied, far from trying to make
Chinese individuals fit our own essentialist agendas, as scholars on both
the left and right of the social sciences are differently inclined to do, Chinese
individuals' skills at turning their objective circumstances to their personal
advantage should inspire us to admire them just as they are. On this basis, it
seems quite wrong to deny Chinese individuals the agency collectively to
determine their own futures, and essentialists who blindly embrace misguided
cultural -isms should examine their role in preventing this.

My later analyses have shown not only how the instantiation of individuality is informed by the particular discourses my research abstracted from
the "language" of social distinction, but also how the "grammar" of those
discourses' consumption has a structuring effect on society in Anshan too:
objectively different individuals have been shown to draw upon exactly the
same discursive axioms in order to assert themselves, just in different ways,
and those ways have themselves been shown to be functions of structured
dispositions to consume discourse in those particular ways.

Specifically, my analysis of rural migrants (Chapter 8) has shown how discourse can be consumed in ways that make its key axioms result in a highly
"individualized" crystallization, where the emphasis is firmly on making your
own way through life, resourceful striving, independence of achievement, and
so on, but ways that are nevertheless structurally shared across a fluid community of similar individuals and openly articulated as such in ways that
bring such individuals together. Further, my analysis of a range of urban
workers (Chapter 9) shows how discourse can be consumed in ways that
though unique to the individual by definition are strongly characterized by an
emphasis on "collectivized" themes, such as the belonging to a particular
social category or situational group, traditional points of moral reference, and
the having of one's way through life determined by others, themes that were
reiterated with remarkable homogeneity at the structural level across a range
of objectively different individuals. Finally, my analysis of a range of professionals
from both the private and public sectors (Chapter 10) shows how discourse can
be consumed in highly differentiated ways which nevertheless unite individuals at
a structural level, but where those individuals are otherwise disparate, do not
know each other, and share very little consciousness of belonging to a group
of individuals or social category, where structural unity is articulated primarily by reference to those other individuals and types of individuals which
these individuals equally are not.

Thus, the dichotomous binaries that positivism generates are shown to
be obsolete: "individualism" versus "collectivism" just doesn't cut it. For
where we allow the capacity of individual agency to consume social structure
to be our paramount analytical principle, and find instances of self-assertion to

be informed not only by particular prior discursive structures but also by socially conditioned ways of consuming those structures too, not only can we conclude that Chinese individuals cannot be as over-determined by the "cultural collective" as Orientalist essentialists imagine, but also that Chinese individuals cannot be as self-determining as the methodological individualist's instrumentally rational actor theoretic would suggest either.

It may seem tautological that my analysis finds that individuals consume the axioms that I had already abstracted in order to assert themselves, but it was made clear in Chapter 1, and again in Chapter 2, that because identity is the consumed product of the interrelation between structure and individual agency, only tautologies are truly true, the dynamics of this interrelation otherwise impossible to capture in language. So if my argument takes a circular form, this is to be expected. Indeed, that tautology – that identity is produced in the interrelation of structure and agency – runs all the way through my entire argument: that is the thesis. What my research has done is to go beyond the postmodern roots of this argument and apply it to contemporary China, disaggregating it in terms of its patterns of manifestation and reconstructing its paradigms to create new knowledge about the way individuality is asserted in the world. There may, of course, be other axioms which this research has neglected to abstract, but enough has been done to show that those it has abstracted are important structural features of the instantiation of individuality in the context from which they were distilled.

Yet the thesis is ultimately that individuals cannot be made to fit into these axiomatic categories: that they can't be classified, atomized, and so on, since they are themselves the agents by which these categorizations are produced. The discourses, indeed, are not perfect in their separation – there is conceptual overlap between them – a fact which itself stands testimony to this argument. However, the process of abstracting them is a highly useful way of interrogating discourse, and of further examining how their consumption functions to structure society. Of course, from a positivist perspective it may seem as if the entire exercise is pointless, for in the end all that is left is the instantiation, but this is exactly where we should hope to be: langue crystallizing into parole, to borrow terms from Structuralism's godfather Ferdinand de Saussure. Although the result enables us to see what is there, what we would expect to find, nothing especially out of the ordinary even, it is precisely by doing this that we can show that there is a structural conditioning that influences the instantiation of individuality above and beyond the autonomy of individual agency, an ordered and ordering force which orders self and society. Indeed, the very fact that we are able to see the links between these discourses and their practice, that we are able to follow their permutations as they inflect and evolve into each other, and yet it is the same logic that is consumed, is evidence of the existence of these discourses: not as things in themselves, but as nevertheless ontologically necessary features of negotiating social interaction.

Yet, though circular in this sense, the research is of course not in another, because it proves its methodological point with an analysis that adds up to much more than the sum of its constitutive parts. The research of course always demanded that readers expect its form to be open-ended, for it was made clear at Chapter 1 that research which offers a "final signified" can only be banal; indeed, my analysis at Chapter 2 which showed the self-referential ambitions of truth and identity to be unsustainable demanded that readers expect its ultimate meaning to derive not from its "conclusion" as such, but from their original consumption of the entire ethnography. Those positivists who believe research should have a conclusion which somehow says everything the study has had to say again, so that readers in fact need only read the conclusion to appreciate everything that the research had to say, will therefore be thoroughly disappointed here. This is a very good sign, for where research does not have such a single, linear conclusion it means that there is the very likely possibility that something genuinely interesting has been said about the world in the process. However, we can nevertheless, of course, relate the "findings" to the argument per se, as we are doing here.

My analyses have shown that individual agencies are both autonomous and co-conditioning. There are, in the end, only these two principles. However, my research has value beyond this meta-level conclusion: that which has been explicated in the preceding chapters. That is to say, that by demonstrating the almost limitless capacity of individual agents to take prior discourses and bend them to suit their projects of individuality, not only does this research broach an entirely new way of thinking about the structuration of Chinese society, it also represents an interpretive platform for engaging Chinese individuals in their consumption. My research furnishes its consumers with a set of discursive axioms and regularities, not a finite list of prescriptions but an active grammar, which taken together can be used to predict individuals' consumption from a range of objective factors (such as age, gender, education), and to predict from individuals' consumption a range of correspondingly likely objective factors. The individual per se remains almost impossible to predict by definition, but where we have not only the langue, but also its "transformative grammar" (Chomsky 1965), we have the tools to make insightful predictions into the way that individuality is asserted within social contexts or situations of practice beyond those examined here.

Circular and non-circular at the same time, like all truly political acts, my research has consistently tried to have everything both ways. Like all truly political acts, my research hasn't stood for anything, except against other things. Where it has appeared to stand for something, it has only really stood for the one thing that has to be: the instantiation of individual agency. For once one has grasped the fact that an individual's standing depends on what that individual is standing upon, there is nowhere solid left to stand, so you keep moving. The research has never seen itself primarily as taking up an easily identifiable position any more than it has seen itself as accumulating towards some singular grand conclusion. Rather, it has seen itself primarily as parsing down, splitting, interrogating that which is obviously variant for its invariant element, and then of that invariant element for that which is much less obviously variant about it. It has pulled apart things that might be best left together, and pulled together things that perhaps make most sense apart. It has spliced discursive logics meticulously, first apart, then together, looking for their internal difference, their points of overlap, reconstructing the internal operations of culture, never taking anything for granted except the fact that the grounds for the ontology of individuality it sought would be there to be seen.

Recognizing that the operations it sought to elicit would stand in direct relation to the operations necessary to elicit them, my research stood primarily on what was seen and heard in the field, rather than on what had already been written. In the process, I have boldly tread across much hallowed academic ground, either explicitly or implicitly, refusing at every turn to alight where other more plodding literatures have lingered, settling anywhere only long enough to allow that position to be itself undermined by the individual agents who informed my enquiry. Thus, though I have at times seemed to lean towards the Right with my emphasis on individual agency, enough should have been done to show that agency is itself determined by particular discursive determinants to satisfy the Left that my research does not harbor a rational actor theorist beneath its interpretivist garb. Indeed, it is only the sway of capitalism on science and the autocratic Chinese State on which the research has come down hard, both for denying individual agency. And rationality has been subject to a significant deconstruction in itself. Certainly I have pushed my analyses towards the edge of meaningfulness in the course of articulating this third way between revolution and evolution, but that's where research is most interesting, the clarity immanent in the chaos.

Overall, then, by looking at the field, and the data collected from it, and by objectifying not only my object but also the relation between myself and that object, my research has found that the grounds for an ontology of individuality in China are simply different inflections of the same discursive apparatus that structures my own mind. That is to say, I have found in my own capacity to explore language, practice, and therefore thought, the very same structures that Chinese consumers use to assert themselves as individuals, thus proving beyond all doubt that Chinese individuals are as agentive, and as individually agentive, as individual agents everywhere. In all sorts of ways, my research has shown that Chinese individuals cannot possibly be the gormless people conjured by Western commentators' objectifications of them: neither the selfless automatons as which Orientalists stereotype them, nor the helpless prisoners of more powerful people's projects for which the social science Left would have us feel sorry. I have found Chinese to be particularly eager to be individuals, to assert themselves as such, to determine their own lives, adept at drawing symbolic boundaries, and so on, even when doing so might also be understood as articulating assimilation or collectivism. I have comprehensively shown that Chinese individuals demand to be treated as having distinct personalities even as they seek intimacy and belonging with their fellows, and even as they conform to the socially constructed rules of social interaction. Though they might in many ways be said to be rather traditional, they are not bound by tradition: unequivocally, they have been shown to have the agency to take all such prior rules and turn them to their own purposes, even where those rules intend to rule this out.

Indeed, just like the agency of the analysis, I have shown Chinese individuals to have the agency to be two things at once – as disposed to take what they need to assert themselves as individuals from other individuals around them as are agents everywhere. Both free to act and at the same time conditioned by objective and intersubjective circumstances, by making their agency to balance this tension as they go about social practice primary, my research has shown how Chinese individuals are human: just like "us" but with locally generated cultural differences. These differences have been demonstrably profound at times, but ultimately it is the familiarity my research has found with Chinese individuals that is the most striking, a finding that points to that which is prior to social construction, that biological and evolutionary capacity to be structurated by discourse which unites individuals everywhere regardless of culture.

At a more straightforwardly sociological, or shall we say political, level, my overall analysis also draws out the ways in which Chinese society is structured in terms of objective factors such as age and gender. There is also a very clear hierarchical or at least "vertical" structuration in what might be understood as "class" terms, which may be usefully related to more conventional sociological studies. My research has somewhat taken these axes for granted from the start, since where every instantiation of individuality is held to signify in both a "vertical" and a "horizontal" dimension, it is only to be expected that society will take a form marked by degrees of legitimacy. What is perhaps most interesting about my results is the way that the "vertical" structuring in my data conforms to the extent to which individuals are individualized as per the processes of "individualization" described by those literatures of that name discussed in Chapter 1 (Yan 2009a; Halskov-Hansen and Svarverud 2010); that is, a structure determined by individuals' capacity to effect themselves in response to shifting discursive and institutional frameworks for processing responsibility and risk (where the two are understood as related), which demand that they be individuals.

My analyses of entrepreneurs, of youthful rural migrants, and the more progressive individuals amongst my professional informants show that discursive competency in the contemporary era emerges as a highly individualized conflation of knowledge (education), civility (a behavioral value code), and the narrative logic of personality (self-cultivation). The consumption of this conflation, moreover, is shown to be discursively opposed to those more explicitly inclusive logics of moral character (family, proximity, etc.), and innately sociable characteristics, both of which, as argued in Chapters 5 and 6, are internally defined by reference to the Socialist past and the collectivized/agricultural economy. Therefore, my research shows how discursive axioms such as formal education, age and generation, proximity to the State-owned enterprise structure and proximity to the land (or rather the non-proximity of these), crystallize to produce a more individualized, reflexive, and existential subject most immanent in those sectors of society most adapting to the demands of State-market transition and the responsibilities this brings. This is perhaps somewhat obvious given the meta-narrative of China's opening up and market reform, but it is all the more significant that I find this diachronic emphasis from a synchronic study which in no way assumed this at the outset.

Perhaps the most striking finding was that for individuals who were on the whole younger, better educated, more competitive at work, and had higher incomes, consumption of discourse became altogether more individualized and aesthetic in ways that eclipsed ethically tinged iterations of China's "proximity altruism" moral discourse. This was a matter of realizing individuality within and in relation to shifting discursive parameters in a way that testified to the political agency of the emergent "middle class", and would suggest that when Chinese individuals transcend the current fascination with urbanization and consumerism they will increasingly demand equal stakes in democratic political reform, where the risks and responsibilities of an individualized society are matched in equal measure.

Space permitting, I could have allowed the axiomatic discourses of my analysis to be crystallized across a whole range of other fields, further drawing out the grammar of the instantiation. A promising avenue for future inquiry would be to examine a range of young urban adults, including the offspring of those mature adults examined in Chapters 9 and 10, to see how these synchronic structures map out onto diachronic processes of social reproduction; that is, to ask how far young people inherit dispositions to consume social structure in particular ways and how far they make these their own. Another fruitful area of inquiry would be to examine how these discursive axioms are inflected in their consumption by individuals of a wealthier and more powerful persuasion than those examined in Chapter 10, a project that could be broached in tandem with a fuller exposition of the Materialism and Status discourses in which the others are realized. Indeed, once those discourses are more fully expounded, there would be increased scope for analyzing how the grammar thus far articulated crystallizes in consumption that is explicitly paid for alone. However, this latter strategy would be increasingly only to show, the analysis becoming almost repetitive simply in order to make its point, the conceptual roots of the findings already sufficiently laid out here.

At that point, however, there would be further scope for examining how the judgment of the individual as such and the judgment of the social classification of the individual are arrived at each by reference to each other, as articulated at Status (see Chapter 7), by examining the interrelationship between the two words for "taste" on which my analysis came to focus: those two words, often confused in their contemporary usage, both of which are pronounced "pinwei", but which are written differently; the first of which has a character meaning "position" and alludes "vertically" to forms of subjectivity that can only be paid for with money, and the second of which has a different character meaning "flavor" and alludes "horizontally" to forms of unique individual taste.[1] Beyond this, my findings may be usefully applied to extant surveys of consumption in China, levering the analytical power developed here to examine why researchers have reached particular conclusions or have neglected to do so, to explain statistical anomalies and other irregularities in the data, and so on.

Indeed, in this latter respect, my research could be used to fuel all manner of further enquiries, relating its active grammar to research on contemporary China most broadly, stimulating further studies in its own right. Further drawn out, the grammar developed here, if carefully and critically applied, might even be used to inform the design of quantitative surveys intended to measure the size and form of consumer markets in China, though it is doubtful if an appropriately objective measure could be agreed upon to operate this undertaking for reasons given throughout.

Notes

1 Introduction

1 Elizabeth Croll, a notable exception to this rule, was gracious enough to take advice from leading China market segmentation expert Berndt Schmitt (Croll 2006).
2 A "form of life" was: "The underlying consensus of linguistic and non-linguistic behavior, assumptions, practices, traditions, and natural propensities which humans, as social beings, share with one another, and which is presupposed in the language they use; language is woven into that pattern of human activity and character, and meaning is conferred on its expressions by the shared outlook and nature of its users" (Wittgenstein 1953: 88).
3 Anshan's official GDP for 2009 was 192 billion CNY renminbi, rising from 3.8 billion in 1980 (Anshan City Statistics and Planning Bureau). Total consumer expenditure was 46 billion CNY renminbi, rising from 24 billion in 2006 (Anshan City Statistics and Planning Bureau).

2 Authenticity

1 Lacan's re-reading of Freud's psychoanalysis is highly relevant here. "Consumption" was understood to actually divorce agency from the "Real" world even as sign-objects were made absolutely "Other" and individual agency was "subjectivized" as "Self". Rather than "revealing" or "representing" truths about the "Real", language was seen to "fill" a "lack" (the presence of an absence,) a solidifying spatial metaphor which in my view reflects Lacan's pragmatist belief in a Realist ontology after language has collapsed on itself.
2 One of my early fieldwork techniques was to experiment with the idea of "definition-by-opposition", a key Structuralist notion (Sanders 2004), by asking respondents to enter on the left-hand side of a piece of paper their comments about a "person of good taste" (*you pinweide ren*), and on the right-hand side their comments about a "person without good taste" (*meiyou pinweide ren*). The exercise was initiated due to a confusion I had noticed in the contemporary use of two words for "taste", both of which are pronounced "pinwei", but each of which is written differently, one substituting a character meaning "flavor" for a character meaning "position". The exercise used the "pinwei" meaning "flavor" but informants clearly interpreted this in terms of both "horizontal" and "vertical", or hierarchical, senses of "position" too. The results of this exercise hardly appear in the final manuscript, but the process greatly informed my analysis of the other, so much richer data gathered through less overt methods as the research progressed.
3 Briefly, for non-specialist readers, the "Long March" was a massive retreat of the Communist armies from Jiangxi and Fujian provinces in southeast China to Yan'an in northern-central Shaanxi Province via a hugely circuitous route through

southwestern China, pursued all the way by the armies of the Kuomingtang in 1934–35. The retreat has become mythologized in Chinese popular/political culture for the extremely spartan conditions the soldiers experienced; most died en route.
4 Relevant parts of Hanser's analysis can be found at pages 123, 134–35, 140–45 of her 2008 book.
5 Some of my other published works have explored the sociological implications of this "reappraisal" of the discursive balance between "urban" and "rural" in greater depth (see, in particular, Griffiths *et al.* 2010). Beth Notar also makes a relevant argument in her book *Displacing Desire: Travel and Popular Culture in China* (2006), which tracks the Orientalist pursuits of Western backpackers in China's southwestern Yunnan Province: the "Lonely Planeteers" seek out a cultural authenticity to counter modernity's alienation, but since they all follow the same well-beaten tracks, the "Orient" they encounter is only ever a hybrid version tailored for them for comfort by profiteering locals.

3 Knowledge

1 70% of people surveyed by Xinhua news agency considered these "grey skills" important on the job market (Bai 2010).
2 Recent research suggests that nearly all the contemporary Chinese economic elite can be traced back through family trees to the old land-based ruling class prior to the Communist Revolution in 1949 and to those who were revolutionaries (i.e. in the Communist Party) at that time. Very few of the contemporary economic elite have family backgrounds that do not fit into either of these categories; indeed, a striking number have antecedents which can be found in both (Goodman 2010).

4 Civility

1 See: "Say thank you to people who serve you" (*dui wei ni fuwu de ren shuosheng 'xiexie'*). *Jiefang Ribao* August 13, 2007. www.godpp.gov.cn/ddjs_2007-8/13/content_10839419.
2 This maxim means that a woman both wants to be an alpha sexual predator but also wants to hang out a sign or memorial archway as a testament to her moral goodness. Before the Qing dynasty these *paifang* were set up to educate people about advanced moral deeds.
3 See, for example, "Rang paidui houche chengwei xiguan" [Let queuing behind the car in front become the norm]. *Beijing Ribao* 27 November 2006. www.godpp.gov.cn/ddjs_/2006-11/27/content_86221168.htm; or "Chengche jianduyuan shaole, zijue paidui de duole" [Beijing: Bus boarding queue monitors have decreased; people are queuing of their own accord]. *Beijing Ribao* 26 February 2007.
4 QQ is an online instant messaging service used by virtually all young Chinese, with their QQ name being their user name.

5 Sociability

1 Aaker and Schmitt (2001) maintain that because Chinese consumers have an "interdependent self-construal" (this is taken for granted on the basis of earlier research), they will be "more likely to hold attitudes that demonstrate points of similarity with their peers", and be "less likely to hold attitudes that allow them to express that they are distinct from others" than US consumers. These same researchers then demonstrate the rare sensitivity to admit that although individuals with different "self-construals" (i.e. "independent" versus "interdependent" in their terms) have different modes of asserting the self, "a singular role of self expression [nevertheless] exists" in both cases (Aaker and Schmitt 2001: 1), which is of course

nothing short of admitting that the "collectivists" are individuals after all! In reaching this conclusion the researchers acknowledge that the questionnaires preferred for data collection in their field have a limited capacity to capture modes of expressing the self that emphasize "assimilation" rather than "differentiation", effectively further confessing that the problem is not just that quantitative survey instruments are poorly disposed to capture Chinese people's "relational" social ethics, but social psychology's entire Cartesian approach to social science.

2 It is not normal to sit on the floor in Anshan. That we would do so on this occasion had evidently been decided in advance of my arriving, by hosts who seemed to feel that "getting down" in a very informal way (not at all like the more formalized setting familiar to the region's Korean restaurants) served to maximize our sociability and iron out any perceived status difference between us.

3 To my wife's credit, I was on doctor's orders to avoid alcohol at the time.

4 The almost subconscious overlap of animal metaphors pertinent to the "Civil Behavior" construct here demonstrates that these structures work at meta-levels of analysis also.

6 Morality

1 *Zuoren*, means "to be a person": the term invokes the sense in which moral value refers only to the individual's actual social relations in China, rather than to a quality (supposedly) inherent in the individual, as is the case in many Western cultures. I tried to avoid using the term "my fieldwork" since it is so highly loaded with "proximity altruism" connotations and I did not want to overtly influence my informants' narratives.

2 Lucien Pye made the argument that the collective "we", which would be *zanmen* rather than *women*, was *tu*, native in the sense of being rooted and bordered, and thus by definition prevented China from modernizing.

3 Wittgenstein's (1953) notion of "family resemblances" is relevant at a structural level here.

4 Indeed, we might note that the penalties for offences such as drug-trafficking and financial crimes in China, even for rape and murder, are precisely related to the amount of narcotics involved, money embezzled or number of people harmed, in "altruistic" style.

7 Personality

1 Though we are very close to Bourdieu's concept of "habitus" here, I reserve that term to describe individuals' configurations of discourse, or the trajectories they chart through their consumption of discourse, in my later chapters on practice. The logic I am outlining here is much more consciously intentional than Bourdieu's "habitus", closer to Foucault's concept of "technologies of the self" (Foucault 1988).

2 Historian Mark Elvin (1985) tracks this self-cultivating thread of discourse across the philosophy of Mencius (*Mengzi*), Buddhism and others. Though his argument is historical, and very different to my synchronic approach, Elvin shares my conviction that it is a mistake to think of Chinese culture only as collectivist, Confucian, and opposed to individual agency.

3 Though I am not concerned to hermeneutically reconstruct the "origins" of these threads of discourse, again, Mark Elvin's discussion of Buddhist rebirth is relevant here (Elvin 1985).

4 With this type of "control", the "done thing" or "taken for granted" modus operandi (cf. Heidegger's notion of "ready-to-hand"), my analysis is coming much closer to Bourdieu's concept of "habitus". Again, I reserve that term to describe individual trajectories through discourse, in the final chapters of my book.

10 Professionals

1 The term "engineer" can be confusing in the Chinese context. It may refer to consulting civil engineers or "mechanic" as it might do in the West, but also to "scientist" in a sense that was not unfamiliar in the Soviet Union. Some cadres refer to themselves as "professors", others as "engineers".

Conclusion

1 On *pinwei*, see also the second endnote at Chapter 2.

Bibliography

Aaker, Jennifer and Bernd Schmitt (2001) "Culture Dependent Assimilation and Differentiation of the Self", *Journal of Cross-Cultural Psychology* 32(5) September: 561–76.

Access China (2010) "CHAMPS: China's Fastest Growing Cities. A Report from the Economist Intelligence Unit's 'Access China' Service". www.eiu.com/public/access china/marketing.aspx.

Agger, Ben (1992) *Discourse of Domination: From the Frankfurt School to Postmodernism.* Evanston, Illinois: Northwestern University Press.

Alvesson, Mats and Dan Karreman (2000) "Varieties of Discourse: On the Study of Organizations through Discourse Analysis", *Human Relations* 53: 1125.

Ambler, Tim and Morgen Witzel (2000) *Doing Business in China.* London and New York: Routledge.

Anagnost, Ann (2004) "The Corporeal Politics of Quality (Suzhi)", *Public Culture* 16(2): 189–208.

Andreas, Joel (2002) "Battling Over Political and Cultural Power in the Chinese Cultural Revolution", *Theory and Society* 31(4) August: 463–519.

Appadurai, Arjun (1988) *The Social Life of Things: Commodities in Cultural Perspective.* Cambridge: Cambridge University Press.

Archer, Margaret (1995) *Realist Social Theory: The Morphogenetic Approach.* Cambridge: Cambridge University Press.

——(1996) *Culture and Agency: The Place of Culture in Social Theory*, revised edition. Cambridge: Cambridge University Press.

Ardener, Edwin (1971) *Social Anthropology and Language. Introduction to Social Anthropology and Language*, ASA Monographs 10. London and New York: Routledge.

——(1989) *The Voice of Prophecy and Other Essays.* ed. Malcolm Chapman. Oxford: Blackwell.

Arnould, Eric J. and Craig J. Thompson (2005) "Consumer Culture Theory (CCT): Twenty Years of Research", *Journal of Consumer Research* 31 March: 868–82.

Arrow, Kenneth J. (1994) "Methodological Individualism and Social Knowledge", *American Economic Review* 84(2): 1–9.

Bai, Xue (2010) "Can You drink? Play cards? 70% of People Think 'Grey Skills' are Important on the Job Market", [Xue hejiu? Dapai? Qicheng ren renwei zhichang "huise jineng" zhongyao]. *Xinhua News Agency* 9 November 2010. news.xinhuanet. com/edu/2010–11/09/c_12751764.htm.

Bao, Yeqing, Chenting Su, and Zheng Zhou (2003) "Face Consciousness and Risk Aversion: Do they Affect Consumer Decision-making?" *Psychology and Marketing* 20(8): 733–55.

Barmé, Geremie R. (1999) *In the Red: On Contemporary Chinese Culture.* New York: Columbia University Press.

Barth, Frederick, ed. (1969) *Ethnic Groups and Boundaries: the Social Organization of Cultural Difference.* Oslo: Universitetsforlaget. London: Allen & Unwin.

Barthes, Roland (1972) *Mythologies*, trans. Annette Lavers. London: Cape.

Baudrillard, Jean (1981) *For a Critique of the Political Economy of the Sign.* St Louis and New York: Telos Press.

——(1994) *Simulacra and Simulation.* trans. Sheila Faria Glaser. Ann Arbor: University of Michigan Press.

——(1996 [1968]) *The System of Objects.* trans. James Benedict. London: Verso.

——(1998 [1970]) *The Consumer Society: Myths and Structures.* trans. G. Ritzer. London: Sage Publication.

Bauman, Zygmunt (2000) *The Individualized Society.* Polity Press.

Beck, Ulrich (1992 [1986]) *Risk Society: Towards a New Modernity*, originally published in German. London: Sage.

Beck, Ulrich and Elisabeth Beck-Gernsheim (2002) *Individualization: Institutionalized Individualism and its Social and Political Consequences.* London: Sage.

Beck, Ulrich, Anthony Giddens, and Scott Lash (1994) *Reflexive Modernisation: Politics, Tradition and Aesthetics in the Modern Social Order.* Cambridge: Polity Press.

Beck, Ulrich and Elisabeth Beck-Gernsheim (2001) *Individualization: Institutionalized Individualism and its Social and Political Consequences.* Sage Publications.

Becker, Jasper (2000) *The Chinese.* London: John Murray.

Belk, Russell W. (1988) "Possessions and the Extended Self", *Journal of Consumer Research* 15(2): 139–67.

Benjamin, Walter (1968) *The Work of Art in the Age of its Technological Reproduction, and Other Writings on Media.* Cambridge, Mass: Harvard University Press.

Berger, Peter L. and Thomas Luckmann (1967) *The Social Construction of Reality.* Anchor Books.

Bian, Yanjie (2002) "Chinese Social Stratification and Social Mobility", *Annual Review of Sociology* 28: 91–116.

Bishop, Matthew (2009) "One Yuan, One Vision: Jet Li talks to Matthew Bishop and Michael Green", *Intelligent Life Magazine* Summer. www.moreintelligentlife.com/content/matthewbishop/one-yuan-one-vision (accessed October 2009).

Blackman, Carolyn (2000) *China Business: The Rules of the Game.* Crows Nest, Australia: Allan & Unwin.

Bond, Michael Harris (1996) *The Handbook of Chinese Psychology.* New York: Oxford University Press.

Bourdieu, Pierre (1977) *Outline of a Theory of Practice.* Cambridge and New York: Cambridge University Press.

——(1984 [1979]) *Distinction – A Social Critique of the Judgement of Taste*, trans. Richard Nice. Cambridge, Mass: Harvard University Press.

——(1992) *The Logic of Practice*, trans. by Richard Nice. Polity Press.

Brandstädter, Susanne (2009) "Fakes: Fraud, Value Anxiety and the Politics of Sincerity". In Karen Sykes, ed. *Ethnographies of Moral Reasoning: Living Paradox of a Global Ages.* New York: Palgrave Macmillan.

Bray, David S. (2005) *Social Space and Governance in Urban China: The Danwei System from Origins to Reform.* Stanford, CA: Stanford University Press.

Brook, Timothy and Michael B. Frolic, eds. (1997) *Civil Society in China.* Armonk, New York: M.E. Sharpe.

Brownell, Susan (2001) "Making Dream Bodies in Beijing: Athletes, Fashion Models, and Urban Mystique in China". In Nancy N. Chen, Constance D. Clark, Suzanne Z. Gottschang, eds. *China Urban.* Durham: Duke University Press.

Campbell, C. (1987) *The Romantic Ethic and the Spirit of Modern Consumerism.* Oxford: Basil Blackwell.

Chan, Anita (2001) *China's Workers Under Assault: The Exploitation of Labor in a Globalizing Economy.* Armonk, London: M.E. Sharpe.

Chan, Anita, Stanley Rosen, and Jonathan Unger (1980) "Students and Class Warfare: The Social Roots of the Red Guard Conflict in Guangzhou (Canton)", *The China Quarterly* 83 September: 397–446.

Chan, Kara and Hong Cheng (2002) "One Country, Two Systems: Cultural Values Reflected in Chinese and Hong Kong Television Commercials", *The International Journal for Communication Studies* 64(4): 385–400.

Chan, Kara and James U. McNeal (2002) "Children's Perceptions of Television Advertising in Urban China", *Young Consumers: Insight and Ideas for Responsible Marketers* (3)3: 69–79.

Chang, Leslie T. (2009) *Factory Girls: From Village to City in a Changing China.* New York: Spiegel & Grau.

Chapman, Malcolm (1992) *The Celts – The Construction of a Myth.* London: Macmillan.

Chen, Baoling (1998) "To be Defined a *Liumang*". In Michael Dutton, ed. *Streetlife China.* Cambridge and New York: Cambridge University Press.

Chen, Nancy, N. Constance, D. Clark, Suzanne Z. Gottschang, and Lyn Jeffery, eds. (2001) *China Urban: Ethnographies of Contemporary Culture.* Durham and London: Duke University Press.

Chen, Xiangming and Jiaming Sun (2006) "Sociological Perspectives on Urban China: From Familiar Territories to Complex Terrains", *China Information* 20(3): 519–51.

Chen, Yang (2008) "Jiaoshi dizhenshi bugu xuesheng xian taoming cheng cishi lian muqin ye bujiu", May 5, 2008. news.sina.com.cn/s/2008-05-25/015115612013.shtml (accessed October 2009).

Cheng, Tiejun and Mark Selden (1994) "The Origins and Social Consequences of China's Hukou System", *The China Quarterly* 139: 644–68.

Chia, Robert and Robin Holt (2006) "Strategy as Practical Coping: A Heideggerean Perspective", *Organization Studies* 27(5): 635–55.

Chinese Culture Connection (CCC) (1987) "Chinese Values and the Search for Culture-free Dimensions of Culture", *Journal of Cross-Cultural Psychology* 18(2): 143–64.

Chomsky, Noam (1965) *Aspects of the Theory of Syntax.* Cambridge, Massachusetts: MIT Press.

Christiansen, Flemming (1993) "The Legacy of the Mock Dual Economy: Chinese Labour in Transition 1978–92", *Economy & Society* 22(4): 411.

Christiansen, Flemming and Ulf Hedetoft, ed. (2004) *The Politics of Multiple Belonging: Ethnicity and Nationalism in Europe and East Asia.* Aldershot and Burlington: Ashgate.

Ci, Jiwei (1994) *Dialectic of the Chinese Revolution: From Utopianism to Hedonism.* Stanford, CA: Stanford University Press.

Clunas, Craig (2004) *Superfluous Things: Material Culture and Social Status in Early Modern China.* Honolulu: University of Hawaii Press.

Cochran, Sherman, (1980) *Big Business in China: Sino–Foreign Rivalry in the Cigarette Industry, 1890–1930*. Cambridge, Mass: Harvard University Press.

——ed. (1999) *Inventing Nanjing Road: Commercial Culture in Shanghai, 1900–1945*. Ithaca: Cornell University.

Coonan, Clifford (2007) "Girl, 10, is Tied up by Father Before Tackling 3-hour Swim". *The Independent*. Friday, 5 October 2007. www.independent.co.uk/news/world/asia/girl-10-is-tied-up-by-father-before-tackling-3hour-swim-396024.html (accessed October 2009).

Croll, Elizabeth (2006) *China's New Consumers: Social Development and Domestic Demand*. Abingdon and New York: Routledge.

Cui, Geng. and Qiming Liu (2001) "Emerging Market Segments in a Transitional Economy: A Study of Urban Consumers in China", *Journal of International Marketing* 9(1): 92–114.

Davis, Deborah S., ed. (2000) *The Consumer Revolution in Urban China*. Berkeley and Los Angeles: University of California Press.

——(2005) "Urban Consumer Culture", *The China Quarterly* 183: 692–709.

Davis, Deborah S., Richard Kraus, Barry Naughton, and Elizabeth J. Perry, eds. (1995) *Urban Spaces in Contemporary China: The Potential for Autonomy and Community in Post-Mao China* (Woodrow Wilson Center Press). Cambridge, New York and Melbourne: University of Cambridge Press.

de Certeau, Michel (1984) *The Practice of Everyday Life*. Berkeley, Los Angeles and London: University of California Press.

Delman, Jørgen and Xiaoqing Yin (2008) "Individualisation and Politics in China: The Political Identity and Agency of Private Business People", *European Journal of East Asian Studies* 7(1): 39–73.

Derrida, Jacques (1976) *Of Grammatology*, trans. from the original French by Gayatri Chakravorty Spivak. Baltimore and London: Johns Hopkins University Press. (Originally published 1967 as *De La Grammatologie*. Paris: Les éditions de minuit.)

Dickson, Marsha A., Sharron J. Lennon, Catherine P. Montalto, Dong Shen, and Li Zhang (2004) "Chinese Consumer Market Segments for Foreign Apparel Products", *The Journal of Consumer Marketing* 21(5): 301–17.

Ding, Yu (2012) 'Negotiating Intimacies in an Eroticized Environment: Xiaojies and South China Entertainment Business', *International Journal of Business Anthropology*, Volume 3(1), 158–175.

Dirlik, Arif (2001) "Markets, Culture, Power: The Making of a Second Cultural Revolution in China", *Asian Studies Review* 25(1) March: 1–33.

Doctoroff, Tom (2005) *Billions: Selling to the Chinese Consumer*. New York: Palgrave Macmillan.

Douglas, Mary (1966) *Purity and Danger*. London: Routledge and Kegan Paul.

Douglas, Mary and Baron C. Isherwood (1979) *The World of Goods: Towards an Anthropology of Consumption*. London: Routledge.

Duara, Prasenjit (2004) *Sovereignty and Authenticity: Manchukuo and the East Asian Modern*. Lanham, Maryland: Rowman & Littlefield.

Dumont, Louis (1992) *Essays on Individualism: Modern Ideology in Anthropological Perspective*. London: University of Chicago Press.

Dunn, Robert G. (2008) *Identifying Consumption: Subjects and Objects in Consumer Society*. Philadelphia: Temple University Press.

Durkheim, E. (1997 [1951]) *Suicide: A Study in Sociology*. The Free Press.

Durkheim, E. and M. Mauss (1967) Primitive Classification, trans. R. Needham. London: Heinemann Educational Publishers.

Dutton, Michael Robert (1998) *Streetlife China*. Cambridge: Cambridge University Press.

Eckhardt, Giana M. (2004) "The Role of Culture in Conducting Trustworthy and Credible Qualitative Business Research in China". In Marschan-Piekkari and Welch, eds. *Handbook of Qualitative Research Methods for International Business*. Cheltenham and Northampton: Edward Elgar Publishing.

Eckhardt, Giana M. and Michael J. Houston (2001a) "Cultural Paradoxes Reflected in Brand Meaning: McDonald's in Shanghai China", *Journal of International Marketing* 10(2): 68–82.

——(2001b) "To Own Your Grandfather's Spirit: The Nature of Possessions and Their Meaning in China", *Asia Pacific Advances in Consumer Research* 4: 251–57.

Eckhardt, Giana M. and Humaira Mahi (2004) "The Role of Consumer Agency in the Globalisation Process in Emerging Markets", *Journal of Macromarketing* 24(2) December: 136–46.

Eco, Umberto (1986) *Travels in Hyperreality*. New York: Harcourt Brace.

The Economist (2007) "Blatant Benevolence and Conspicuous Consumption: The Evolutionary Selfishness of Charity", *The Economist* 2 August 2007. www.economist.com/sciencetechnology/displaystory.cfm?story_id=E1_JVRTGVG (accessed October 2009).

Eimer, David (2008) "China Outlaws Lip-synching after Olympics Row", *The Telegraph* 14 November 2008. www.telegraph.co.uk/news/worldnews/asia/china/3457263/China-outlaws-lip-synching-after-Olympics-row.html (accessed October 2009).

Elias, Norbert (2000) *The Civilizing Process: Sociogenetic and Psychogenetic Investigations*. Oxford and Malden: Wiley-Blackwell.

Elvin, Mark (1985) "Between the Earth and Heaven: Conceptions of the Self in China". In Michael Carrithers, Steven Collin, and Steven Lukes, eds. *The Category of the Person: Anthropology, Philosophy, History*. Cambridge: Cambridge University Press, 156–89.

Ewing, Michael T., Julie Napoli, Leyland F. Pitt, and Alistair Watts (2002) "On the Renaissance of Chinese Brands", *International Journal of Advertising* 21(2): 197–216.

Fairclough, Norman (1989) *Language and Power*. Longman.

——(1995) *Critical Discourse Analysis*. Harlow: Longman.

Fang, Tony (2003) "A Critique of Hofstede's Fifth National Culture Dimension", *International Journal of Cross Cultural Management* 3(3): 347–68.

Farquhar, Judith (2002) *Appetites: Food and Sex in Post-socialist China*. Durham and NC: Duke University Press.

Farrer, James (2002) *Opening Up: Youth Sex Culture and Market Reform in Shanghai*. Chicago and London: University of Chicago Press.

——(2008) "From Passports to Joints Ventures: Intermarriage Between Chinese Nationals and Western Expatriates Residing in Shanghai", *Asian Studies Review* 31(1): 7–29.

Farrer, James and Zhongxin Sun (2003) "Extramarital Love in Shanghai", *The China Journal* 50 (July): 1–36.

Fei, Xiaotong, Gary G. Hamilton, and Zheng Wang (1992) *From the Soil, the Foundations of Chinese Society: A Translation of Fei Xiaotong's Xiangtu Zhongguo, with an Introduction and Epilogue*. Berkeley: University of California Press.

Festa, Paul E. (2006) "Mahjong Politics in Contemporary China: Civility, China, Chineseness, and Mass Culture", (Duke University Press) *Positions* 14(1): 7–35.

Firat, A. Fuat and Alladi Venkatesh (1995) "Liberatory Postmodernism and the Reenactment of Consumption", *Journal of Consumer Research* 22(3): 239–58.

Fiskesjö, Magnus (2012) "The Animal Other: China's Barbarians and their Renaming in the Twentieth Century", *Social Text* 109. 29(4) Winter.

Fong, Vanessa L. (2007) "Morality, Cosmopolitanism, or Academic Attainment? Discourses on 'Quality' and Urban Chinese-Only-Children's Claims to Ideal Personhood", *City and Society* 19(1): 86–113.

——(2008) *Only Hope: Coming of Age Under China's One-Child Policy.* Stanford, CA: Stanford University Press.

Forney, Matthew (2008) "China Mourns: In Tragedy, a New Kind of Unity", *The Washington Post* 18 May 2008. www.washingtonpost.com/wp-dyn/content/article/2008/05/15/AR2008051502737.html (accessed July 2009).

Foucault, Michel (1970) *The Order of Things.* Tavistock/Routledge. (Originally published 1966 as *Les mots et les choses.* Paris: Editions Gallimard.)

——(1972) *The Archaeology of Knowledge.* Tavistock Publications. (Originally published 1969 as *L'Archéologie du savoir.* Paris: Editions Gallimard.

——(1975) *Discipline and Punish: the Birth of the Prison.* New York: Random House.

——(1988) "Technologies of the Self". In L.H. Martin, H. Gutman and P.H. Hutton, eds. *Technologies of the self.* Amherst: University of Massachusetts Press, 16–49.

Fram, Eugene H., Lu Le and David Mchardy Reid (2004) "Consumer Behaviour in China: An Exploratory Study of Two Cities", *Journal of Asia-Pacific Business.* Binghamton 5(4): 25–42.

Gadamer, Hans-Georg (1975) *Truth and Method*, trans. from the original German by William Glen-Doepel. London: Sheed and Ward.

Gamble, Jos (2003) *Shanghai in Transition: Changing Perspectives and Social Contours of a Chinese Metropolis.* London: Routledge Curzon.

Garner, Jonathan (2005) *The Rise of the Chinese Consumer.* Chichester, UK: John Wiley and Sons.

Geertz, Clifford (1975) *The Interpretation of Cultures.* London: Hutchinson.

Ger, Güliz and Russell W. Belk (1996) "I'd Like to Buy the World a Coke: Consumptionscapes of the 'Less Affluent World'", *Journal of Consumer Policy* 19.3.

Gerth, Karl (2004) *China Made: Consumer Culture and the Creation of the Nation.* Cambridge and Mass.: Harvard University Press.

Giles, John, Albert Park and Fang Cai (2006) "How has Economic Restructuring Affected China's Urban Workers?" *The China Quarterly* Vol. 185, March: 61–95.

Goffman, Erving (1959) *The Presentation of Self in Everyday Life.* Garden City, New York: Anchor.

Gold, Thomas B. (1985) "After Comradeship: Personal Relations in China Since the Cultural Revolution", *The China Quarterly* 104 December: 657–75.

Gold, Thomas, Doug Guthrie, and David Wank (2002) *Social Connections in China.* Cambridge: Cambridge University Press.

Goodman, David (2010) "New Economic Elites: The Social Basis of Local Power". Working paper, Chinese Studies Centre, Institute of Social Sciences, University of Sydney, given at the Worldwide Universities Network Virtual Seminar Series, Tuesday 7 December.

Griffiths, Michael. B. (2009) "Eating Bitterness: Re-enacting the Primitive Rural". In L. Hernández and S. Krajewski, eds. *Crossing Cultural Boundaries: Taboo, Bodies and Identities.* Cambridge Scholars Press, 159–73.

——(2010) "Lamb Buddha's Migrant Workers: Self-assertion on China's Urban Fringe", *Journal of Current Chinese Affairs* (China Aktuell) 39, 2: 3–37.

Griffiths, Michael B., Flemming Christiansen, and Malcolm Chapman (2010) "Chinese Consumers: The Romantic Reappraisal", *Ethnography* September, 11: 331–57.

Griffiths, Michael B. and Jesper Zeuthen (2012) *Bittersweet: Bitter Civilization*. Under review, June 2011.

Halskov-Hansen, Mette and Cuiming Pang (2008) "Me and My Family: Perceptions of Individual and Collective among Young Rural Chinese", *European Journal of East Asian Studies* 7(1): 75–99.

Halskov-Hansen, Mette and Rune Svarverud, eds. (2010) *iChina: The Rise of the Individual in Modern Chinese Society* (Nias Studies in Asian Topics), Foreword by Ulrick Beck and Elisabeth Beck-Gernsheim.

Hamilton, Gary G. and Chi-kong Lai (1989) "Consumerism Without Capitalism: Consumption and Brand Names in Late Imperial China". In Henry J. Rutz and Benjamin S. Orlove, eds. *The Social Economy of Consumption: Monographs in Economic Anthropology*. New York: University Press.

Hanser, Amy (2004) "Made in the P.R.C.: Consumers in China", *Contexts* 3(1): 13–19.

——(2005) "The Gendered Rice Bowl: The Sexual Politics of Service Work in Urban China", *Gender and Society* 19(5): 581–600.

——(2006) "Sales Floor Trajectories: Distinction and Service in Post-Socialist China", *Ethnography* 7(4): 461–91.

——(2008) *Service Encounters: Class, Gender, and the Market for Social Distinction in Urban China*. Stanford, California: Stanford University Press.

Hauerwas, Stanley and Samuel Wells (2006) *The Blackwell Companion to Christian Ethics*. Wiley-Blackwell.

Heidegger, Martin (1962) *Being and Time*, trans. from the original German by John Macquarrie and Edward Robinson. Malden, Oxford and Carlton: Blackwell.

Heimer, Maria and Stig Thøgersen, eds. (2006) *Doing Fieldwork in China*. Copenhagen: Nordic Institute of Asian Studies Press.

Hird, Derek (2009) *White-Collar Men and Masculinities in Contemporary Urban China*. PhD thesis, University of Westminster. westminsterresearch.wmin.ac.uk/8026.

Hjelmslev, Louis (1963) *Prolegomena to a Theory of Language*, trans. Francis J. Whitfield. Madison: University of Wisconsin Press.

Ho, Suk-Ching (2001) "Growing Consumer Power in China: Some Lessons for Managers", *Journal of International Marketing* 9(1): 64–83.

Hofstede, Geert (1991) *Culture and Organizations: Software of Mind*. Maidenhead, UK: McGraw-Hill.

——(2001) *Culture's Consequences: Comparing Values, Behaviours, Institutions and Organisations Across Nations*, second edn. London: Sage.

Holt, Douglas B. (1997) "Poststructuralist Lifestyle Analysis: Conceptualizing the Social Patterning of Consumption in Postmodernity", *Journal of Consumer Research* 23(4) March: 326–50.

Hook, Brian, ed. (1996) *The Individual and the State in China* (Studies in Contemporary China). Oxford: Oxford University Press.

Hooper, Beverly (1998a) "Keeping Up with the Wangs: Consuming Desires in Post-Mao China", *The Asia Pacific Magazine* 9(10): 17–22.

——(1998b) "From Mao to Market: Empowering the Chinese Consumer", *Harvard Asia Pacific Review* 2(2): 29–34.

——(2000) "Globalisation and Resistance in Post-Mao China: The Case of Foreign Consumer Products", *Asian Studies Review* 24(4) December: 439–70.

Hsu, Carolyn L. (2005) "A Taste of 'Modernity': Working in a Western Restaurant in Market Socialist China", *Ethnography* 6(4): 543–65.

Hsu, Francis L.K. (1953) *Americans and Chinese: Two Ways of Life.* New York: Abelard-Schuman.

——(1971) "Psychological Homeostasis and *ren*: Conceptual Tools for Advancing Psychological Anthropology", *American Anthropologist* 73: 23–44.

——(1985) "The Self in Cross-Cultural Perspective". In A.J. Marsella, G. DeVos and F.L.K. Hsu, eds. *Culture and Self: Asian and Western Perspectives.* New York: Tavistock, 24–55.

Huang, Kwang-Kuo (2002) "Chinese Relationalism: Theoretical Construction and Methodological Consideration", *Journal for the Theory of Social Behaviour* 30(2): 155–78.

Hubbert, Jennifer (2005) "Revolution is a Dinner Party: Cultural Revolution Restaurants in Contemporary China", *China Review* Vol. 5, No. 2.

Hung, Eva P.W. and Stephen W.K. Chiu (2003) "The Lost Generation: Life Course Dynamics and *Xiagang* in China", *Modern China* 29(2): 204–36.

Hung, Kineta H., Stella Yiyan Li, and Russell W. Belk (2007) "Glocal Understandings: Female Readers – Perceptions of the New Woman in Advertising", *Journal of International Business* 38: 1034–51.

Hwang, Alvin, Anne Marie Francesco, and Eric Kessler (2003) "The Relationship between Individualism-collectivism, Face and Feedback and Learning Processes in Hong Kong, Singapore, and the United States", *Journal of Cross-Cultural Psychology* 34(1): 72–91.

Hwang, Kwang-Kuo (1987) "Face and Favor: The Chinese Power Game", *American Journal of Sociology* 92(4): 944–74.

——(2000) "Chinese Relationalism: Theoretical Construction and Methodological Considerations", *Journal for the Theory of Social Behaviour* 30(2): 155–78.

Hyde, S.T. (2001) "Sex Tourism Practices on the Periphery: Eroticizing Ethnicity and Pathologising Sex on the Lancang". In N. Chen, ed. *China Urban: Ethnographies of Contemporary Culture.* Durham, NC: Duke University Press, 143–62.

Ikels, Charlotte (1996) *Return of the God of Wealth: The Transition to a Market Economy in Urban China.* Stanford: Stanford University Press.

Jacka, Tamara (2006) *Rural Women in Urban China: Gender, Migration and Urban Change.* Armonk, NY: M.E. Sharpe.

——(2009) "Cultivating Citizens: Suzhi (Quality) Discourse in the PRC", *Positions: East Asia Cultures Critique* 17(3): 523–35.

Jankowiak, William R. (1993) "Sex, Death, and Hierarchy in a Chinese City: An Anthropological Account", *The China Quarterly* 140: 1180–81 (Columbia University Press).

Jenkins, Richard (1992) *Pierre Bourdieu*, revised edition. Key Sociologists Series Editor: Peter Hamilton. London and New York: Routledge, Taylor & Francis Group.

Johansson, Perry (1998) "White Skin, Large Breasts: Chinese Beauty Product Advertising as Cultural Discourse", *China Information* 13(2–3): 59–78.

Kant, Immanuel (1996) *The Metaphysics of Morals* (Cambridge Texts in the History of Philosophy), by Immanuel Kant, Mary J. Gregor, and Roger J. Sullivan.

Khu, Josephine M.T. (2001) *Cultural Curiosity: Thirteen Stories about the Search for Chinese Roots.* Berkeley, Los Angeles and London: University of California Press.

Kipnis, Andrew (1997) *Producing Guanxi: Sentiment, Self, and Subculture in a North China Village.* Durham, NC: Duke University Press.

——(2007) "Neoliberalism Reified: Suzhi Discourse and Tropes of Neoliberalism in the People's Republic of China", *Journal of the Royal Anthropological Institute* 13(2): 521–400.

——(2011) *Governing Educational Desire: Culture, Politics and Schooling in China.* University of Chicago Press.

Kirke, Charles (2010) "Orders is Orders ... Aren't They? Rule Bending and Rule Breaking in the British Army", *Ethnography* 11: 359–80.

Knight, Deirdre Sabina (2003) "Shanghai Cosmopolitan: Class, Gender and Cultural Citizenship in Weihui's Shanghai Baby", *Journal of Contemporary China* 12(37): 639–53.

Konrád, Gyorgy and Ivan Szelényi (1979) *The Intellectuals on the Road to Class Power: A Sociological Study of the Role of the Intelligentsia.* Brighton: Harvester Press.

Kozinets, Robert V. (2002) "Can Consumers Escape the Market? Emancipatory Illuminations from Burning Man", *Journal of Consumer Research* 29(1) June: 20–38.

Krajewski, Sabine (2009) "Spitting – The Emergence of a Taboo". In L. Hernandez and S. Krajewski, eds. *Crossing Cultural Boundaries.* Cambridge: Cambridge University Press, 81–91.

Kraus, Richard Curt (1977) "Class Conflict and the Vocabulary of Social Analysis in China", *The China Quarterly* 69 March: 54–74.

Lacan, Jacques (1977) *Écrits: A Selection*, transl. Alan Sheridan. New York: W.W. Norton & Co.

Lamont, Michèle (1992) *Money, Morals, and Manners: The Culture of the French and American Upper-Middle Class.* Chicago: University of Chicago Press.

Lamont, Michèle and Virág Molnár (2002) "The Study of Boundaries in the Social Sciences", *Annual Review of Sociology* 28: 167–95.

Lee, Ching Kwan (2000) "The Revenge of History: Collective Memories, Unemployment and Labor Protests in Northeastern China", *Ethnography* December, Vol. 1, No. 2: 217–37.

——(2007) *Against the Law: Labor Protests in China's Rustbelt and Sunbelt.* Berkeley, CA: University of California Press.

Lee, Gregory (1996) "Fear of Drowning". In Gregory Lee. *Troubadours, Trumpeters, Troubled Makers.* Durham, NC, and London: Duke University Press and C. Hurst & Co.

Lee, Gregory B. (2007) "Chinese Migrants and the 'Inundation' Metaphor", *East-AsiaNet Workshop*, "Framing Risk: Hazard Perceptions as a Crucial Factor in Imagining East Asia", Suède. hal-univ-lyon3.archives-ouvertes.fr/view_by_stamp.php?&halsid=anmgbrrvh76ebnm53em4fhjl47&label=UNIV-LYON3&langue=fr&action_todo=view&id=halshs-00188544&version=1 (accessed July 2009).

Lee, Leo Ou-fan (2000) *Shanghai Modern: The Flowering of a New Urban Culture in China 1930–45.* Berkeley: University of California Press.

Lei, Guang (2003) "Rural Taste, Urban Fashions: The Cultural Politics of Rural/Urban Difference in Contemporary China", *Positions* 11(3): 613–46.

Lévi-Strauss, Claude (1975) *The Raw and the Cooked.* New York: Harper & Row Publishers.

Li, Conghua (1998) *China: The Consumer Revolution.* New York: John Wiley.

Lin, Carolyn A. (2001) "Cultural Values Reflected in Chinese and American Television Advertising", *Journal of Advertising* 30(4): 83–94.

Liu, Xinyan (2009) "Zhu Jianqiang pei yuyong siyangyuan, anmoshi, bannian tizhong zhang sanbei". 26 January 2009. news.sohu.com/20090126/n261953969.shtml (accessed October 2009).

Lowe, Sid (2001) "In the Kingdom of the Blind, the One-Eyed Man is King", *International Journal of Cross-Cultural Management* 1(3): 313–32.

——(2002) "The Cultural Shadows of Cross-Cultural Research: Images of Culture", *Culture and Organization* 8(1): 21–34.

Ma, Dali and William L. Parish (2006) "Tocquevillian Moments: Charitable Contributions by Chinese Private Entrepreneurs", *Social Forces* 85(2): 943–64.

Ma, Lawrence J.C. (2006) "The State of the Field of Urban China: A Critical Multidisciplinary Overview of the Literature", *China Information* 20(3): 363–89.

Madsen, Richard (1998) "Chinese Catholics". In Richard Madsen, ed. *China's Catholics: Tragedy and Hope in an Emerging Civil Society.* (Excerpts reprinted in: *China: Adapting the Past, Confronting the Future*, 2002, ed. Thomas Buoye, Kirk Denton, Bruce Dickson, Barry Naughton, and Martin K. Whyte. Michigan: Center for Chinese Studies. Ann Arbor: The University of Michigan.)

Marcuse, Herbert (1964) *One-dimensional Man: Studies in the Ideology of Advanced Industrial Society.* London: Routledge and Kegan Paul.

Markus, Hazel R. and Shinobu Kitayama (1991) "Culture and the Self: Implication for Cognition, Emotion, and Motivation", *Psychological Review* 98(2): 224–53.

McCracken, Grant (1990) *Culture and Consumption: New Approaches to the Symbolic Character of Consumer Goods and Activities.* Bloomington: Indiana University Press.

McMillan, Joanna (2006) *Sex, Science and Morality.* London: Routledge Press.

Mealey, Ann Marie (2008) *The Identity of Christian Morality.* Farnham, UK: Ashgate Publishing.

Miller, Daniel (1987) *Material Culture and Mass Consumption.* Oxford: Blackwell.

Murphy, Rachel (2004) "Turning Chinese Farmers into Modern Citizens: 'Population Quality' (*suzhi*), Demographic Transition, and Primary Schools", *The China Quarterly* 177: 1–20.

Murray, Jeff B. (2002) "The Politics of Consumption: A Re-inquiry on Thompson and Haytko's (1997) 'Speaking of Fashion'", *Journal of Consumer Research* 29(3) December: 427–40.

Murray, Jeff B. and Julie L. Ozanne (1991) "The Critical Imagination: Emancipatory Interests in Consumer Research", *Journal of Consumer Research* 18(2) September: 129–44.

Nee, Victor (1989) "A Theory of Market Transition: From Redistribution to Markets in State Socialism", *American Sociological Review* October (54): 663–81.

Nietzsche, Friedrich Wilhelm (1994) *On the Genealogy of Morality, and Other Writings*, Keith Ansell-Pearson, ed. Carol Diethe, trans. Cambridge: Cambridge University Press.

Notar, Beth (2006) Displacing Desire: Travel and Popular Culture in China. University of Hawai'i Press.

Ong, Aihwa (1999) *Flexible Citizenship: The Cultural Logics of Transnationality.* Durham, NC: Duke University Press.

——(2005) "Anthropological Concepts for the Study of Nationalism". In Pál Nyíri and Joana Breidenbach, eds. *China Inside Out: Contemporary Chinese Nationalism and Transnationalism.* Budapest: Central European University Press.

——(2006) *Neoliberalism as Exception: Mutations in Citizenship and Sovereignty.* Duke University Press.

Ouyang, Ming, Hongxia Zhang and Nan Zhou (2002) "Does Nationalist Appeal Affect Chinese University Students' Product Evaluation? A Conjoint Analysis", *Asian Journal of Marketing* 9(1): 31–37.

Paek, Hye-Jin and Zhongdang Pan (2004) "Spreading Global Consumerism: Effects of Mass Media and Advertising on Consumerist Values in China", *Mass Communication and Society* 7(4): 491–515.

Perry, Elizabeth J. and Mark Selden (2010) *Chinese Society: Change, Conflict and Resistance*. Abingdon: Taylor & Francis.

Pieke, Frank N. (1996) *The Ordinary and the Extraordinary: An Anthropological Study of Chinese Reform and the 1989 People's Movement in Beijing*. London and New York: Kegan Paul International.

Pine, B. Joseph, II and James H. Gilmore (2007) *Authenticity: What Consumers Really Want*. Harvard Business School Press.

Pritchford, Paul (1993) *Healing with Whole Foods: Oriental Traditions and Modern Nutrition*. Berkeley, CA: North Atlantic Books.

Propp, Vladimir (1985) *Theory and History of Folklore*. trans. Anatoly Liberman and Richard P. Martin. Minneapolis: University of Minneapolis Press.

Pun Ngai (2003) "Subsumption or Consumption? The Phantom of Consumer Revolution in 'Globalizing' China", *Cultural Anthropology* 18(4): 469–92.

——(2005) *Made in China: Women Factory Workers in a Global Workplace*. Durham: Duke University Press.

Pye, Lucien (1990) "China: Erratic State, Frustrated Society", *Foreign Affairs*, New York: Fall, Vol. 69, Iss. 4.

——(1993) "How China's Nationalism was Shanghaied", The Australian Journal of Chinese Affairs 29(1): 107–33.

——(1996) "The State and Individual: An Overview Interpretation". In Brian Hook, ed. *The Individual and the State in China (Studies in Contemporary China)*. Oxford: Oxford University Press.

Ricoeur, Paul (1971) "The Model of the Text: Meaningful Action Considered as a Text", *Social Research* 38.

Rolandsen, Unn Malfrid H. (2008) "A Collective of Their Own: Young Volunteers at the Fringes of the Party Realm", *European Journal of East Asian Studies* 7(1): 101–29.

Rose, N. (1996) *Inventing Our Selves: Inventing Our Selves: Psychology, Power and Personhood*. Cambridge: Cambridge University Press.

Said, Edward W. (2003) *Orientalism*. London: Penguin.

Sanders, Carol, ed. (2004) *The Cambridge Companion to Saussure*. Cambridge: Cambridge University Press.

Schatzki, Theodore R. (1996) "Practices and Actions: A Wittgensteinian Critique of Bourdieu and Giddens", *Philosophy of the Social Sciences* 27(3): 283–308.

Schein, Louisa (1994) "The Consumption and the Politics of White Skin in Post-Mao China", *Social Text* 41 (Winter): 141–64.

Schell, Orville (1989) *Discos and Democracy: China in the Throes of Reform*. New York: Anchor Press.

Schmitt, Berndt (1997) "Who is the Chinese Consumer? Segmentation in the People's Republic of China", *European Management Journal* 15(2): 191–94.

Scott, James C. (1999) *Seeing Like a State: How Certain Schemes to Improve the Human Condition Have Failed*. New Haven: Yale University Press.

Sen, Amartya (1997) "Human Rights and Asian Values", *The New Republic*, 14 July–21 July.

Singelis, Theodore M. (1994) "The Measurement of Independent and Interdependent Self-construals", *Personality and Social Psychology Bulletin* 20(5): 580–91.

Solinger, Dorothy J. (2002) "Labour Market Reform and the Plight of the Laidoff Proletariat", *The China Quarterly* 170: 304–26.

——(1999) *Contesting Citizenship in Urban China: Peasant Migrants, the State and the Logic of the Market*. University of California Press.

Spiggle, Susan (1994) "Analysis and Interpretation of Qualitative Data in Consumer Research", *Journal of Consumer Research* 21(3) December: 491–503.

Stafford, Charles (1992) "Good Sons and Virtuous Mothers: Kinship and Chinese Nationalism in Taiwan", *Man* 27(2): 363–78.

Stening, Bruce W. and Marina Y. Zhang (2007) "Methodological Challenges Confronted when Conducting Management Research in China", *International Journal of Cross Cultural Management* 7(1): 121–42.

Sturrock, John, ed. (1979) *Structuralism and Since: From Lévi-Strauss to Derrida*. Oxford: Oxford University Press.

——(2003 [1986]) *Structuralism*. Malden and Oxford: Wiley-Blackwell.

Sun, Catherine Tien-Lun (2008) *Themes in Chinese Psychology*. Cengage Learning Asia.

Tapp, Nicholas (2008) "Romanticism in China? – Its Implications for Minority Images and Aspirations", *Asian Studies Review* 32, 4.

——(2010) *The Impossibility of Self: An Essay on the Hmong Diaspora*. Berlin: Lit Verlag.

Thøgersen, Stig and Anru Ni (2008) "'He is he, and I am I': Individual and Collective Among China's Rural Elderly", *European Journal of East Asian Studies* 7(1): 11–37.

Thompson, Craig, William Locander, and Howard R. Pollio (1989) "Putting Consumer Experience Back into Consumer Research: The Philosophy and Method of Existential-Phenomenology", *Journal of Consumer Research* 16(2): 133–46.

——(1990) "The Lived Meaning of Free Choice: An Existential-Phenomenological Description of Everyday Experiences of Contemporary Married Women", *Journal of Consumer Research* 17(3): 346–61.

Tse, David K., Russell W. Belk, and Nan Zhou (1989) "Becoming a Consumer Society: A Longitudinal and Cross-Cultural Content Analysis of Print Ads from Hong Kong, the People's Republic of China, and Taiwan", *Journal of Advertising Research* 15(4) March: 457–72.

Tse, Edward, Kevin Ma, and Yu Huang (2009) "Shan Zhai: A Chinese Phenomenon". Booz & Co. white paper.

Tu, Wei-ming (1994) *The Living Tree: The Changing Meaning of Being Chinese Today*. Stanford: Stanford University Press.

——(2005) "Cultural China: The Periphery as the Centre", *Daedalus* 134(4): 145–67.

Unger, Jonathan and Geremie R. Barmé (1996) *Chinese Nationalism*. Armonk, NY: M.E. Sharpe.

Veblen, Thorstein (1954 [1899]) *The Theory of the Leisure Class*. New York: Penguin Press.

Veeck, Ann (2000) "The Revitalization of the Marketplace: Food Markets of Nanjing". In Deborah S. Davis, ed. *The Consumer Revolution in Urban China*. Berkeley and Los Angeles, California: University of California Press.

Vogel, Ezra F. (1965) "From Friendship to Comradeship: The Change in Personal Relations in Communist China", *China Quarterly* No. 21 (Jan.–Mar.): 46–60.

Wagner, Roy (1981) *The Invention of Culture*. Chicago: University of Chicago Press.

Walder, Andrew George (1986) *Communist Neo-Traditionalism: Work and Authority in Chinese Industry*. Berkeley: University of California Press.

Walder, Andrew (2009) *Fractured Rebellion: The Beijing Red Guard Movement*. Harvard University Press.

Walters, Peter G.P. and Saeed Samiee (2003) "Marketing Strategy in Emerging Markets: The Case of China", *The Journal of International Marketing* 11(1): 97–106.

Wang, Chenglu and Zhenxiong Chen (2004) "Consumer Ethnocentrism and Willingness to Buy Domestic Products in a Developing Country Setting: Testing Moderating Effects", *The Journal of Consumer Marketing* 21(6): 391–400.

Wang, Fei-Ling (2005) *Organising Through Division and Exclusion: China's Hukou System.* Stanford: Stanford University Press.

Wang, Jing (2008) *Brand New China: Advertising, Media and Commercial Culture.* Cambridge, Mass. and London, England: Harvard University Press.

Wang, Wei (2006) *The China Executive: Marrying Western and Chinese Strengths to Generate Profitability from Your Investment in China.* Bretton, Peterborough: 2W Publishing.

Wang, X.Y. (2002) "The Post-Communist Personality: The Spectre of China's Capitalist Market Reforms", *The China Journal* 47(1-17).

Watson, James L., ed. (1998) *Golden Arches East: McDonald's in East Asia.* Stanford, California: Stanford University Press.

Weber, Ian (2002) "Shanghai Baby: Negotiating Youth Self-Identity in Urban China", *Social Identities: Journal for the study of Race, Nation and Culture* 8(2): 347–68.

Wei, Ran (1997) "Emerging Lifestyles in China and Consequences for Perception of Advertising, Buying Behaviour and Consumption Preferences", *International Journal of Advertising* 16(4): 261–75.

Wei, Ran and Pan Zhongdang (1999) "Mass Media and Consumerist Values in the People's Republic of China", *International Journal of Public Opinion Research* 11(1): 75–96.

Weick, Karl E. (1999) "Theory Construction as Disciplined Reflexivity: Tradeoffs in the 90s", *Academy of Management Review* 24: 797–806.

Weiss, Gilbert and Ruth Wodak, eds. (2003) *Critical Discourse Analysis: Theory and Interdisciplinarity in Critical Discourse Analysis.* London: Palgrave.

Whyte, Martin King (1975) "Inequality and Stratification in China", *The China Quarterly* 64, December: 684–711.

Williams, Rowan (2007) "Christianity in the Reinvention of China", *China Review* (40): 1–3.

Wilson, Scott (2002) "Face, Norms and Instrumentality". In Thomas Gold, Doug Guthrie, and David L. Wank, eds. *Social Connections in China: Institutions, Culture, and the Changing Nature of Guanxi.* Cambridge: Cambridge University Press.

Wittgenstein, Ludwig (1953) *Philosophical Investigations.* Oxford: Basil Blackwell.

Wodak, R. and Michael Meyer (2002) *Methods for Critical Discourse Analysis.* Sage.

Won, Jaeyoun (2005) "The Making of the Post-Proletariat in China", *Development and Society* December, Vol. 23, No. 2: 191–92.

Wong, Stephen (2009) "No Stopping China's Cheaters", *Asia Times* 22 August. www.atimes.com/atimes/China/KH22Ad01.html (accessed October 2009).

Wu, Yanrui (1998) *China's Consumer Revolution: The Emerging Patterns of Wealth and Expenditure.* London: Edward Elgar.

Xin, Liu (2002) *The Otherness of Self: A Genealogy of the Self in Contemporary China.* Ann Arbor: University of Michigan Press.

Yan, Hairong (2003a) "Neoliberal Governmentality and Neohumanism: Organising Suzhi/Value Flow through Labor Recruitment Networks", *Cultural Anthropology* 18(4): 493–523.

Yan, Yunxiang (1996) *The Flow of Gifts.* Stanford: Stanford University Press.

——(1998) "McDonald's Beijing: The Localisation of Americana". In T. Buoye, K. Denton, B. Dickson, B. Naughton and M.K. Whyte, eds. *China: Adapting the Past, Confronting the Future.* Michigan: Center for Chinese Studies, University of Michigan, Ann Arbor, 255–59.

——(2003b) *Private Life Under Socialism: Love, Intimacy and Family Change in a Chinese Village, 1949–1999.* Stanford: Stanford University Press.

——(2009a) *The Individualization of Chinese Society.* Berg Publishing.

——(2009b) "The Good Samaritans New Trouble: A Study of the Changing Moral Landscape in Contemporary China", *Social Anthropology* 17(1): 9–24.

Yang, Mayfair Mei-hui (1994) *Gifts, Favors, and Banquets: The Art of Social Relationships in China.* New York: Cornell University Press.

Yao, Souchou (2002) *Confucian Capitalism: Discourse, Practice and the Myth of Chinese Enterprise.* New York: Routledge.

Yau, Oliver H.M. (1988) "Chinese Cultural Values: Their Dimensions and Marketing Implications", *European Journal of Marketing* 22(5): 44–57. news.xinhuanet.com/edu/2010-11/11/c_12760741.htm.

Zeuthen, Jesper W. and Michael B. Griffiths (2011) "The End of Urban-Rural Differentiation in China? Hukou and Resettlement in Chengdu's Urban-Rural Integration". In Björn Alpermann, ed. *Politics and Markets in Rural China.* Routledge Press, 218–32.

Zhan, Mei (2009) *Other-Wordly: Making Chinese through Transnational Frames.* Duke University Press.

——(2005) "Civet Cats, Fried Grasshoppers, and David Beckham's Pyjamas: Unruly Bodies after SARS", *American Anthropologist* Vol. 107(1): 31–42.

Zhang, Jing and Sharon Shavitt (2003) "Cultural Values in Advertisements to the Chinese X-Generation: Promoting Modernity and Individualism", *Journal of Advertising* 32(1): 23–33.

Zhang, Li (2001) *Strangers in the City: Reconfigurations of Space, Power and Social Networks within China's Floating Population.* Stanford, CA: Stanford University Press.

Zhang, Lijia (2011) "How Can I be Proud of my China if We Are a Nation of 1.4bn Cold Hearts?" *The Guardian*, 22 October. www.guardian.co.uk/commentisfree/2011/oct/22/china-nation-cold-hearts.

Zhao, Xin and Russell W. Belk (2008) "Politicizing Consumer Culture: Advertising's Appropriation of Political Ideology in China's Social Transition", *Journal of Consumer Research* Vol.35, August: 231–44.

Zheng, Tiantian (2008) "Commodifying Romance and Searching for Love: Rural Migrant Bar Hostesses' Moral Vision in Post-Mao Dalian", *Modern China* 34(4): 442–76.

Zhou, Lianxi and Michael King-man Hui (2003) "The Symbolic Value of Foreign Products in the People's Republic of China", *Journal of International Marketing* 11(2): 36–58.

Zhou, Nan and Russell W. Belk (2004) "Chinese Consumer Readings of Global and Local Advertising Appeals", *Journal of International Advertising* 33(3): 63–76.

Zhou, Xiaohong, ed. (2005) *Zhongguo zhongchan jieceng diaocha* [Survey of the Chinese Middle Strata]. Beijing: Social Sciences Academic Press.

Zhou, Xueguang (2004) *The State and Life Chances in Urban China: Redistribution and Stratification, 1949–1994.* Cambridge: Cambridge University Press.

Index

Aaker, J. and Schmitt, B. 5, 78
abilities, respect for 157–58
Abrahamic divine referent 96
advertising in China 13
age, considerations of 49, 50, 51, 64, 70–71, 82, 116, 132, 134, 139, 146, 155–56, 157–58, 163
Agger, Ben 11
altruism 122, 162, 163, 184–85, 186, 188; altruistic deference 97–102; conspicuous altruism 100; proximity altruism 96–97
Alvesson, M. and Karreman, D. 18
Ambler, T. and Witzel, M. 36
Anagnost, Ann 10, 72, 73, 75
Andreas, Joel 2
animals and civil behaviour 61–63
Anshan city 20–23; consumer culture 21–22; economic stimulus 22; fieldwork in 20–23; international retailers 22; material inequalities and cultural distinctions 22–23; minorities in 22–23; pollution 21–22; population growth 21, 22–23; shopping malls and upscale apartments 21; Showa Steelworks 20; steel and mining industries 20–21; upmarket restaurants in 39; wealth differentials 21
Appadurai, Arjun 9
Archer, Margaret 19
Ardener, Edwin 30
Arnould, E.J. and Thompson, C.J. 8
Arrow, Kenneth J. 4, 5
aspiration and aspirationary moves 163–66
authenticity 24–43; branded clothes 24–25; categorical anomaly 35; categorical legitimization of "authentic" individuality 25–28; Chinese context 24; coarse grain,

peasant tastes and urban consumption of the hyper-rural 39–42; cosmetics 32; definition of 36; "flow" concept of 30–31; free space and categorical legitimization of "authentic" individuality 25–28; hyper-rural, local products and marketing of 37–39; hyper-rural, urban consumption and ideas of 39–42; individuality, authenticity in categorical legitimization of 25–28; iterations of the authenticity discourse 24–25, 32–33; legitimate inauthenticity 37; local products and 38; originality and 31; peasant tastes and urban consumption of the hyper-rural and ideas of 39–42; reality and 24–25; reality and personal perceptions of 25–28; social value invested in 32–33; socially constructed ideal of 42–43; solid sight, visual metaphors and perceptions of 28–30; temporal priority and 30–32; Traditional Chinese Medicine 35, 79; true lies, legitimate inauthenticity and 36–37; urban consumption of the hyper-rural and ideas of 39–42; visual metaphors and perceptions of 28–30

Bai, Xue 206n1
Bao, Y., Su, C. and Zhou, Z, 4, 6
Barmé, Geremie R. 3, 30, 104
Barth, Frederick 8
Barthes, Roland 17
Baudrillard, Jean 8, 16, 18, 32, 41, 42
Bauman, Zygmunt 15
Beck, U. and Beck-Gernsheim, E. 15
Beck, U., Giddens, A. and Lash, S. 152
Beck, Ulrich 15, 152
Becker, Jasper 2

human practice 4–5, 20, 35
Hung, E.P.W. and Chiu, S.W.K. 21, 154
Hung, K.H., Li, S.Y. and Belk, R.W. 9
Hwang, A., Francesco, A.M. and
   Kessler, E. 5
Hyde, S.T. 29
hyper-rural: local products and
   marketing of 37–39; urban
   consumption and ideas of:
   authenticity 39–42

identity 3, 14, 16, 18, 20, 78, 112–13,
   136–37; collective identity formation
   10; consumption and 9–10, 199;
   private selves and social identity 5;
   production of 95, 195, 199; regional
   identity 87; social identity 188; socio-
   historical product 95, 195; structuralist
   and post-structuralist ideas on 15–16
Ikels, Charlotte 63, 89
in *(nei) versus* out *(wai)* boundaries
   104–5
inclusion-*versus*-exclusion dynamic
   162–63
individual agency 5, 11, 14–15, 16, 20,
   27, 28, 44, 73, 78, 79, 95, 123, 125,
   132, 183, 194, 195–96, 197, 198–99,
   199, 200–201; comradeship,
   imposition over 1; configuration of
   30; individual mastery and 129–31;
   social construction of 17–18
individual autonomy, importance for
   individuals 14–15
individual–collective, East–West binary
   oppositions 7–8
individualism mistaken for individuality
   13–14
individuality: Asian concept of 'personage'
   6; categorical legitimization of
   authenticity in 25–28; Chinese
   medicine and approach to 79;
   comradeship, imposition over
   individual agency 1; consumer-agents,
   actions of 8; consumerist culture and
   3, 6–7; diversity of 175; dynamics of
   social and cultural practice and 7;
   educational system and 78–79; free
   space and categorical legitimization
   of "authentic" individuality 25–28;
   individual agency, social construction
   of 17–18; individualism mistaken
   for 13–14; individuals' practices of
   196–97; instantiation of 195, 198–204;
   Maost era standardization of 1–2;

methodological individualism and
   4–5; private selves and social identity
   5; self-assertion and social interaction
   18; social and cultural, reconciliation
   with individual agency 5; sociological
   and psychological perspectives on
   5–6; 'standing out' and 13–14; status
   agencies, manipulation of 1–2; stifled
   projects of 159–60
individualization, processes of 14
individuals' practices of individuality
   196–97
"innate" character or personality
   (xingge) 178
innocent socialist paradise, nostalgia
   for 162
insecurity 78, 151, 155, 160
instantiation of individuality 195,
   198–204
intent, intentionality and 115–18
internality, externalization of 135–37
international retailers 22
interrelations, sociability and 77
intimacy and social distance, boundary
   between 196
intimate sphere civility and 64–65
iterations of authenticity discourse
   24–25, 32–33

Jacka, Tamara 72, 75, 122, 134, 141
Jankowiak, William R. 89
Jenkins, Richard 16, 20
Jiang Zemin 184, 185
Johansson, perry 25, 30

Kant, Immanuel 96
Khu, Josephine M.T. 34
Kipnis, Andrew 10, 11, 45, 72, 82, 92,
   93, 103, 115
Kirke, Charles 54
Knight, Deirdre S. 113
knowledge 44–58; engagement, rules of
   44–45; knowledge economy 45–48;
   knowledge politics 48–50; law and
   practical order 53–56; practicability
   51–53; and rules, value of 196; rules
   and ruling 56–58; rules of engagement
   44–45
knowledgeability 155
Konrád, G. and Szelényi, I. 2
Kozinets, Robert V. 45
Krajewski, Sabine 60
Kraus, Richard C. 1
kung fu 118–20